The Hum1   ᴊ s
Journey to God

Perspectives on San Pedro,
the Cactus of Vision & Andean Soul
Healing Methods

First published by O Books, 2009
O Books is an imprint of John Hunt Publishing Ltd., The Bothy, Deershot Lodge, Park Lane, Ropley,
Hants, SO24 0BE, UK
office1@o-books.net
www.o-books.net

Distribution in:

UK and Europe
Orca Book Services
orders@orcabookservices.co.uk
Tel: 01202 665432 Fax: 01202 666219
Int. code (44)

USA and Canada
NBN
custserv@nbnbooks.com
Tel: 1 800 462 6420 Fax: 1 800 338 4550

Australia and New Zealand
Brumby Books
sales@brumbybooks.com.au
Tel: 61 3 9761 5535 Fax: 61 3 9761 7095

Far East (offices in Singapore, Thailand,
Hong Kong, Taiwan)
Pansing Distribution Pte Ltd
kemal@pansing.com
Tel: 65 6319 9939 Fax: 65 6462 5761

South Africa
Alternative Books
altbook@peterhyde.co.za
Tel: 021 555 4027 Fax: 021 447 1430

Text copyright Ross Heaven 2008

Design: Stuart Davies

ISBN: 978 1 84694 242 6

All rights reserved. Except for brief quotations
in critical articles or reviews, no part of this
book may be reproduced in any manner without
prior written permission from the publishers.

The rights of Ross Heaven as author have been
asserted in accordance with the Copyright,
Designs and Patents Act 1988.

A CIP catalogue record for this book is available
from the British Library.

Printed by Digital Book Print

O Books operates a distinctive and ethical publishing philosophy in
all areas of its business, from its global network of authors to
production and worldwide distribution.
This book is produced on FSC certified stock, within ISO14001
standards. The printer plants sufficient trees each year through
the Woodland Trust to absorb the level of emitted carbon in
its production.

The Hummingbird's Journey to God

Perspectives on San Pedro, the Cactus of Vision & Andean Soul Healing Methods

Ross Heaven

BOOKS

Winchester, UK
Washington, USA

CONTENTS

Dedications and Thanks

Thank you to Lesley and Miguel for your help with this book and to the other shamans and participants on my Cactus of Vision journeys for sharing your insights and for permission to use your words.

This book is for my children, Jodie, Mili, Ocean, and Javen, with love, and for the spirit of San Pedro, with gratitude.

Love and welcome too to our plant spirit babies Kai and Freddie. The former joined us *in utero* for our 2007 Magical Earth journey, while the latter was conceived as the result of a vision.

Cleansing the Doors of Perception
Introduction by Dr David Luke

This book is essentially about healing, but healing of a very different kind to that which we may ordinarily understand.

The conception of illness and medicine we have in the West – what we call the 'medical model' – goes back to the ancient Greeks and the philosophy of Hippocrates. The current view, continuing from that tradition, is that all physical illnesses have a physical cause.

This view of medicine seems to work well with some types of illness, particularly physical trauma, but has only limited success in the treatment of much physical and mental disease (a word which might be better thought of by its constituent parts: dis-ease).

Within the medical model, psychological processes are, from time to time, thought to play a significant role in healing, such as recently, but then only to a moderate degree. However, these psychological processes are eventually hoped to be explained by physical factors, such as genetics. Spiritual factors are generally rejected outright unless they constitute some sort of secondary psychological component.

This medical perspective seems odd given that, with many disorders, the beneficial effect of drugs amounts to only a small fraction of the healing that actually occurs through the placebo effect, thereby indicating the importance of belief over medicines alone.

Throughout all this time the medical model has also managed to conduct itself without any real definition of what *life* actually is, and has conveniently omitted to consider the existence of any kind of life force or energy, like the Eastern chi, or ki of traditional Chinese medicine or practices such as chi-gong.

1

Elsewhere in the world, older and more magical conceptions of healing can still be found. There, illness might be considered to be the physical manifestation of psychological or spiritual issues, and may even extend itself to other people unintentionally through 'energetic' or spiritual means. It is also thought that malice may be sent intentionally through sorcery or the evil eye, causing illness; and, by the opposite means, prayer can help heal or cure someone. Furthermore, diagnoses of illness may be sought through psychic means, or, through divination, future events might be foretold.

In many traditional worldviews thoughts can become manifest and knowledge can be accessed without the need for the intervening physical mechanics we understand as necessary in our 'Western' scientific worldview. But, how unscientific actually is this magical worldview? Certainly it conflicts with the traditional and, currently, the dominant materialist notion of science that considers that the world is only composed of mathematically-understood factors like matter, energy, force and time. Consciousness itself is often supposed to be merely illusory or, at best, an awkward side-effect of physical brain processes.

But even the most fundamental and robust of all sciences, physics, is at a loss to explain the ultimate nature of everything, and various respectable interpretations of quantum physics sound even more magical than any so-called 'primitive' worldview.

For instance, one understanding of quantum physics, concerned with what is called the collapse of the state vector, holds that the observation of an unknown physical state is necessary for it to become known – so that *consciousness itself* causes physical reality to occur.

Furthermore, defying what was once considered possible by classical (Newtonian) conceptions of physics we now know that two particles once joined together continue to *simultaneously* act together, even when they are separated by vast distances in space. However, physicists continue to argue over what is the best interpretation of quantum physics. So, perhaps magical conceptions of how the universe works are not so implausible after all. Traditional 'primitive' doctrines that consider that everything in the universe is connected shouldn't seem so intellectually juvenile anymore, and nor should ideas that 'two things once connected remain connected', which is the basic principle of what was once derided as 'contagious magic' by Western anthropologists studying other cultures some 100 years ago.

When the English novelist Aldous Huxley was given mescaline (seemingly the most important psychoactive constituent of the San Pedro cactus) by the English physician Dr Humphrey Osmond in 1953, he said that it allowed man access to mystical states by overriding the brain's 'reducing valve'. Huxley was a proponent of the ideas of the French philosopher Henri Bergson, who had, in the previous century, supposed that the brain acted as a filter of memory and sensory experience so that our conscious awareness wasn't overwhelmed with a mass of largely useless information, irrelevant to the survival of the organism.

Bergson suggested that if these filters were bypassed, man would be capable of remembering everything he had ever experienced and of perceiving everything that is happening everywhere in the universe, i.e. clairvoyance.

Huxley then applied this theory to mescaline and other similar substances – which he and Osmond called 'psychedelic', meaning 'mind manifesting' – and suggested that they override the reducing valve of the brain, bypassing the filters that stop us from potentially perceiving everything.

Huxley paraphrased this notion by quoting the English poet and mystic, William Blake: 'If the doors of perception were cleansed, every thing would appear to man as it is, infinite.'

In my late teens I took psychedelic substances and experienced the world in a completely different way to that of my ordinary waking consciousness. I became extremely curious as to how these seemingly magical experiences occurred and so I went back to school to study psychology, and then went on to university to do a degree in the subject so that I might better understand these experiences.

I learned a lot about normal, and what psychologists call 'abnormal', states of consciousness but felt that the exceptional states experienced with psychedelics didn't really fit either of these categories. If anything, in the end, studying mainstream psychology made me very cynical about everything other than the normal state of consciousness, and even that couldn't be trusted it seemed.

After my degree, partly in an attempt to get away from this narrow and hardened scientific way of looking at the world, I followed a naïve 'calling' to go to Mexico in 1998, though I knew practically nothing about this country.

While I was there I took the psychoactive peyote cactus in the desert and this triggered a whole series of what I can only call visionary and shamanic experiences, involving various profound synchronicities, esoteric discoveries, escape from death, and a spontaneous shamanic initiation into hummingbird wisdom.

The entire story of that journey would probably need its own book so I won't go into it here, but it was an interesting surprise when Ross, who knew nothing of my hummingbird story and travels in Mexico, asked me to write the introduction to this book merely because of my current scientific research.

After a year and a half in Mexico I decided to continue my studies and returned to the UK to start a PhD in parapsychology, the study of the psychology of the paranormal, which at that time was the branch of science that I felt could most help to me to understand the incredible experiences of the psychedelic state, because they are neither normal nor abnormal.

Having finally completed my doctorate I am resuming the research that partly began in 1950 by Humphrey Osmond's colleague Dr John Smythies, who conducted one of the first mescaline experiments into clairvoyance – the ability to transcend space to access otherwise unobtainable information.

That original experiment by Smythies had some success, as did a number of other psychic experiments with mescaline over the years, but by today's standards those studies were not tightly controlled enough to rule out explanations other than psychic abilities.

So, currently I find myself in South America, scientifically researching people's ability to obtain information from outside space and time through the use of the San Pedro cactus, because, independently of Huxley, Osmond and Smythies, we know from anthropologists that South American people use San Pedro for psychic purposes too.

For instance, one Peruvian folk healer described how he used San Pedro to induce '...the telepathic sense of transmitting oneself across time and matter...', and in this book you will find a number of similar such accounts from both San Pedro healers and from Europeans and North Americans (who we might loosely call Westerners) experiencing such things with the cactus themselves.

You will also find a great many stories in this book that challenge our orthodox 'Western' conceptions of healing and the bounds of reality; stories which, with the growing discoveries in physics, biology, psychology and parapsychology, should not, perhaps, seem so scientifically implausible these days.

Science may be one path to truth, but it is a path that was only allowed to consider the truths we might access through altered states of consciousness for about a decade between the late 1950s and late 1960s, before governmental mandates dictated what kind of truths could be explored through science, or, for that matter, by any other means of investigating reality.

Fortunately, however, that restriction on science now appears to be receding and once again scientists are beginning to ask questions about the function of psychedelics in the brain, about their potential for healing, and about their capacity for inducing genuine mystical and so-called paranormal experiences.

For instance, survey research I conducted with a colleague, Dr Marios Kittenis, has found that there are some typical 'transpersonal' experiences (either of the mystical or paranormal type) that most commonly occur with mescaline-containing cacti (e.g. peyote and San Pedro). The most common of these is the experience of perceiving an aura around living things, followed by the experience of sensing the intelligence or spirit of the cactus, and then the sense of connecting with the universal consciousness of all things. For those who reported these experiences, they were said to occur often, or even more frequently, upon taking the cactus.

Less frequently and less commonly, in descending order of the number of people reporting them, experiences also included dissolving into energy, powerful long-lasting religious awakenings, out-of-body experiences, clairvoyance, death and rebirth experiences and/or past life memories, psychokinesis (influencing objects or people with one's mind), encountering a divine being, encountering a (non-animal) intelligent entity, and the sense of the loss of causality (where A causes B).

For scientists, whether or not these experiences are 'real' is a matter of ongoing debate between those who believe that these phenomena *may* be possible and those who reject them out of hand because they do not fit within their confined 'physicalistic' worldview.

For the people who experience these phenomena, however, they are often considered 'more real than real', and, although they challenge what we 'Westerners' think we know about the world, those experiencing these extraordinary events often find it very difficult to reject them as mere hallucinations. This is because these experiences often have such a depth of meaning and can stimulate such a wealth of personal change and healing that they cannot be ignored – and nor should science continue to ignore or dismiss them.

David Luke, PhD
Lecturer in Psychology, University of Greenwich, London
(Villcabamba, Ecuador, December 2008)

Following the Flight of a Hummingbird
Introduction by Ross Heaven

It seems to me that, for the last several years, I have been following the flight of a hummingbird; its bright trajectory leading me, through coincidence and odd events, to places and outcomes wholly unexpected. This book is one of the stopping points on that journey which begins with the chance telling of a tale about a hummingbird – a simple story; a fable and little else that has now come to mean much more. That phase of the journey ended just days ago when I received the introduction to this book from Dr Luke, and the manuscript was complete.

A lot has happened in-between, including encounters with 'miracles', meetings with remarkable men and women, and the dawning of a completely new understanding of the world: that it is deeper, richer, and more mysterious than we have been led to believe. Parts of this journey have been dramatic and marvellous, others more subtle, containing meanings I still need to explore, but all of it has been extraordinary and I am grateful to San Pedro for making it possible.

One of the more 'subtle' coincidences along the way was how David Luke came to write his introduction at all. It is also an example of what I mean by an 'odd event' linked by the hummingbird as a symbol or metaphor.

In November 2008, I had just returned from Peru, a country I visit each year to lead Cactus of Vision retreats where participants are able to meet and receive healing from the shamans and curanderos of the Andes and to experience their extraordinary medicine, San Pedro.

My schedule was busy when I got back: first a trip to Spain and then to Norfolk, England, to lead two plant spirit workshops and six ayahuasca ceremonies with the Shipibo maestro,

Guillermo Aravelo, who was making his first visit to Britain to introduce people to the 'vine of souls'.

During my travels I had not paid much attention to my emails but, just prior to my Norfolk trip, I was able to check them and, via a forwarded mail from an associate, I received a message from Dr Luke.

He was about to embark on a research project to explore whether ayahuasca was a natural enhancer of human psychic and ESP capabilities, he said. The visionary brew was once known by the scientific name *telepathine* because of its noted abilities to do so, and he wanted to find out more. He had heard about my workshop with Guillermo and wondered if it might be possible to administer tests to some of my participants during the ceremonies which would take place.

As he says in his Introduction, very little scientific research has been done into psychedelics since the 1960s as government legislation has made it difficult even for scientists, and research grants for this sort of work are also almost impossible to come by.[1] To gain research funding, for example, scientists typically have to phrase their grant applications and frame their experiments to 'prove' that drugs are harmful and, that by better understanding their mechanisms, we might be able to prevent their 'abuse' or help those who have 'fallen prey to them'. Such experiments, then, are biased from the start (they have to be to get funding) and their outcomes are almost certain: more results that 'prove' the government's position and uphold its 'war against drugs'.[2] We should also remember that the few scientists who are fortunate to be given approval for such research are, indeed, studying 'drugs': synthetic substances created and distributed, by and large, for the purposes of entertainment and 'getting out of it'. What they are not studying is spiritual sacraments and medicines.

In my opinion (and Strassman would agree), there is a vast difference between injecting a volunteer with a chemical in the clinical setting of a sterile research lab or hospital, where they are analysed, probed, and connected to monitoring devices, and offering them a cup of ayahuasca in a beautiful rainforest setting as part of a ceremony guided by shamans with a defined healing purpose. In the latter circumstances, my experience of taking groups to Peru and partaking in probably a hundred ceremonies myself suggests that the benefits of psychedelic plants (as opposed to 'drugs') are profound but that set, setting, and sacred intent are vital to the healing process – and all of these are lacking in laboratory studies of 'drugs'.

What interested me about Dr Luke's research, therefore, was that it seemed to echo the spirit of the early psychedelic pioneers who were prepared to get out into the field, consider the ceremony and its intent as well as the psychedelic agent involved, and to deal with the whole plant, instead of a chemical administered to a 'subject' in an unpleasant and inappropriate environment.

Circumstances and the limits of time, however, meant that I could not accommodate Dr Luke's requests, as much as I would have liked to. I wrote instead to say that I'd be pleased to help at a later date, perhaps during one of my journeys to Peru and, almost as an after-thought, I asked if he had considered extending his research to look at the healing and divinatory qualities of San Pedro, a plant with some similar effects to ayahuasca, but one which has been far less studied or written about.

He wrote back with one of those emails that begin 'funnily enough...' and attached an outline proposal for almost exactly the study I had suggested.

Another coincidence, as it turned out, is that Dr Luke is a guest lecturer at the Centre for the Study of Anomalous Psychological Processes at the University of Northampton, the same university I had attended in the 1970s and 80s when I took my own degree in psychology.

That was the least of it, though. In exchange for the information Dr Luke sent me I forwarded him a draft of this book. As he says in his Introduction, 'it was an interesting surprise' when he received it and saw its title, for he too had been led to his current studies by the appearance of a hummingbird.

He had taken peyote (another mescaline cactus) some years ago, he told me, and, with that, the hummingbird had entered his life. He writes about this in an unpublished account of his experiences, that he later sent me, and about what he calls a 'spontaneous shamanic initiation' and 'calling of the hummingbird', after which he seemed to share an affinity with these birds and they would even land in his hands if he held them out in front of him.

At the time of his initiation, Dr Luke was already a psychologist and, of course, familiar with the work of Jung and others who regard such synchronous moments as a fortuitous step to better understanding the self, so he undertook a little web research into the symbolism of the hummingbird. It said:

Sometimes an animal or bird will mysteriously come into our life and begin to haunt our consciousness. The image of that animal becomes associated with our sense of who we are and where our values come from...

Hummingbirds awaken us to the beauty of the present moment. They bring us medicine to solve the riddle of duality. They also awaken us to the medicinal properties of plants.

They teach us how to use flowers to heal and win hearts in love. They teach us to fight in a way where no one really gets hurt. They teach us simple courage.

There are different ways that a totem animal can be discovered: in Native American tradition they may make their appearance while one is on a vision quest. They also come in dreams, meditations, and shamanic spirit-journeys.

'The Native American mythology continually alluded to the bird's connection between humans and plants,' wrote Dr Luke. This is as well as connections between 'this world and the world of the dead ancestors, the upperworlds and the underworlds. The section on mythology summarised that one of the widespread beliefs amongst indigenous people of the Americas is that hummingbirds, in some way, are messengers between the worlds.'

It is a small bird and, perhaps, a small symbol but the impact of these connections was immense. Dr Luke writes that 'I began a mission of discovery, driven by a vision of my own future, and I have grown and expanded beyond what I thought was possible.' As a direct result, he is now pursuing his research into the psychic and healing effects of plants like San Pedro.

So, perhaps the hummingbird is indeed a messenger between worlds and the means by which the wisdom of San Pedro is pollinated so it can spread hope and healing and change people's lives.

Some of Dr Luke's realisations, as a result of his mescaline experiences, were that: 'Everything is permissible; nothing is impossible' and, simply, 'Relax! We're all God.' These are conclusions similar to my own, as you will read, and, no matter how 'new age' they may seem to you now, you will hear them from many other people in this book too as they share their stories of how they have been helped and healed by San Pedro. *Something is going on* – and the hummingbird knows what it is.

Despite the miracles that may be possible through San Pedro, amazingly little has been written about this plant. It is a mystery why, given the benefits it reportedly brings. I regard my own book, therefore, as a *starting point* in our understanding of San Pedro, not as a definitive statement, and I hope that other studies will follow. I offer a range of perspectives within it, in the desire to explore and perhaps unravel some of the mysteries of San Pedro: how it works, the benefits it bestows, and, finally, what its message may be. I hope that, as a result of reading it, you will be inspired to look more closely at San Pedro too, and to explore its wisdom for yourself. It is, in my opinion, the medicine most needed for our times.

I offer this book to the spirit of San Pedro and the small bright bird that is its guardian, in thanks for its healings and teachings, and I encourage you to follow its trajectory too and allow the hummingbird into your own life.

Ross Heaven
(Brighton, England, December 2008)

Small, superlative being
You are a miracle
And you blaze

From *Ode to the Hummingbird* by Pablo Neruda

Chapter 1

The Condor and the Hummingbird
An Andean Fable

Storytellers clothe the naked body of myth in their own traditions so that listeners can relate more easily to its deeper meaning
Joan D Vinge

Iquitos, the strange jungle town on the banks of the Amazon, has a sense of fever and muted madness about it that began at least 500 years ago with the arrival of Francisco Pizarro.

The Conquistador Pizarro came to Peru in search of El Dorado, the fabled city of gold. Red and not gold is what he discovered, however, in the blood of the natives that fell before his sword as he carved Spain's insignia into the land and his dreams turned into obsessions.

As is so often the case in matters of karma and madness, having lived by the sword, Pizarro was also to die by it when, in 1541, twenty assassins entered his home one night, intent on revenge and riches of their own.

His life ebbing out of him, Pizarro, then 70, found only the strength to paint a cross in his own blood on the cold stone floor before him and to cry for absolution from Christ. Then, gathering his sword – 'the companion of all my deeds' – he left this world and his aspirations for gold behind him.

Pizarro's dreams were for nothing, for no gold has ever been found in Iquitos. Three hundred years later, however, in the years between 1880 and 1912, riches did flow into the town from the jungles around it, in the form of latex, a product of the jebe tree.

The invention of vulcanisation by Goodyear had created a

huge demand for latex and, following Pizarro's lead, the town of Iquitos was birthed by rubber barons as a base for their own excesses. From an almost standing start Iquitos had 20,000 inhabitants by the mid-1880s, many of them Europeans who became fabulously wealthy by enlisting (or, rather, enslaving) local tribes to work their plantations for them.

Their opulent bubble burst thirty years later when it was discovered that greater profits could be made in the plantations of Malaya (now Malaysia) than in the wild forests of the Amazon. The traders left Iquitos as quickly as they had arrived.

The town's colours are faded now but in its day it stood for a certain kind of 'excellence', 'modernity', and the 'genius of man' as he employed science and slavery to transform and tame the forest, turning it from a 'wilderness' ('red in tooth and claw') into something far removed from its true nature and more akin to his taste for order and opulence.

Only a few reminders of past glories remain. The town retains its promenade on the banks of the Amazon River, for example, where Victorian gentlemen would take their evening strolls. In the shadows of some moonlit nights you may even glimpse their tuxedoed ghosts with their arms around their wives dressed in ball-gowns and evening dresses, looking out across the jungle to survey their kingdoms as lightening flashed in the forest and the sweat of the air made their dress-shirts stick to their backs.

Other follies, reflective of long-gone wealth, can also be seen. One is a house – now a restaurant (The Casa de Fierro or 'Iron House') – made entirely of iron, that was built by Monsieur Eiffel, the designer of Paris' famous Tower. Iron, of course, is subject to rust and you must wonder what a building like this is doing in a place of baking heat, rainforest downpours, and humidity so extreme that the air itself can rot the clothes from your back. The reason for its presence is explained by the one-time spirit of those Victorian gentlemen: 'It can be built, so why not build it? We have money to spare, after all.'

The eccentric rubber baron, Carlos Fermin Fitzcarrald had a base near here. Fitzcarraldo, as he is better known, was also driven by dreams of gold and longed so passionately to instal an opera house deep in the jungle that some say his dreams, in their turn, drove him mad. One of the stories told of him and his consuming need for profit and opera relates how he purchased the only remaining parcel of forest that might still yield rubber, in a remote area of the Amazon cut off by treacherous rapids, with the intention of building a plantation, a fortune, and an opera house (not necessarily in that order). To avoid the problems of the river, Fitzcarraldo had the natives physically carry his 30-ton steamship through the jungle, across an isthmus of land from one part of the river to the next.

The vainglorious driving force behind his actions was, he said, "not to undertake an adventure, but to offer this land to mankind so we can find a new home for the disinherited of the world". In return for their labour, he promised the natives gunpowder and bullets and guns to tame the beasts", so they could conquer the natural world, just as he intended to do.

It seems that nature was not so anxious to be conquered, however, and Fitzcarraldo died in the rapids of the Urubamba River on July 9, 1897.[1]

Nowadays, with few hints of its former wealth or the madness that has historically fuelled its accumulation (except for those few monuments that remain), Iquitos still buzzes with frenetic energy and the desire for profit. At any time of the day or night, for example, it is almost impossible to sit quietly in the main square (the Plaza de Armas or 'Place of Arms') or sip coffee in one of its restaurants or cafes without attracting vendors and craftswomen who will try to sell you Shipibo textiles, that have taken them days or weeks to make, for just a few American dollars, or shoeshine boys who will clean your boots (whether they need it or not) for just one sol (about 15 pence). The desire for money lives on, but driven now by the poverty of a town abandoned to its fate.

James Redfield, in *The Celestine Prophecy*,[2] writes that there are two roads into Iquitos: the 'high' and the 'low' road. In fact, there are no roads in, just a river and an airstrip littered with the rusting carcasses of small planes that did not quite make the landing.

There are roads out, however, and we had taken one of these a few days before, leaving the strange beauty of the town to journey deeper into the jungle.

Here in the forest a quieter river flowed, dyed red by the tannins in the leaves of the trees along its banks that turn it the colour of tea when they drop from the branches and sink below the surface of the water. They are good for the skin, having toning, astringent, and antiseptic qualities, but those are not their only virtues: more romantically, they make the water look like rose wine. The river was low, after several days of jungle sunshine.

The people with me, unlike Fitzcarraldo's enslaved community, *were* here to experience an adventure. They had joined me to live with a Shipibo tribe for a few weeks and experience their legendary visionary brew: ayahuasca, the vine of souls. There were twenty or so of us in this rainforest camp by the river: people who had come to search for visions, magic, and healing, or a new direction in their lives.

It was a few hours before our final ceremony. A little distance away our shaman was preparing his ayahuasca medicine and his icaros – the plaintive and prayerful songs sung by shamans to the spirits of the plants – drifted softly in the air around us.

As had been customary since our arrival, I had given the group some time for meditation and reflection in the afternoon before our ceremonies began in the darkness of the evening. Some were in their rooms, but there were a dozen of us relaxing by the river.

The day was dreamy and drowsy and, it occurred to me, the

perfect time for a story: a fable, or a lullaby, really… about a hummingbird. Like all fables, it also contained a current of truth to it, which had a depth like a river.

Lying on my back, eyes closed against the sun, I began to speak, to no one in particular.

A very long time ago, it was only the condor who was able to visit God because his great strength and powers of endurance meant that he alone could make such a journey across the face of the Sun, the Milky Way, and through the vastness of space to Paradise, where God would wait to receive him. He carried the prayers of the people with him so they could be heard and – God willing – granted.

All the time, as he recited these requests and earnest wishes, the humble condor turned his face away from God so He would not be offended. Then he made his way back to Earth so he could circle the sky and collect more prayers from the people below, gathering them in with his wingtips and storing them in his feathers until the time came for his next audience with God.

As I said, that was all a long time ago and things are different now – because of a hummingbird.

This tiny bright wisp of a bird so yearned for God that he spent his days in prayer, darting from flower to flower and garden to garden, hoping that one might be the first garden, which he had heard men call Eden, and that God might be found in its brightest flower.

Every day his Eden eluded him, but he still would not give up on his quest to know God. So what do you think he did, this little bird, to attain his burning desire?

He became a stowaway.

One day, when the sun was at its highest, he crept into the condor's feathers and tucked himself away amongst the prayers, knowing that the condor had great strength and could make a journey to God that a hummingbird never could.

The sun was bright in the condor's eyes that day and the hummingbird so still and quiet that he went unnoticed as the great bird made his flight. Finally, they arrived at the palace of God, and the condor, his head turned away, began to recite the prayers of his people.

It was then that the hummingbird flew out from the condor's feathers and, for the first time, saw what he had most longed for: the face of God and the radiance that surrounded Him.

The condor was immediately fearful at what God might do to a bird so small who had presumed to look upon Him. But God just smiled.

'Welcome, little one,' He said. "I have been waiting a long time for you to make this journey. You and the one who brought you are both welcome here, but because your love is so strong and your courage so great, it is to you that I will reveal My greatest secrets.'

And so now it is the condor and the hummingbird who are both most precious to God: the first for his strength and service, the second for his bravery and passion.

But, still, to this day, it is the hummingbird who carries the wisdom of God in his soul.

It is an Andean more than an Amazonian story, but its principles are universal, I think: that courage, faith and love are our most important allies, and that through these we can discover the deepest spiritual truths.

That was probably why I had chosen to tell this story just prior to our ayahuasca ceremony; that and the lyrical nature of the afternoon and the murmurs of the river close by. Actually, I had no idea why I'd told it; it just seemed like the perfect tale.

It would be time for the ceremony soon, so I wandered back to my room while the others stayed behind, dreaming in the sun.

A few days later our adventure with the Shipibo people and their vine of souls would be over and our circle would be broken – in this reality anyway. Of course, it is never an accident that brings people together for an experience like this and so, once formed, a circle of pilgrim-souls who have shared a journey of the spirit can never really be broken. We would all meet again, in life or in dreams.

For now, though, amid smiles and hugs, I would say goodbye to our group in Iquitos as they began their more mundane journeys back to America, Australia and Europe, while I prepared for a different onward journey: to the Andes and – as events, life or the spirits would have it – to another adventure I could never have dreamed of, not even while telling the story of the hummingbird that day.

Chapter 2

Sunlight and San Pedro
A Healing Ceremony in the Andes

Los chupaflores juntan
The hummingbirds gather
Todos los dolores malos y enfermedades
All the bad pains and sicknesses
Juegan con sus encantos
They play with their enchantments
Eduardo Calderon, Andean healer

Night in the Andes doesn't so much fall as crash down around you. I close my eyes and when I open them again, in a matter of seconds the day has gone and I am lying in a pool of shadows as darkness swirls around me, consuming the ground I am on.

Miguel is trying to rouse me. He speaks ever-so softly, aware that any word out of place will be jarring, and what he says is deliberately paced and practical, with no emotion and nothing 'spiritual' about it. He wants to know if I'd like some water, a blanket, or if a walk in the mountains would interest me.

I can't walk, though. I can't even speak. My body hasn't reformed yet. I shake my head, no, and even that is an effort. Then I close my eyes again and return to the desert.

This all began ten or twelve hours ago, on a different planet, in a different life, it seems now.

It was then that Miguel Silva Guttierres, a shaman (or as he prefers, a *guia*, or guide) from Cusco in the south of Peru, unwrapped a blue and red blanket and made it his *mesa*: an altar containing objects called *artes*, which, for him, hold a special power and healing significance. With that gesture, he created a channel through which the energies of the cosmos could travel 'from the mind of God to the core of your soul'.

Miguel moved to Cusco in 2003. Before that he lived in the capital, Lima, where he suffered from pneumonia three times in a row and became so ill that he lost the function of a lung and nearly died. His doctors told him that if he got sick again the illness would be his last.

He was also an alcoholic. 'I'd wake up, drink... then shower and drink; I'd even drink in the shower!' he laughed, in his mixture of Spanish and broken English which he calls Spanglish. 'Then, throughout the day, I'd... drink.'

In Cusco, though, apparently by chance, he met a woman – a sorceress – who said she could cure him if he drank a special plant medicine. He did so, of course, and the next day his pneumonia was gone. It is years later and his illness has never returned.

The alcoholism took a little longer and was only finally cured after he had drunk the same plant a number of times and it showed him the cause of his problems: a family who had, in his childhood, devalued him while, at the same time, providing the love he needed through their gifts of whisky. It took him two years, with the aid of the sorceress' plant, to make the connection between his early years and his adult problems, but then he threw away the bottle and has stayed away from it ever since.

Miguel was so excited by the powers of this plant, which he saw as truly miraculous, that he began immediately to train with the woman who had helped him and to learn all he could about the plant that had saved his life.

'I have been the assistant of this plant for the past five years,' he continued, 'and it is my pleasure to make this healing available for you too.' I thought it was an interesting choice of words. Even though he would guide the ceremony to follow, Miguel saw himself as an assistant – and not to the woman who had saved and then trained him, either, even though he remained her apprentice, but to the plant itself: San Pedro.

We were sat in the walled garden of a private house in the hills above Cusco as Miguel told us his story. Our surroundings had a fairytale quality to them. The walls to the garden were entered through a large wooden gate, as if guarding a fortress of secrets. It looked as though it had stood here for years growing ever-more bleached by the sun.

In contrast to the rugged landscape outside, the garden, once entered, was an explosion of colour as red, gold, and yellow flowers rose up in beds that bordered bright lawns. It was like stepping into another land: a scene from the English countryside, perhaps – an impression reinforced by an open-sided marquee that stood on one of the lawns, as if drinks were about to be served there after a genteel game of bowls or croquet. The stillness of the day was palpable and the silence of the garden so absolute that not even the wind carried whispers.

Just outside the gate – though it may as well have been part of a different world – was the Temple of the Moon, a place of power and mystery, full of ancient caves and rock carvings, which takes its name from the way moonlight radiates into its subterranean chambers at night. At the centre of one of these caves there is a throne carved from rock and, beside it, steps that lead deeper into the Earth. No anthropologist really knows why or what it was used for.

By chance, and some weeks before I knew I would be coming to Cusco or sitting so close to this temple, I had been reading a book by Alberto Villoldo[1], an American apprentice to a shaman from Cusco. In it, he describes his own experiences at the Temple of the Moon.

According to Villoldo, there are undead things here: zombies made by sorcery. Once they were human, but they allowed themselves to be caught in a web of magic and now they are no longer living and not dead either, but something in-between. Their stalking ground was right outside our gates, Villoldo said, although the peace of the day and the beauty of the Temple provided no evidence for it at all. My companions, Donna and Mark, knew nothing of this, however, and I resolved to keep it to myself.

Donna had been a friend of mine for years, since I first met her on a workshop I was giving in England. We had experienced several adventures together since then. Most recently she had joined me on my rainforest trip where we had drunk ayahuasca together in the red river camp.

Mark was a participant on that journey too. An artist more familiar with dreams than the 'real world', he was a young 28: a child in and of the spirit, with a fragility and vulnerability to him and a sense of innocence and wide-eyed wonder at the world that was the envy of those around him.

I made a mental note that, whatever happened, Mark would need my attention more than Donna, who I knew could take care of herself. I suppose now that by even having that thought I must have sensed that something *would* happen.

As for me, I had first journeyed to Peru in 1998 to drink ayahuasca, the legendary vine, and San Pedro, the cactus of vision, and, in some way through this to 'find myself'.

Despite that cliché, and much to my surprise and even amusement, I *did* find myself. Ayahuasca provided me with exactly what I needed to make the changes my soul was demanding and, like Miguel, I had been so inspired by the magic of the plants that I wanted others to experience them too so they could wake up to their lives. Eventually, I had begun to organise journeys to Peru so that others could explore the vine's potential for healing and magic.

That had been the purpose of our stay at the Shipibo camp and, as ever, ayahuasca had woven its spell. Just days after our group disbanded I had started to receive emails from those who had arrived safely home, still enraptured by what ayahuasca had given them:

I am the happiest man I know! You can't imagine how this has changed the person I am or brought out the real me! (Heath, Australia)

The stillness I feel and the lack of rush is incredible. What we experienced was something so special and life just keeps getting better. (Linzi, UK)

An experience that changed my life. I will draw from this forever. (Annette, USA)

My previous experiences with San Pedro, on the other hand, had never been quite so powerful, partly because the shamans in the north of Peru, where I had drunk the brew, had a rather different approach to that of the jungle's ayahuasceros.

In contrast to the more laid-back and gentle rituals of the latter, for example, San Pedro maestros are often very demanding and expect participants to take part in long and arduous activities as a component of their visionary work.

One of my first San Pedro shamans, Juan Navarro, was in this mould. In the ceremonies I had attended with him some years ago, he had first given me another plant to drink, a *contrachisa* which caused me to empty my stomach through vomiting. Then I was required to snort tobacco macerated in alcohol: a practice called *singado*, which is designed to cleanse the body spiritually and change one's luck, but which is very much an acquired taste, to say the least. He had also beaten me and his other participants with wooden sticks called *chonta* and 'bathed' us in holy water and flowers (that is, more or less, poured cold water over us) at various points throughout the ceremony.[2] The point of these activities, the shamans say, is healing. But as beautiful as some of these rituals are – such as being bathed in perfumed water – they were also distractions that meant that I and Juan's other partici-pants could not fully relax and allow the plant to do its work so the visions could unfold.

Instead, our thoughts and inner reflections were constantly

interrupted as we were made to stand, sit, strip down to bathing wear for the cold water baths, dry ourselves off and dress again, all under the influence of the plant.

The anthropologist, Bonnie Glass-Coffin, describes similar ceremonies she has attended in Peru in her book, *The Gift of* Life,[3] where 'Patients (and the family members/friends they have brought with them to the ceremony) will actively participate in all aspects of the mesa (healing ritual) and will not be allowed to sit or rest until sometime near dawn'. And yet, as her shaman, Yolanda, remarks in the same book, without faith and 'attention to a spiritual state in which one is completely with God, there is nothing' and no healing will ever take place. 'We have to concentrate with all our hearts to be able to help others, and in this way to liberate them,' she continues.

This being the case, I couldn't help but wonder at the apparent contradiction inherent in these San Pedro ceremonies, which included so many activities that the necessary concentration on one's healing and spiritual state was almost impossible. All of this is quite different to the ayahuasca experience, where those who drink it are asked only to sit quietly and listen to the songs of the shaman as they lead him or her in gentle lullabies to realms of visionary healing.

I had taken part in a number of San Pedro ceremonies, with Juan and with other shamans over the years, perhaps hoping for something different and for the cactus to make good on its promise as a 'plant of the Gods'. But my experience was always the same; whatever wisdom San Pedro held it was, for me, overwhelmed by the rituals surrounding it.

Despite its seeming failures, however, there was something about San Pedro that kept drawing me back, so now, here I was again, in this walled garden by the Temple of the Moon, about to drink once more the sacrament that had saved Miguel's life before changing its course so dramatically.

I was certainly willing to concede that I had missed

something with San Pedro if it could have such a huge effect on people like Miguel. Because of my earlier experiences, however, I still half-expected that nothing much would happen in this ceremony either, apart from a healing spectacle delivered by our shaman.

This subconscious expectation of nothing may also be why I had felt comfortable in inviting my friends to join me; at least the ceremony would be 'safe', I reasoned, and an interesting event for them to be part of, even if no great visions resulted.

Now, though, as we sat together on mattresses beneath the marquee, I wasn't at all sure that nothing would happen. There was a sense of difference about this ceremony, underlined by the departures in procedure I had already noticed between this and the other rituals I had attended.

There had been no lengthy rounds of prayers, for example, no formal seating, contrachisa or singado. In fact, the objects that accompany these things in ceremonies by other shamans – the snail shells which hold the singado and the wooden staffs of the chonta – did not even play a part in the mesa at our centre.

And then there was Miguel himself, who didn't seem the sort of person to ever go by the ritual book. His long hair, designer stubble, sunglasses, jeans and jewellery made him look more rock star than shaman.

As if aware of my thoughts, he began to speak again.

In many San Pedro ceremonies the shaman demands certain things from participants: that they are cleansed by water and purges, and so on. These things are, in our view, unnecessary. They get in the way of the healing San Pedro offers.

In the tradition I am now part of, we do not expect such things. The reason is simple: we have faith in San Pedro. We are fortunate, through this plant, to be granted an audience with God, and we do not expect you look the other way or ignore what is given in favour of cold baths and beatings with sticks!

In our ceremony, therefore, I will protect you, watch over you, and offer you assistance if you request it, but there will be nothing for you to do and I will disturb you and the plant as little as possible.

If you are familiar with San Pedro, you will know that most ceremonies take place at night. Another difference is that this one, of course, does not.

It was true that every other ceremony I'd attended, including those of Juan Navarro, was an all-night affair that did not begin until the sun had dropped well behind the mountains.

Bonnie Glass-Coffin explains in her book that this is because (for her shamans, at least)

> the light of the night sky is always associated with God and humankind. As Isabel [another San Pedro shaman] told me, stars are the eyes of God. Just as she must see to heal her victims of the evil from which they suffer, God will guide her mesa services so long as He can see. She never begins her ritual until she can see at least one star in the sky above and know that God is watching over her actions.

The Andean healer, Eduardo Calderon, had a similar perspective about how and when ceremonies should proceed.

> One sings from ten until midnight. The cure is from one in the morning, the beginning, the genesis of the day, until three or four in the morning. At six in the morning everything terminates. Six is the opening of the new day. At this moment the 'third eye' closes because it is now that the force of the sun flowers, in the same sense as did the San Pedro, which bloomed in the night, giving its own light, its own vital energy.[4]

29

Here with Miguel, however, we were bathed in sunlight and it was barely 11am. Miguel continued:

What some shamans keep hidden is that the power of San Pedro comes from the sun. The cactus grows in dry landscapes and in sunlight. Daytime is its active phase, when it draws power from the Earth and sky. Night is its dreaming phase, when it uses this power for regeneration. We work *with* this natural cycle and with the spirit of San Pedro, not against them. That is why our ceremonies take place by day.

This also means that the world around you, no longer masked by darkness, will come fully to life under the guidance of this plant. Colours are brighter when your eyes are opened and the world takes on its real form, so you will see and sense its energies around you. These things are always there, of course, but in shadow. Sunlight and San Pedro reveal them.

The third difference – and perhaps more important for today's work – is that San Pedro is cooked by most shamans for eight or even four hours in order to liberate its spirit.[5] The brew you are about to drink, however, has been cooked for twenty and is unparalleled in its power.

In short, what you are about to receive is true San Pedro and an authentic ceremony of healing, not a tourist performance.

With that, he held up a bottle in front of him, presented it to the four directions, and offered a half-whispered prayer before pouring its thick green contents into three mugs. Each vessel, decorated with ritual designs, held around a pint of the mucousy fluid. It looked similar to, but unlike, the thinner, more watery brews I had drunk before. 'The taste is not delightful,' said Miguel. 'I suggest you drink it quickly.'

I had already decided that I would drink first since the others were here at my suggestion and I felt a sense of responsibility towards them. This was just as well as it turned out because Miguel, without knowing my thoughts on the matter, had arrived at the same idea and handed the first cup to me.

San Pedro has the taste and consistency of snot. That was how I'd described it before when people had asked. It is nowhere near as unpleasant as ayahuasca, however, which can, at times, taste like the worst kind of Chinese medicine blended with something indescribable but recognisably vile. By contrast, the cactus is only slightly salty, earthy, and a little bitter, but mostly it is bland.

It is its texture that most people find more of a problem. If not snot, then frogspawn or pond slime would be apt descriptions; an impression reinforced by its light green colour and lingering aftertaste, which is ever-so-slightly that of stale water.

I gagged once, halfway through, but before I could throw up I conquered my body's urges – just. Then, through an act of will more than a desire to finish, I swallowed the rest. Mark and Donna struggled too, but we all kept it down.

Miguel wished us a good journey then left us to sit a distance away where he could watch over our group but not intrude on the experiences we were bound for. Touched by the sun, we found our shade and lay down, giving ourselves to what dreams might come.

Chapter 3

The World beyond Paradise
A Personal Perspective: The Healing
Experience of San Pedro

One frightens oneself.
It is not the shadow that frightens one
Eduardo Calderon

Some time passed and I began to feel cold.

Part of me knew that I couldn't actually *be* cold, however, because the sun was hot and the air so warm around us. I checked myself again and noticed I was sweating. But if I wasn't cold, then why were my muscles cramping?

It was a simple question but even this, and the words I was using to ask it, began to confuse and overwhelm me. It was like I couldn't think straight or find the *right* words and was becoming entangled by definitions.

If the cramping wasn't 'cramping'... then what was it? More a tightening and relaxation of the muscles, like the movements of a snake. There was no pain (it was almost sensual, in fact), but its unceasing regularity – and the sensation itself, which was like small jolts of electricity pulsing through my legs – was unfamiliar and uncomfortable, and I grew irritated as the cycle repeated itself and I began to anticipate and then wait for the next jolt to arrive.

I was also frustrated at myself for getting caught up in so much thought, so much trying and failing to find the right word to describe what I was feeling, as if I had no control over my own mind. I willed myself to relax and end my pointless mental chatter so I could let go and just experience.

To get myself 'out of my head', I turned my attention to my body. The cramps – if that is what I was choosing to call them – began in my feet, then my calves, and spread upwards to my thighs, stomach and torso. By the time they reached my shoulders I had forgotten my irritation and was fascinated. I sat up and held my arms out in front of me so I could study them, convinced I would be able to see my skin and muscles moving.

What I saw, though, was even more intriguing. My arms – along with my legs and body – were no longer 'me' at all; no longer even human. My skin had become yellow-green and my arms had grown ridges and furrows from which brittle hairs were sprouting. Their appearance reminded me of something but it took me a while before I knew what it was. Then it dawned on me: a cactus. I had *become* a cactus.

I understood what was happening then and what these cramps were all about: San Pedro, the cactus brew I had drunk, had become an electrical charge moving through my body, transforming me until I became San Pedro itself, possessed by it. From the feet up, it was 'checking me out' and resolving areas of weakness it found in me. The cramps in my muscles were a response to its gentle surgery, like something passing through me and being shaken off and expunged.

This was a wholly new experience for me, even after years of working with other plant teachers and even with San Pedro itself: a total awareness on every level that the cactus was really *in* me. Or, rather, it *was* me, absorbed into who or whatever 'I' thought I was.

For what now felt like the first time in my life, I was aware – without the shadow of a doubt – that plants have a consciousness that is unique to them and that I was in the presence of a whole and other intelligence that was more powerful than me and had its own agenda for my healing.

The wisest action I could think of was to do nothing, and

certainly not interfere with whatever San Pedro's intentions were, especially as I had invited it into my body for precisely this purpose. Although they are odd words to use, to do anything else, it seemed to me now, would appear rude and ungrateful and I did not want to offend the plant.

Frankly, however, I doubted that there was much I *could* do to control the experience anyway given the power of San Pedro so far, so I laid back down instead and tried to relax while the cactus did its work, resolving to put up with the... not discomfort exactly, but the unusual sensations that accompany a healing on this scale.

I must have drifted then and time as measured by clocks must have passed because I 'came to' again at some point later with a vague awareness that my conscious mind – that which I think of as 'me' – was no longer a part of my experience. Instead, it felt as if 'I' was standing behind myself, observing calmly as my body went through its changes.

This sense of calm detachment increased until something happened that is hard to describe. It was as if San Pedro gathered together all of my energy and swept it into the wind. A more prosaic, but no more elegant or descriptively useful way of putting this would be to say that my soul left my body. From that moment, for what seemed like hours, I *became* the wind, unaware of anything else except being.

If the wind can have feelings, it felt wonderful to be this free. Wind is everywhere and blows where it wishes, from one side of the world to the other in an instant. It moves like a fluid, like water, its atoms uncontained like ours, so that one drop is all drops, even if they are separated by an ocean.

The writer, Kurt Vonnegut, once described Paradise as a place where 'Everything is beautiful and nothing hurts'. That is how it is to be wind. You breathe the sky, are breathed, and are breath itself – all of it at once. You are vast and connected to everything and, at the same time, wholly and totally free.

Somehow, from the perspective of the wind, you understand – not gradually, but with a gentle immediacy – that the meaning of truth is to view all eventualities and things from a place beyond space, time, and comparisons or judgements of any kind. All judgements are, after all, self-centred, ambiguous, meaningless and ultimately irrelevant. They are also ridiculous, hilarious, and faux, even if they are the stuff by which we manufacture our daily realities. And so, of course, 'reality' is therefore suspect too.

My rational mind, normally filled with its usual roster of conceits, deceits, denials, affirmations, questions, judgements, and busy, self-absorbed concerns about what was real and unreal in the world had been put firmly on hold by San Pedro, and some new intelligence – one not my own –propelled me to a new understanding. The simplest of concepts – those I had learned to take for granted in the familiar world which I had consumed and been consumed by – became unfathomably complex or obviously false while those that philosophers have struggled with for centuries – the meaning of life, the nature of truth, and the destiny of souls, among them – revealed themselves in answers that were suddenly incredibly simple.

Time (as a concept, at least, rather than something felt and experienced) shifted again and, at some other point in my San Pedro journey, I started to feel more 'human' again as it dawned on me that this wind I had become was also contained by my lungs and that it was my breath – and my thoughts contained within it – which was everywhere. It was as if my lungs were great bellows, pumping my life force, desires, and intentions into the world where they flowed across landscapes as a presence in the clouds, the mountains and trees.

I read some years ago that while we may vanish from the Earth at our deaths, our breath never really does so that everyone who has ever lived leaves some part of themselves in the air. Every time we inhale, therefore, we may be filling our lungs with fragments from the last breath of Christ or the sad remonstrations of a dying Caesar.

When I first come across this idea it intrigued me but only really as a concept: something to throw out at dinner parties and spark a conversation. Now that I had *experienced* the intelligence of the wind, however, I understood the power of this 'living breath' and the energy it contained: the wisdom that is available to me simply by breathing. I was aware, too, of the responsibility I carried for my own breath and the thoughts – good or bad – that it may contain.

Many religions speak of the 'breath of life' and many shamans of the presence of spirit around us. The intelligence of air and the wisdom (or otherwise) it holds may therefore still, in some small way, continue to influence us through the currents that eddy around us and the ideas and philosophies contained there which, simply by breathing in, become an everyday part of us.

My thoughts were interrupted by a new body sensation as San Pedro led me out of my head and back to the physical world. I *felt* my lungs and then other organs forming around them. More magical than my realisation that the air was filled with spirit was this simple truth: *I have a body*!

With that, it was as if a lightening bolt hit me full in the back. I felt it first and then, in my mind's eye, saw it: crackling white and electric blue energy coursing through my lungs, spine, torso, and up into my skull.

The force of it jolted me to my knees, threw open my arms, and compelled me to inhale more deeply than I knew I could. The air tasted like honey, mint, and mist – like the first breath I ever took when I came into this world – and with it the breathlessness of the altitude sickness that had bothered me since my arrival in Cusco was completely gone.

In its place was fresh air that I could breathe with absolute ease. Later (in a rather pathetic attempt at 'scientific enquiry'), I would have four cigarettes in a row to test this new ability. Every one tasted like air and, through that, I came to understand two things: firstly, that for the first time in days, my lungs were completely clear, and my wheezing and struggle to breathe at altitude had left my body entirely. Secondly, that every illness I have ever had, including this altitude sickness, was absolutely a matter of my own choice.

Before San Pedro, I had been resigned to sickness because 'I always get ill when I travel at altitude' and, without even a fight, my beliefs had allowed the spirit of sickness to consume me. San Pedro had expelled this spirit – along with my self-limiting beliefs – and taught me that *nothing* in life, including illness, is automatic or necessary but demands an agreement from us to *be ill*, to define ourselves in that way.

After this, the visions deepened. I found myself in a desert, beside a great white wall of stones. It was so tall that the top could not be seen and it ran on forever in both directions. It knew that it was the wall to Paradise and I was outside it in the desert of the 'normal world'.

It was terrifying. There was nothing there, just a desert; remote, barren, and bleak. I had turned my body away from it, trying to make myself as small as possible so that the world would not notice me, and I was even holding my breath in case I was heard. Inside, though, my soul was screaming to be let back into Eden.

Saint Peter held the keys and from him there was a gentle, but definite and insistent, no. His answer was delivered as if by a parent who knew what was best for his child. I realised then that I had *chosen* to walk outside his gates, like a child leaving home, to experience, explore and to know life, or perhaps for a lesson to be learned, and my pleadings now were a form of reneging on the decision I had made. That understanding did nothing to stop my terror however; it only added to the futility of my situation in the face of these desert surroundings.

And then I noticed something: a figure in the desert, standing on a low hill, overlooking the empty sand, with his back to me. He was dressed in black, in a sort of matador's costume, and in his hand was a sword.

A quiet strength and confidence radiated from him and I had a sense that this was the spirit of San Pedro, sent to help me with my fears. The words of a Stephen Crane poem began to echo, some distance off, in my brain:

I walked in a desert.
And I cried,
'Ah, God, take me from this place!'
A voice said:
'It is no desert.'
I cried, *'Well, But –*
The sand, the heat, the vacant horizon.'
A voice said:
'It is no desert.'

I pulled myself together and walked towards the matador-spirit and stood alongside him. For the first time since I had found myself beyond the gates of Paradise, I didn't feel afraid any more but, rather, an odd mix of resignation and confidence, perhaps even excitement. If I had to find a single word for it, I would say I felt dignity.

I understood then that everyone on Earth is alone and excluded from Paradise, just as I was, whether by their own decisions or not, and we were all utterly terrified deep within our souls. In the face of our fear, however, there is still a correct way to act and that is with strength, impeccability – and dignity – not by holding our breaths and trying to make ourselves small. By doing so, I now realised, I had caused my own illness. My negative beliefs had created a negative – and very real – outcome for my body.

The matador-spirit drew a line with his sword in the sand: a circle of protection around us that the world could not pass. 'This is how we control our fears and how we preserve our power,' I heard him say (although he spoke without words if he actually spoke at all). 'By knowing our centre and holding it with quiet esteem and gratitude for our lives, we honour the experiences we have chosen.'

I saw myself then drinking San Pedro a thousand times in a thousand different lifetimes... all of my soul's long history drawn back to this place again and again to hear the same message. I'd been here before, I had no doubt, but San Pedro had somehow enabled me to forget, so I would return in this lifetime and drink again – and maybe in the next lifetime too – until its message finally became part of my soul.

I opened my eyes then and found that the garden had come to life and changed every aspect of its nature. Things around me were shining with an iridescence I had never seen before. A flower border in front of me had become a river of chocolate where diamonds sparkled that before had been dirt and stones. The yellow of a flower was so bright that I withdrew from it in shock. There was a beauty to the world that was not fearful at all but amazing and almost beyond my ability to take it in. Everything was fresh and remarkable... and nothing hurt.

I turned to Mark who was sitting up now, staring at the grass and its million shades of green. His body was shaking with energy and he was saying something about a hummingbird... about hummingbird energy flowing through him. No sooner had he said it than four of them flew into the garden and danced like bright darts between the shimmering flowers. I pointed them out to him.

Later, we would have to agree on the strange and wonderful poetry behind the appearance of these birds. Firstly, because San Pedro has for millennia been associated with the hummingbird, which the shamans regard as its guardian spirit. Secondly, because I had, seemingly by chance alone, told the story of the hummingbird and the condor only a few days before. Its moral – that faith, courage, surrender, and the desire to know God are sometimes more important than strength – was the message of the matador-spirit too: that dignity not fear, confidence not arrogance, and power not force, are the keys to seeing the world as divine and ensouled.

The appearance of these birds could not just be dismissed as coincidence, then, but felt more like a sign: a reflection of the true order of reality that San Pedro had revealed to us but which is always there, as Miguel had said, just below the surface of everything.

I closed my eyes again at the brightness of the sun and its energy which rippled like waves and when I opened them again, what felt like a second later, it was night and Miguel and Donna were standing before me. They had been walking on the hillside at the Temple of the Moon, where they had watched the sky turn red and then black. The ceremony had ended and Miguel had arranged a taxi home for us.

I had no idea how I was going to stand or put my shoes and coat back on. I began to prepare for problems of co-ordination, effort and struggle, and then I stopped myself. Wasn't this exactly what San Pedro had taught me about illness: that it was dependant on my thoughts and the way that I saw things? Yet, here I was again, imagining – and so, literally creating – new problems for myself.

More of Kurt Vonnegut's words rattled around in my brain: 'Be careful what you pretend to be – because you *are* what you pretend to be'.

I decided on a new choice then: that standing would be easy and dressing would be simple – and they were. Both were perfect and effortless. So was walking. It felt like the first steps I'd ever taken: amazing, exciting, and fascinating. My body just knew how to do it and even when the path became uneven my feet adjusted to it all by themselves. Walking was a joy and my body felt full of brilliance and power.

Up on the hillside, the sky arced around us, completely filled with stars. I marvelled at them and watched the light from each one mingle with that of its companions, as if greetings and secrets were being exchanged.

'How was your journey?' Miguel asked, bringing me back to Earth in his quiet and gentle way. I just looked at him. I couldn't speak yet – or perhaps I just didn't want to, because I knew I would be able to if I chose. Anything was possible now.

'Ah, I understand,' he said. 'You are not so strong now, eh, Mr Ross!'

He meant it well and I understood that he was talking about the different power that San Pedro imparts, stripping away the fake-strength we surround ourselves with as a protection from our fears of the world and replacing it with genuine power and a sense of awe at who we really are, what we are capable of, and the true nature of creation and the world. It is a softer strength: power not force that blends humility with the knowledge that this world – in a good way – is *ours*.

Below us, the lights of Cusco sparkled like Atlantis as our taxi made its way down the hill. Miguel came with us to our lodgings and said his goodbyes when we were safe inside.

Mark went to his room but Donna and I stayed up to talk. She, too, had seen a matador-spirit exactly like my own. She, too, had felt San Pedro reshape her and watched the breath of the world as it passed across the mountains.

We had shared almost the same vision on a journey that, in the blink of an eye, had lasted for more than eight hours and was still continuing now.

With ayahuasca, it is not uncommon for people to share a visual image. The brew was once known by the scientific name telepathine for its abilities in this respect. Jeremy Narby writes of one common image, the cosmic serpent, in his book of the same name.[1] Dr Benny Shanon, professor of psychology at the Hebrew

University of Jerusalem, records others in his exhaustive book, *The Antipodes of the Mind*;[2] among them images of the natural world and the aliveness of nature, pictures of palaces and healing temples, and scenes from the participant's own life that are invested by the plant with new meaning. Some of these images are similar to those I had experienced with San Pedro, and in many previous ayahuasca ceremonies.

What is less common with ayahuasca though, I think, is for people to share a *vision*, as Donna and I had done: an *understanding*, *realisation* and *transmutation* of visual imagery into a wholly *felt* and *experienced* sense of the world and the self that was not so much personal as transpersonal in nature.

'Overall,' says Shanon, 'it seems that ayahuasca leads people to the conclusion that the world contains both good and evil, that the two are intertwined, and that the ultimate reality is beyond good and evil.' This, again, is not dissimilar to the understanding that Donna and I had arrived at with San Pedro. But I think we would both argue from experience – if this does not sound too grand – that ayahuasca tells you something very personal about yourself and your standing in the eyes of the universe, whereas San Pedro reveals the laws of the universe itself. The experience is less *personal*, less about *you*, and more about truth, reality, and your relationship to it.

To me, the qualitative difference between the two plants seemed clear though it is, of course, hard to express in words, especially if you have not experienced these plants for yourself.

Firstly, with ayahuasca, the information and images received are, in my experience and that of the participants I have worked with, more fleeting, more 'serpentine' – undulating and less direct – and they take place more frequently and with greater intensity with the eyes closed so that one is more deeply involved with what arises *within the mind* as a consequence of contacting the spiritual world.

San Pedro, by contrast, does not create fleeting images but

rather one overriding image or philosophical point that it explores in singular depth. In this way it appears to reveal *practical truths* that can be applied directly to the world, to life, and to healing.

The journey is, of course, also longer (with ayahuasca perhaps four hours; with San Pedro perhaps ten or more) as we are led by the cactus towards this single truth and held there until we have explored it in all of its aspects and felt it deeply in our bodies and souls.

The key difference, then, it seems to me, is that ayahuasca takes us *out* of our bodies and into the unseen world, where we may be taught by spirit and return to reflect upon what we have learned. San Pedro, meanwhile, is of *this world*. It teaches us to see the spirit and beauty already around us and apply its lessons to the business of living.

The closest parallel to my experience with San Pedro, in fact, is not ayahuasca, strangely enough, but chemical DMT, in the account of a participant (Sara) in Rick Strassman's book, *DMT: The Spirit Molecule*.[3]

I was terrified. I felt abandoned. I'm completely and totally lost. I have never been so alone. How can you describe what it feels to be the only entity in the universe?

The essence of who I am was alone in the void, back in the staging area for life where souls wait to incarnate. The singing angels were there only to observe me, not to comfort me.

Sara's experience, similar to my own where I found myself outside the walls of Paradise in the presence of an unrelenting Saint Peter, ultimately resolved itself and was positive, as was mine. The biggest difference between the two is really only the agent involved. Perhaps there is something, then – some intelligence within all psychedelics – that can, in some cases and under certain conditions, reveal to us common and fundamental truths about the world.

San Pedro is not just about spiritual healing or a change in our life's philosophy and choices, however. At the perfect moment, about two hours after Miguel's ceremony ended, I felt a need to purge.

Other shamans had taught me that when we vomit it is not just matter that leaves our bodies but toxic thoughts and energies we are holding on to from unsatisfactory events in our lives. When we purge it is a blessing and a healing and sometimes as we vomit we can see what is leaving our bodies and know what is being removed.

The puke in my sink looked like rust and old relationships and the assumptions and expectations from these that had become so ingrained in me that they had been central to who I was – like the urge to see problems before beauty. As I threw up, these toxic thoughts and their effects on my body were removed and now I felt completely at peace.

For the next day, all three of us – Mark, Donna and I – were on a high and the information we had been given, which had changed us all in some way, continued to pulse in our bodies. We felt healthier and more whole than we had since leaving the jungle or, perhaps, than ever before.

San Pedro shamans say – and I have noticed this in myself – that the information the cactus provides never really leaves us once given, and the changes it brings can be permanent... if we choose.

My thoughts and behaviour are different now because I know, as I never quite did before, that I have *choice* – and I understand the power of that and what it really means.

I *choose* not to see problems in the world any more but to reconnect with the matador-spirit of San Pedro who is still somewhere inside me, and to live with the dignity and strength to honour the teachings I was given.

As for Donna, she later wrote down her recollections of her

experience with San Pedro and her conclusions from it. They are similar to my own.

> It was the most powerful, profound experience of my life. Before this, I had *intellectually* understood about us coming from, and one day returning to, energy; I had even glimpsed it in the past. But on this occasion I *became* energy. I completely dissolved – no room for ego! I breathed with the sky. I *became* the Breath of Life, Infinite and Eternal Love.
>
> I now dedicate my life to walking with honour and integrity and to accepting life's path rather than trying to dictate it.
>
> If everyone experienced this the world would be very different. It has become better for me already.

Because of my past experiences with Juan Navarro and others, I never expected to receive so much from San Pedro and perhaps that in itself is significant; one key to its power – that letting go of expectations and relaxing fully into the pure experience of the plant without all the ritual distractions of the past – is itself vitally important. By doing so, after ten years of 'failures', I finally came to know its essence and I discovered a remarkable healer.

And so, in a way, all the times I had drunk San Pedro before and received so little from it were in preparation for this moment... so I would approach it with no agenda and allow its spirit to show me what I most needed to know.

As a result of my experience, a few months later I purchased a copy of Aldous Huxley's book, *The Doors of Perception*, a work I had first read perhaps twenty years before but felt relatively little connection to at the time because I did not then have a frame of reference by which to fully understand it.

The book is an account of Huxley's personal experiences and realisations following his own ingestion of mescaline. Reading it again now, several passages found resonance with me.

'We live together, we act on, and react to, one another, but always and in all circumstances we are by ourselves. The martyrs go hand in hand into the arena; they are crucified alone. Embraced, the lovers desperately try to fuse their insulated ecstasies into a single self-transcendence; in vain. By its very nature every embodied spirit is doomed to suffer and enjoy its solitude... From family to nation, every human group is a society of island universes.' And yet, 'The urge to transcend self-conscious selfhood is, as I have said, a principal appetite of the soul.'

For Huxley, mescaline was one of the routes to this transcendence. He writes of the world when seen through its eyes that 'I was seeing what Adam had seen on the morning of his creation – the miracle, moment by moment, of naked existence... flowers shining with their own inner light and all but quivering under the pressure of the significance with which they were charged... a transience that was yet eternal life... the divine source of all existence.

'I continued to look at the flowers, and in their living light I seemed to detect the qualitative equivalent of breathing – but of a breathing without returns to a starting-point, with no recurrent ebbs but only a repeated flow from beauty to heightened beauty, from deeper to ever deeper meaning.'

That feeling of aloneness and, once reconciled, the awareness of the majesty and beauty of the world and the significance of the breath that blows through it were all suddenly familiar to me – and to Donna who had *become* "the Breath of Life" during her own journey. These things, these insights and sensations, these crucial realisations were a *part* of San Pedro, it seemed: the message its spirit was there to deliver.

But could there be a deeper significance to this message, I wondered. What was it exactly that San Pedro wanted us to *know*?

Chapter 4

Hummingbird Medicine
The History and Use of San Pedro

God won't lie to you. He is. He exists.
He is a spirit in your heart and in your thoughts.
Only He is there. And He, in your subconscience, is going to tell
you:
Yes, yes, yes, you are going to be cured
Isabel, Andean healer[1]

After my experience with San Pedro at the Temple of the Moon, I was alive for days and I knew that I had to find out more about this incredible teacher that, to my great shame, I had so overlooked before.

My enthusiasm waned, however, as I discovered just how little information there was to discover. A Google search produced next to nothing and, having explored other avenues, I was amazed that almost no research had been done into San Pedro or its effects and, indeed, that almost nothing had been written about it.[2] Here was a miracle plant that no one seemed interested in. Given the experience I had been through, the concordance of that with the healings that Donna and Mark had received, and the new life that Miguel had been given (a 100% success rate among the four who had drunk that particular brew – a limited sample, admittedly, but still an impressive result), it seemed bizarre that no one had taken San Pedro seriously before.

At least in part, this lack of information is no doubt a reflection of the fact that the most ancient healing traditions of Peru, like those of other pre-Christian cultures, are transmitted orally. Not much is ever written down by the shamans and healers themselves, so where such records exist they have tended to be made by European explorers, invaders or missionaries who have brought their beliefs with them and denigrated indigenous practices that did not, on the face of it, sit well with their notions of God.

As professor of cultural anthropology, Irene Silverblatt, puts it:

> History making (which includes history denying) is a cultural invention... History tends to be 'made' by those who dominate... and then universalised to celebrate their heroes and silence dissent.[3]

Such commentaries have always tended to distort the native experience. One 16th century conquistador (quoted by the ethnobotanist, Richard Evans Schultes), for example, described San Pedro as a plant used by heathens to 'speak with the devil', not God; a devil who apparently answered them via 'certain stones and in other things they venerate'.[4]

A Spanish missionary described San Pedro similarly, as:

> A plant with whose aid the devil is able to strengthen the Indians in their idolatry; those who drink its juice lose their senses and are as if dead; they are almost carried away by the drink and dream a thousand unusual things and believe that they are true.[5]

Another, Father Olivia, part of a 17th century Church-sponsored scheme to 'extirpate idolatries', wrote in 1631 that:

> After they drink it they [participants in San Pedro ceremonies] remain without judgement and deprived of their senses and they see visions that the Devil represents to them and consistent with them they judge their suspicions and the

intentions of others.[6]

Fundamentalism like this rarely results in any pure or useful critique and, as Jim DeKorne remarks in *Psychedelic Shamanism*[7], rather than trying to understand native customs, 'the Spanish Inquisition reacted with characteristic savagery to anyone who dared to break their laws by eating it [San Pedro]'.

As a result of their attempts to maintain a connection to their own gods 'a great many Indians were flogged and sometimes killed when they persisted in using [San Pedro]... [One man's] eyeballs were said to be gouged out after three days of torture; then the Spaniards cut a crucifix pattern in his belly and turned ravenous dogs loose on his innards'.[8]

The anthropologist and ethnobotanist Wade Davis may well understate the case, therefore, when he suggests that the result of such prejudices and pressures was that indigenous practices, including the original rituals and ceremonies surrounding the use of San Pedro, 'undoubtedly were transformed'.[9]

'Transformed' may not be the half of it. As Jim DeKorne remarks, 'This level of response to the ingestion of... San Pedro in Peru effectively drove the use of [the cactus] underground for hundreds of years'.[10]

Even the current name of the re-emergent sacred plant may owe more to Catholicism than to its original personality, meaning or intention, as understood by the shamans of the Andes, for the cactus, as DeKorne relates, was renamed after Saint Peter, 'guardian of the threshold for the Catholic Paradise... an apparent strategy of the Indians to placate the Inquisition'.

The ceremonies that emerged from its years of underground usage may have been so radically altered that the post-colonial use of San Pedro possibly bears little resemblance to its ritual first form, which might well have been closer to the ceremony performed by Miguel than versions by shamans like Juan

Navarro that incorporate far more Catholic symbolism, procedures, meanings, and artefacts in their healing.

Neither the oral tradition nor the distortions by Europeans
fully explain the absence of information on San Pedro, however.
After all, the same situations apply to ayahuasca and the other
planta maestros (or 'master teacher plants') of Peru.

The training of ayahuasca shamans (*ayahuasceros*) and the
nature of their ceremonies is also part of an oral tradition, for
example, and the use of ayahuasca has been equally demonised
by non-native observers – and yet scientists and others have been
exploring the vine of souls and writing about it for years. Some,
like Dr Jaques Mabit, have even succeeded in popularising the
brew and having it at least debated within mainstream medical
circles, following his observations that remarkable healings are
possible through its use, including a 70% recovery rate from
alcohol and drug addiction.[11]

More fundamentally, and more so than with ayahuasca, there
is a sort of mystery surrounding San Pedro and a sense that
knowledge of the plant must remain secret or, at least earned
through preparation, participation, and the worthiness of those
who drink it.

Juan Navarro, with whom I drank San Pedro in the 1990s, says
something similar: that it has 'a certain mystery to it' – and I
wondered if Miguel may not have been right that shamans like
Juan perform their rituals with crosses and staffs and hold their
ceremonies at night as a sort of mask, to retain a degree of secrecy
about the way things really were (and perhaps still are) done
within the tradition.

A similar situation exists in Haiti, as I discovered during
research for my book, *Vodou Shaman*.[12] During the slave trade,
thousands of Africans were transported to this Caribbean island
and baptised at the point of a gun into the Catholic religion of
their new Spanish owners. As a form of social control, their old
gods were denied to them and their ceremonies prohibited.

The average life expectancy for a slave on Haiti was just two years and, in fear of death, they marched their bodies into Catholic churches to pray to God and the Virgin. Their spirits were not so easily controlled, however, and the souls of the slaves remained in Africa with their old traditions.

Thus, the houngans (priests and healers) I have spoken to are clear that the Catholic symbols for God and the Virgin mean something very different to them than the slave owners would recognise. God is Bondye, the sun and the cosmos; the Virgin is Erzuli, the spirit of love and abundance; Ogoun is the spirit of power, equivalent to Saint Peter (or San Pedro) in the Vodou, Santeria, and Palo traditions. For every Catholic saint there is a parallel in the African system of belief.

The slaves knelt before Christian icons and even incorporated them into their ritual practices, changing forever the nature of their original ceremonies and methods of prayer, but, still, the God to whom a Haitian prays is not the God of the Spanish and the cross does not signify Jesus but the meeting of spirit and matter.

By the same token, when Juan Navarro performs a ceremony, he prays to God, the saints, the Virgin, and to Jesus, and he holds the cross aloft, but these emblems have a different meaning to him than to a European. Some anthropologists suggest, for example, that the Virgin of Guadalupe, whose image is ubiquitous in Andean healing rituals, is in fact a Christianised version of the Aztec lunar goddess, Tonantzin, so whoever Juan is praying to, it is not the Virgin we know.

At the same time, and irrespective of all of these symbols and their ambiguous meanings, Juan is clear that 'The cactus is a powerful teacher [and] the healer must be compatible with it.' It is *the cactus* and not the Virgin – however she is conceived of or represented – that teaches and heals and for whom the shaman must have a love and affinity and with whom he must undergo a blending of power.

Juan's rituals are a merging of beliefs, symbols and practices. The form they take may be the mask they wear but their true power comes from something beyond Earthly symbols: the world opened up by San Pedro.

If these speculations are correct then Miguel's ceremonies, stripped of Christian symbols, are a return to a sort of ritual first form and a quiet revolutionary statement in their own right. I resolved to put these questions to Miguel later – or to his teacher if I could meet her – and for now discover what I could about San Pedro, the cactus of vision and mystery.

Physically, San Pedro (*Trichocereus pachanoi*) is a tall blue-green cactus reaching heights of seven metres or more. Its cylindrical branches produce a funnel-shaped flower of green-tinged white, which itself can grow to ten inches or so. It enjoys a tough, desert-like environment and grows readily in the highest parts of Peru such as the Yunga and Quechua regions (2,300 metres and 3,500 metres above sea level respectively) between Piura, Lambayeque, and La Libertad, and in the Huancabamba Valley.

It has many names among shamans and healers, including *cardo, chuma, gigantón, hermoso, huando, pene de Dios*[13], *wachuma*, and, simply, *El Remedio*: The Remedy – the latter referring to its healing powers and its ability to help those who drink it let go of 'the illusions of the world'.

Another Quechua name, *punku*, also suggests this quality. The word means 'doorway', since the cactus is considered able to open a portal into a world beyond illusion so that healing and visions can flow from the spiritual to the physical dimensions.

Even its more common name, San Pedro, has similar connotations. It refers to Saint Peter, who holds the keys to Heaven, and is suggestive of the plant's power to open the gates between the visible and invisible worlds, the sacred and profane, so those who drink it enter a realm where they can heal, know their true natures, and find purpose for their lives. 'Just as the saint called San Pedro is "keeper of the keys... and guardian of the doors of

Heaven", so the San Pedro plant is called "guardian of the doors of remedy",' as Olinda, an Andean curandera put it.[14]

Some of the shamans I have spoken to, no doubt informed by their country's colonial history, believe that Saint Peter, appalled at the behaviour of the Spanish, hid the keys to Paradise so only those who renounced their violence and lust for gold would ever find them and truly know God. Saint Peter's somewhat ironic hiding place was the cactus, a pagan sacrament that existed for centuries before the coming of Catholics and Conquistadors.

According to these shamans, however, it was not necessarily Saint Peter's intention that the invaders should renounce their religion and return to pagan beliefs in order for them to meet God. On the contrary, San Pedro recognised no one 'true religion' and required only that people find the *'spirit* of God', as an energy or cosmic force within themselves, and act in a reverent and dignified manner instead of giving in to the frenzied desire for riches which so seemed to drive them.

The curandero, Eduardo Calderon, defined this force or 'spirit of God' in the following way:

Many think of God the way the Christians depict him: as a bearded man with the world in his hands. Others in other forms. But God is the cosmic energy within ourselves. Yes, we are part of God because we have that energy and this energy is an elemental force that allows us to converge at an important point, which is curing.[15]

What the cactus demanded, then, was not religious adherence but purity: a return to a first state where love and healing replaced Earthly illusions and the lust for gold that seemed to dictate the Spaniards' actions.

Among healers, San Pedro is also known as *huachuma* and the shamans who work with it are called *huachumeros* if male and *huachumeras* if female. Its use as a sacrament and in healing rituals is ancient. The earliest archaeological evidence so far discovered for this is a stone carving of a huachumero found at the Jaguar Temple of Chavín de Huantar in northern Peru which is almost 3,500 years old, dating to at least 1300 years before the origins of the religion brought to Peru by the Spanish.

Textiles from the same region and period of history depict the cactus with jaguars and hummingbirds, its guardian spirits, and with stylised spirals representing the visionary experiences brought on by the plant.

A decorated ceramic pot from the Chimú culture of Peru, dating to AD 1200, has also been unearthed which shows an owl-faced woman holding a cactus. In the Andes, the owl is the tutelary spirit and guardian of herbalists and shamans, and the woman depicted is therefore most likely a curandera and huachumera.

Some of the reasons that San Pedro ceremonies were (and continue to be) held are: to cure illnesses of a spiritual, emotional, mental or physical nature; to know the future through the prophetic and divinatory qualities of the plant; to overcome sorcery or *saladera* (an inexplicable run of bad luck); to ensure success in one's ventures; to rekindle love and enthusiasm for life; and to restore one's faith or find meaning by re-experiencing the world as divine.

San Pedro can perform healings like these because, in the words of a shaman quoted by Schultes, it is

in tune with the powers of animals and beings that have supernatural powers... Participants [in ceremonies] are set free from matter and engage in flight through cosmic regions... transported across time and distance in a rapid and safe fashion.[16]

He also describes the effects of the plant as this healing takes place:

First, a dreamy state... then great visions, a clearing of all the faculties... and then detachment, a type of visual force inclusive of the sixth sense, the telepathic state of transmitting oneself across time and matter, like a removal of thoughts to a distant dimension.

Like ayahuasca, San Pedro is always taken as part of a shamanic ceremony with the intention of healing; it is never taken lightly, and never as a 'recreational drug' in the way that some Westerners have been known to use similar plants of power.

Healing, in a ceremony like this, is defined more widely than a Western doctor might understand the term and means an ultimately beneficial or positive change in the mental, emotional, or spiritual dimensions of one's life, as well, often, as a physical cure or change.

Wade Davis described a ceremony performed in 1981, for example, where the people present included a girl who had been paralysed and was suffering from back and stomach pains, members of a family whose cattle had become diseased, a person seeking healing for a relative who had gone mad, a man who had become unstable after seeing his wife with her lover, and a businessman wanting to know who had stolen money from his company.

To us, the last reason for attending may appear to bear little or no similarity to the first, but, in the Andean view of healing, the ability to bring order to one's financial and business affairs is just as valid in terms of restoring balance to the soul and peace to the mind as relieving the pains of a paralysed girl. Both are healing in this sense.

Many of these ceremonies, like Juan Navarro's – and perhaps for the reasons we have discussed (of masking the true nature of San Pedro or because of the imposition of Catholic ideas and procedures) – involve their participants in lengthy and challenging procedures. Others, like Miguel's, are less demanding so that the 'true healer', the spirit of the plant, is given the freedom to work directly with participants in the way that it sees fit. In the latter case, the shaman defers to San Pedro, which he regards as the real healing force, rather than conducting a stylised ritual that in effect puts the shaman centre-stage.

Whatever the inclination of the shaman, however, the mesa is always involved. According to Eduardo Calderon,

> The mesa is the important part of a curing session for the simple reason that it is the panel where all the elemental forces are computed.[17]

The mesa (the word literally means 'table') is an altar that may be elaborate or simple, again, depending on the shaman. Most are woven fabrics laid directly on the earth.

In their field of power they contain objects (or artes: 'arts') that hold spiritual energy; these may include artefacts from archaeological or ritual sites to represent the power of the ancestors, herbs and perfumes in ornate or antique bottles that bring good luck and healing, swords and statues, or stones from cemeteries and sacred sites which stand as emblems for powers conferred on the shaman by his guides and allies in the Land of the Dead.

Other objects, in Davis' experience, include wooden hardwood staffs, bones, quartz crystals, knives, toy soldiers (for the powers of opposition or victory), deer antlers and boar tusks (for strength in the face of challenges), shells, and photographs or paintings of saints.[18]

I have also seen torches (for spiritual illumination), mirrors (for self-reflection or the return of evil forces) and carvings of various animals that are symbolic of particular qualities. Participants may also place an offering of their own on the altar.

There are three fields to the mesa and where artes are placed in relation to these may also be significant. The left is the negative or 'extraction' field ('the Field of Evil', in Calderon's words), while the right is positive and life-giving ('the Field of Justice'), and 'the Mediating Centre' is the neutral and/or transformative space in the middle.

It is important to qualify our terms, however, since negative and positive have different connotations for us in the West and may suggest a quality or intent that is simply not present in Andean healing.

Most shamans do not consider the two sides of the mesa to be 'good' or 'bad', per se, for example, and, in a sense, they are not 'sides' at all but parts of a continuum where every field is harmonious and, through their relationship to each other, ensure that the world remains in balance.

Although Calderon uses emotive terms like 'justice' and 'evil', for example; to him the Field of Justice is really 'the primordial axis that moves everything in accord with my criteria, with my feeling, with my religion, most of all with my faith', while the Field of Evil is 'where one looks for the cause of a problem'.[19] Rather than a repository for, or representation of, negative and positive forces, then, the fields on the left and right complement more than oppose each other. Thus, for example, 'good' and 'bad' luck go hand-in-hand because without each we could not recognise the other.

In one way, then, the mesa can be regarded as a representation of divine (rather than human) scales of justice where the goal is equilibrium and order, not a weighted outcome in favour of 'light' or 'dark'; or, as Calderon puts it, it is 'a control panel by which one is able to calibrate the infinity of accesses into each person'.

This balance is important because, as shamans know, the more 'good' luck we have (right side), the more 'bad' luck (left side) can sometimes also result as the same energy manifests in different forms, flowing from one to the other and back again. An example might be a man who has the good fortune to be wealthy and because of this indulges in fine foods and wines to the point that his desires take him over and he becomes ill or addicted as the energy of causality circulates.

Another way of understanding the mesa, therefore, despite the linearity of its layout, is as a cosmic circle that brings everything back to its rightful place and represents the circularity of human experience.

Within this framework of understanding, the measure of a truly successful life is not riches or fine food but a correct attitude, a moderate approach, and a harmonious relationship to the physical and spiritual worlds.

To signify this, the neutral field in the centre of the mesa is the point of balance on which the world turns. 'Everything is stabilised by the Mediating Centre which computes the other two zones,' says Calderon. 'It is the balance of the other fields, the stability of the mesa.'

It is also the place of transformation, where illness can be cured by finding a point of equilibrium between negative and positive forces. Herbs that bring strength and energy may be placed by the shaman in this zone, along with images of the sun (for light, brilliance, and regeneration), or reflective materials and lodestones to draw in appropriate energies and dismiss others so that balance is restored.

Once the mesa is assembled the ritual can begin with the altar as the point of focus: a portal through which all energies can flow and a visual reminder to participants that the purpose of the ceremony is to heal imbalances so that order prevails and the will of God is done.

I have heard shamans say that San Pedro ceremonies are 'always and only performed at night' (or on certain nights – Tuesdays and Fridays, most notably, when supernatural energies are said to be most potent and able to flow more freely), while others (like Miguel) say that, in their original form, these ceremonies were 'always performed in daylight'. I have attended both and clearly, therefore, neither of these statements is wholly true in Andean healing today.

My preference is for the daytime and Miguel's explanation that San Pedro draws its power from the sun and is stronger during the day makes sense to me and is borne out by my experience.

Miguel's views and my preferences aside, however, it seems that all we can sensibly say about the timing of San Pedro ceremonies – or of what may or may not take place during them – is that it varies and there is room for creative expression by the shamans who run them.

In contrast to Miguel's rituals, for example, which involve a minimum of intervention by the shaman, Juan Navarro's are delivered in a much more regimented and structured ceremonial fashion.

Juan is a healer from the highland village of Somate, department of Piura. Now in his sixties, he is the descendant of a long line of San Pedro maestros and first drank the medicine himself at the age of eight. His practices reflect what he has learned from his family.

The first time I attended a ceremony with him (and at the times subsequent to it), it involved a lengthy opening ritual which consisted of prayers, invocations and chants addressed to the spirits of San Pedro, the land, and his guides and super-natural allies, as well as the Catholic saints. This was followed by a purification where participants took other plant medicines to cleanse them before the San Pedro could be drunk. The first was a contrachisa (a sour potion made from the outer skin of the cactus) that causes vomiting so that spiritual and physical toxins are removed from the body.

'This is a healing,' said Juan. 'It also cleans out the gut to make room for San Pedro so the visions will come.'

Next was the singado (tobacco macerated in aguardiente: 'fire water' alcohol), which participants inhaled through their nostrils. In Juan's philosophy, how this functions depends on the nostril into which it is snorted.

When taken in the left nostril it will liberate the patient from negative energy, including psychosomatic ills, pains in the body, or the bad influences of other people. When taken through the right nostril it is for rehabilitating and energising so that all of that patient's projects will go well. Afterwards he can spit the tobacco out or swallow it, it doesn't matter.[20]

The experience of contrachisa and singado, despite the blessings they may bring, is never pleasant. The former is a bitter, thick liquid that sits heavily in the stomach, churning like bile. Its impact is not immediate as the plant first 'checks out' the gut for impurities or excess food. Only after about 45 minutes, when its explorations are complete, is it ready to gather together the 'poisons' it finds there and prepare the body to purge them.

As with ayahuasca, this purge, when it comes, may be through vomiting or diarrhoea, but Juan is rigorous in ensuring it does. He works with his two sons and, armed with chonta which they use to beat and scrape the bodies of participants or trap limbs to squeeze them and release harmful energies, he and his assistants police their patients second-by-second until the contrachisa has taken its course.

Purging over, almost immediately it is time for the singado. As with the contrachisa, participants stand before Juan's mesa to receive this. It is handed to them in a snail shell; a red-black liquid which feels like fire when snorted into the nostrils and tastes peppery and acidic as it drips down the back of the throat. Just when you think the agony is over the shell is refilled for the other nostril and only when both have been taken can the participant return to his chair to sit upright and watch in silence as the other members of the congregation step up to take their medicine.

With an empty, aching stomach, and with tobacco juice and

alcohol pounding in my head, I felt anything but ready for San Pedro when I had taken part in these preliminaries with Juan. Still, I needn't have worried about my readiness or lack of it as there was further chanting and prayers before the San Pedro could be drunk and it was only at around midnight that we were finally given the sacrament.

By then the ritual had already taken some hours and feeling tired, sick, and with a headache from the alcohol I had snorted, I was bored and cold and probably not in the right frame of mind to receive the visions San Pedro might bring. I felt sure that Juan's medicine would have no impact, and I was right.

Their cultural interest aside, rituals like these just seem like hard work. I have experienced them in other parts of the country and with other shamans as well and, while I appreciated the healing they offered and the efforts and attentions of the curanderos who led them, the procedures they employed always overshadowed the power of San Pedro by far. Drinking the cactus became a minor part in a lengthy process or 'show' instead of the central reason for being there: to receive the blessings of the sacrament at their heart.

Perhaps, in a way, though, that is the intention of healers like Juan. Asked to explain the nature of the cactus, he remarked once that 'it helps the maestro [i.e. the shaman] to see what the problem is with his patient'.

For more 'traditionalist' shamans,[21] San Pedro is a diagnostic tool for *the shaman* to use; it is there to help *him* do *his* work, and not to heal the patient directly. Juan continues:

The maestro has a special relationship with its [San Pedro's] spirit. When it is taken by a patient, it circulates in his body and, where it finds abnormality, it enables the shaman to detect it. It lets him know the pain the patient feels and where in his body it is. So it is the link between patient and maestro.

Clorinda, another of Bonnie Glass-Coffin's informants, says something similar; that San Pedro provides 'the vista' she needs 'to see into other worlds'.[22]

As regards the spiritual and revelatory powers of San Pedro, Juan feels that 'It won't work for everybody' but as a healing plant or herbal remedy it is always effective: 'It purifies the blood of the person who drinks it and balances the nervous system so people lose their fears and are charged with positive energy.'

Thus, San Pedro, in 'old school' traditions like Juan's, is a medicine more than a sacrament; a herbal cure more than a divine healer and, if it has an impact on a spiritual level at all, it is for the benefit of the shaman more than the patient because of the 'special relationship' between the healer and the brew. Once in the patient's body, if San Pedro finds an illness or abnormality it enables *the shaman* to detect it so that he, rather than San Pedro, can do the healing.

Just as a Catholic priest stands as an intermediary to God for the members of his congregation, so Juan stands between his participants and their experience of the divine.

Peter Furst, in *Flesh of the Gods*, relates San Pedro ceremonies that are in many ways similar to Juan's.[23] At the beginning the participant stands before the left side of the altar to drink the medicine as the shaman chants his name and looks for the form that the illness in his body or the problems in his life have taken. Often these have the shape of threatening or frightening animals; an idea consistent, generally, with the shamanic vision of illness as an intrusive spiritual force which reveals itself in animal or insect form.

Having seen the intrusion, the shaman sometimes massaged or sucked on parts of the patient's body or used his chonta to extract the source of the affliction. In serious cases he might take a sword from his mesa and charge out beyond the circle of participants to conduct a battle with the spiritual forces he saw as attacking his patient. In one spectacular ceremony Furst's shaman performed seven somersaults in the form of a cross while grasping the sword in both hands with the sharp edge held forward. This was intended to drive off invading spirits and shock the sorcerer who was sending them to release his hold on the patient.

I have seen similar shows as well but, after experiencing the power of San Pedro as a healer in its own right during my ceremonies with Miguel, I now find them at best anachronistic and quaint, and at worse unimportant and farcical.

There is one thing though: such performances do demonstrate the efforts for healing made by the shaman on his patient's behalf. The exertions by Juan (and, indeed, the participants at his ceremonies) may go on for hours, and something life-affirming and positive must therefore surely result after an investment of energy and heart on a scale as grand as this.

But it can also come as no surprise that, while healing may take place, the visions that ceremonialists like this are able to invoke are limited in the midst of such distractions. Personal realisations and more powerfully healing insights that might lead to deeper and more prolonged recovery are also restricted because the participant is never able to fully relax and experience them, and nor does the shaman allow the plant to do its visionary work.

In the next part of Juan's ceremony, participants, having drunk San Pedro, are required to stand again before the mesa while he performs a diagnosis for them and identifies herbs and plants that he believes will help them to heal. This diagnosis takes the form of a visionary 'tuning in' to the participant's energy field, which may also be confirmed by throwing shells to divine causes and cures.

As a consequence of the diagnosis, immediate actions are often taken to begin the healing. Specific flowers and herbs may be placed into containers, for example, to which are added icy waters from Las Huaringas, the sacred lakes that have been

revered in Peru for their healing properties since the earliest civilisation. The participant is then 'bathed' by having the cold water
poured over his head and body.

Agua florida (perfumed 'water for flourishing') may also be
sprayed onto and over the participant, along with holy water,
magical powders, and sugar to add 'sweetness' to his life. Juan
explains:

> If you bathe in [water from] the lakes it takes away your ills.
> You bathe with the intention of leaving everything negative
> behind...
>
> The maestro [also] cleanses you with artes, swords, bars,
> chontas, and even *huacos*.[24] They flourish you – spraying you
> with agua florida and herb macerations, and giving you
> things like honey, so your life will be sweet and flourish.

Participants may also be presented with bottles of sacred herbs
called *seguro*, which are not to be taken, but placed on altars in
their homes so that the magical power of the plants they contain
will infuse their daily lives and good fortune will surround them.
Juan describes the seguro as 'a friend', a confidante or an ally that
participants can talk to and which will hear their problems and
take them away so they are removed and given to spirit.

There is a final benediction or prayer and then Juan's night-
time ceremony, which has probably lasted a marathon number of
hours by now, is ended and the circle is closed as the dawn brings
the brightening sun.

It is fair to say that few of the people who attended Juan's
ceremonies with me received visions from his San Pedro – but
that doesn't mean that his medicine does not work.

I have often cautioned my own participants during ayahuasca
ceremonies not to expect great revelations or be disappointed if
they do not receive them because plant medicines often work
subtly and in other ways. The visual pyrotechnics sometimes

expected of teacher plants may be a distraction in themselves, in fact, from the greater healing which is taking place and the gentler insights where the real information lies.

By the same token, it is important that participants do not get wholly lost in their visions either but follow the threads of healing through their bodies so the experience is as full as it can be.

I was not disappointed, therefore, not to have had extraordinary visions with Juan because his healing had a value in itself. The nature of his ceremonies, however – for me, at least – do little to introduce the participant to the reality of San Pedro or the power of this sacred plant.

Dr Valentin Hampejs is a different and more unusual Andean shaman in that he also has a doctorate in psychiatry and neurology from a European university. What he has learned from his Western training and degrees, however, is, according to him, 'pre-kindergarten' stuff. San Pedro is 'the real school'.

Using San Pedro, he claims, for example, to be able to cure anyone of depression or schizophrenia 'within three weeks': cures that still elude us in the West. But then, 'Psychiatrists do not know what causes it [mental illness]. I do. And using the sacred medicine I can cure it.'

Sunday Times Lifestyle writer Caspar Greeff attended San Pedro ceremonies with Dr Hampejs in 2007 and records his experiences in his Blog.[25]

We were in the ceremony and by now I was pretty familiar with it. Prayers, chants, mantras and invocations in English, Spanish and Sanskrit; the syringe-load of tobacco juice [singado] up each nostril... the vomiting in the bushes, the blessing of the cardinal points and their archangels. Michael, Gabriel, Uriel, Raphael.

We sang songs of praise to all four in turn, and we blessed each direction with our cigar smoke, and we blessed the sky and we knelt down and we blessed the earth – La Pacha Mama – and all the singing and all the blessing made *me* feel blessed...

Valentin blessed the medicine with smoke and we each drank a glass of a dark, bitter brew. The shaman downed a mixture of ayahuasca and San Pedro; my glass contained only San Pedro.

After about 40 minutes the medicine kicked in but had an outsider been observing us she would have not have noticed anything out of the ordinary. She would have seen two guys sitting around a fire, talking, singing and smoking. Of course, had a member of the Galactic Council of Elders been present, he would have seen the spirit of Mescalito (aka San Pedro) and the spirit of Grandmother Ayahuasca. Two very different entities.

The invocations in Sanskrit appear to be a personal addition by Dr Hampejs, and sitting round the fire (which I have never experienced in any San Pedro ceremony) seems more familiar to a peyote ritual. San Pedro, as I remarked, does allow for a degree of individual creative expression.

What is consistent, however, is the perspective that shamans have of San Pedro and its (male) spirit. It is 'as straight as an arrow', according to Dr Hampejs. 'San Pedro will never deceive you and he will never lie to you... ayahuasca [by contrast] is more like a snake: slippery, tricky and winding all over the place. It takes much more experience with ayahuasca to know what is true.'

Hampejs then began to work with Greeff to help him explore the issues that may have brought him to San Pedro. The approach is more direct than any I have experienced but the question, perhaps, is the same one asked in some form or another by every person who has ever attended a ceremony. Maybe the question is in the nature of the cactus itself: 'So, Caspar, who are you?'

'I am a pure angel of God,' replied Greeff.

Hampejs shook his head. 'No. You are not a pure angel of God. You are deluding yourself. If you were a pure angel of God, you would not have a physical body. So, I ask you again: Who are you?'

'Caspar.'

'And who is Caspar? It is a simple question. Who are you?'

'It is not a simple question,' Greeff said. 'Philosophically and existentially it is one of the most difficult questions of all to answer.'

'Now you are masturbating with your mind,' said the ex-psychiatrist, puffing on his pipe. 'We are not talking philosophy or existentialism. I am asking you a simple question: Who are you?'

'I am I,' said Greeff, somewhat frustrated with the way this was going.

Valentin nodded. 'Yes. That is good. I am I. You are you and you always have been and you always will be. I am I. Good. You are starting to learn...'

'Who am I – *really*?' is a question I have watched many participants ask in San Pedro ceremonies (or even to have answered without needing to ask the question at all), and the information they have received in response (as you will read in a forthcoming chapter) has often been life-changing.

The point, I think, is that our sense of identity (and a whole raft of associated emotions and concepts, like self-worth, shame, purpose, and possibility) so often goes unquestioned in daily life and we end up acting from habit, or as a consequence of what we have learned of ourselves from others or been conditioned by them to believe. San Pedro opens our minds and invites us to reconsider. Inevitably, our relationship to ourselves and to the world then changes as our habituated self-limitations are stripped away.

So important does this question seem to be in connection with

San Pedro, in fact, that Bonnie Glass-Coffin[26] found herself force-fully on the receiving end of it from her shamans, Isabel and Olinda. She writes:

> During one mesa, Isabel made this point graphically when she asked me, "You are Bonnie *y que* ['and what else']?" I thought she was asking for my middle name, so I responded, "My middle name is Kay".
>
> "That's fine," she told me. "You are Bonnie Kay, but from now on you will be Bonnie *y que*." I didn't understand the reference so I asked her what she meant by '*y que*'.
>
> Olinda replied, "*Y que* is like saying, *Y que mierda te importa* ['what the hell should it matter to you']?" The implication was that I should not be concerned with what other people might think... the important thing is to find validation and worth within.

For Greeff, the healing of San Pedro proceeded in a way that I am now very familiar with from my own experiences and those of others, to an outcome that I also know well:

> I felt joy, ecstasy and love in my heart... a reconnection with the divine. I felt whole. I felt healed. I felt happy. "I wish all my friends were able to be here to experience this," I said. "It seems unfair that not everyone can do this."
>
> It was a beautiful morning. Mist rolled down the green mountains. Droplets of rain hung from the tips of bamboo leaves. Dragonflies hovered. The birds came out, and swooped and dived and sang... I went to Bolivar Plaza and saw a green hummingbird on the branch of a tree.

Greeff had been able to experience the world – the real and enchanted world – just as I had, simply and through quiet communion with the plant, not participation in showmanship and complicated rituals. San Pedro, as he discovered, has an essence, a personality, and a healing intent of its own, which the wisest shamans allow simply to be.

In his account, too, the cactus and the hummingbird appear. In some strange way, the two are always joined.

Chapter 5

'Paradise is in the Plant'
The Perspective of Science

Taking it apart and seeing how it works may be antithetical to the most fruitful applications of psychedelic drugs
Rick Strassman

Researchers of a more scientific than spiritual persuasion have found that San Pedro contains mescaline at around the one percent level[1], about a third of the mescaline content of peyote, although some San Pedros can match the peyote concentration[2]

San Pedro is not just mescaline, however, and, in my experience, it is usually of limited value and does not aid our understanding much to equate a plant in its totality with a summary of its constituent parts and then extrapolate from these in an attempt to explain its effects. Something gets lost when we do so, which is the spirit or personality of the plant. By the same token, for example, the life of a man cannot be wholly described or explained just by taking a sample of his blood and listing the values and qualities found there.

Nonetheless, scientific studies into the effects of peyote and San Pedro (such as they are – for there are few enough of them) have tended to do just that, concentrating on the mescaline and not the plant as a whole.

Mescaline was first isolated from the cactus which contains it by German scientists in the 1890s. However, as Huxley points out in *The Doors of Perception*, by 1953, 'in spite of seventy years of mescalin research, the psychological material... was still absurdly inadequate'. Strassman agrees. 'Medical and psychiatric interest in mescaline was surprisingly restrained, and researchers published only a limited number of papers by the end of the 1930s.' A little while later, 'LSD made its revolutionary appearance' and mescaline was all but forgotten.[3]

The early research conducted into mescaline tends to be rather 'mechanical' in nature. It suggests, for example, that mescaline stimulates the visual areas of the cortex and it is this that causes the brain to experience an altered state of consciousness and perception, producing 'visual phenomena' that tend, on the whole, to be consistent and take the form of geometric patterns, grids, lattices, tunnels and spirals.

Those who have taken mescaline in one form or another might disagree that the experience is wholly about 'visual phenomena' rather than meaningful *visions,* or that these 'phenomena' can be easily compartmentalised and labelled as grids or spirals (as Huxley, again, writes: 'The mind [under the influence of mescaline is] primarily concerned, not with measures and locations, but with being and meaning') but that is the way the research has gone.

Heinrich Klüver was one of the first to study the effects of mescaline, for example, and, in his *Mescal and Mechanisms of Hallucinations* (1928 and 1966), attempted to account for the (supposed) similarity of the 'visual phenomena' it produced by referring to the structure of the brain and eye itself.

He organised the images reported by mescaline users into four groups he called 'form constants':

1. Tunnels and funnels
2. Spirals
3. Lattices, including honeycombs and triangles, and
4. Cobwebs

From this, he concluded, in effect, that mescaline 'hallucinations' are the result of seeing patterns on the retina under the influence of the drug, with the images interpreted by (and generated in) the brain.

As the title of Klüver's book suggests, he was looking for a *mechanism* – something mechanical, physical and nothing much to do with spirit or even with personal experience – and this, inevitably, is what he found. At the time, his research was pioneering but these days we might say that the Observer Effect also played a part in it – the process by which an experimenter changes the nature of the experiment, its outcome or its findings by virtue of being part of the process himself. Or, put more simply, whatever we look for we will find.

A related problem, even for today's researchers, is what has come to be known as the Research Effect. Strassman, who experienced the problem himself during his administration of DMT to volunteers in laboratories, explains it like this:

> In the research setting there is the expectation of getting data from your subjects. This affects the relationship between those who administer and those who receive psychedelics. Volunteers know they need to give something to the project, and scientists want something from them.
>
> For the person under the influence, just having his or her trip is not enough. For the investigator, helping that person have the best possible outcome isn't fully adequate, either. This sets up expectations, with the inevitable possibility of disappointments, resentment and miscommunication. The interpersonal setting is fundamentally altered.[4]

Then there is the 'problem' of Klüver himself. Heinrich Klüver was born in 1897 and took his doctorate in physiological psychology – a discipline that also has a more 'mechanistic' approach to human behaviour than, say, the humanistic or psychoanalytic fields. He went on to make his mark in the study of animal behaviour, a field where animals (and human beings) are, in the main, considered more-or-less automata, devoid of spirit and reduced to components capable of analysis and conditioning based on physical processes, as demonstrated by the leading lights of Behaviourism, Skinner and Pavlov. With this sort of background, perhaps Klüver was, in a way, conditioned himself to find a physical (rather than a spiritual, emotional or experiential) basis for mescaline effects.

I am not dismissing his work, however; simply pointing to the limitations of its time and the belief that visions can be reduced to a series of lines and spirals. In fairness, too, Klüver's work did extend beyond a purely mechanistic agenda. He coined the term *presque vu*, for example (literally: 'almost seen'), to describe the sensation that accompanies mescaline visions that one is receiving a great insight or revelation which is ever-so slightly beyond the ability of the rational mind to fully comprehend.

Some of the people who reported their experiences to Klüver demonstrated this. One said that he saw fretwork, for example, but then that his arms and hands, and, finally, his entire body *became* fretwork so there was no difference between him and it: 'The fretwork is I,' he wrote.

As with many revelations by teacher plants there is, no doubt, more philosophically to this statement than is captured by the words. The experience of *being* fretwork and realising that there is no difference between I and That, for example, implies a sense of the numinous and of the connection between us and all things, which is beyond the simple reporting of an image. In the same vein, Huxley concurs that 'the typical mescalin or lysergic acid experience begins with perceptions of coloured, moving, living geometrical forms', but for him the emphasis is on the word *living*: the sense, that is, that these forms are alive, aware and purposeful; in a way no different to ourselves. 'The visionary... is not inventing them; he is looking on a new creation. The raw material for this creation is provided by the visual experiences of ordinary life; but the moulding of this material into forms is the work of someone who is certainly not the self'.

In *Miserable Miracle*, the Belgian artist and poet, Henri Michaux (1899-1984) describes a similar experience with mescaline, where he realised that 'one is nothing but oneself'.[5]

> Hundreds of lines of force combed my being. Enormous Z's are passing through me (stripes-vibrations-zigzags?). Then, either broken S's, or what may be their halves, incomplete O's, a little like giant eggshells... I have once more become a passage, a passage in time.

The last line is, I believe, key to Michaux's experience. It is not the shapes or patterns that are of importance in themselves but the information they carry and the realisations they bring; for we are all just a passage in time, a breath on the wind, vital to the world and, at the same time, a whisper or an insignificant thought, of no more – or less – value or substance than a cloud or a blade of grass.

The sensation of being bathed or bombarded with intense colours is also common to San Pedro, as the reports of Klüver's other mescaline explorers, in their way, confirm. Once again, however, it is not the colours in themselves that are important but the conduits they provide for new revelations about the beauty around and within us, which is present in even the most mundane of worldly forms, and the realisation that our gift of life is special.

> As I gazed, every projecting angle, cornice, and even the face of the stones at their joinings were by degrees covered or hung with clusters of what seemed to be huge precious stones... green, purple, red and orange...
>
> All seemed to possess interior light, and to give the faintest idea of the perfectly satisfying intensity and purity of these gorgeous colours is quite beyond my power... everywhere the vast pendant masses of emerald green, ruby red, and orange

began to drip a slow rain of colours. Here were miles of rippled purple, half transparent and of ineffable beauty. Now and then soft golden clouds floated from these folds.

[I saw] red, brownish, and violet threads... gold rain falling vertically... regular and irregular forms in iridescent colours resembling shells and sea urchins... such singular brilliancy that I cannot even imagine them now.

As Huxley again remarks, the perception of these brilliantly luminous gems and stones is once more secondary to their meaning. 'Reading these accounts, we are immediately struck by the close similarity between induced or spontaneous visionary experience and the heavens and fairylands of folklore and religion. Praeternatural light, praeternatural intensity of colouring, praeternatural significance – these are characteristic of all the Other Worlds and Golden Ages... Most paradises are... bright with gems.

'In this context the words of Socrates in the *Phaedo* take on a new significance. There exists, he tells us, an ideal world above and beyond the world of matter. In this other earth the colours are much purer and much more brilliant than they are down here... 'The view of that world', says Plato, 'is a vision of blessed beholders'; for to see things 'as they are in themselves' is bliss unalloyed and inexpressible'.

As beautiful as the descriptions offered by Klüver's subjects are, then, there remains a problem for the scientific method in trying to explain the impact and effects of mescaline (or San Pedro) as simply visual. Klüver, for example, was interested in what people *saw*, and explained their visions by reference to physical processes and biological or chemical *mechanisms*. The *experience* of mescaline was not sought and so is never fully captured (although some of his accounts come close). He asked his subjects to recount what they had *seen* and because seeing was regarded as a physical action, the temptation was to reduce and thereby 'explain' their visions by reference to the architecture of the eye or the (supposed) powers of the brain, without asking what these experiences *meant* to the subjects themselves.[6]

Another problem is that of Klüver's inherent, though perhaps not deliberate, bias. He begins, for example, from the premise that mescaline experiences are, first and foremost, *hallucinations*; it is there in the title of his book.

The word suggests that these visions contain no information or have little value in themselves. This, in turn, implies that our 'normal' and everyday way of looking at the world is more important, significant or 'real' than anything mescaline or San Pedro might show us. But is this really the case?

The psychedelic explorer, Terence McKenna, writes in one of his books, for example, that there may well be '*true* hallucinations', where what we receive from visions is *more real* and operates at a deeper level than the things seen (or often not seen) in our habitual way of perceiving and processing information from the world.

One example of such a 'true hallucination' may well have been the discovery of the structure of DNA and its double helix by the Nobel Prize winner Francis Crick.

Crick wrote that he was struggling to understand how DNA worked one day and entered what he called a dreaming state while he had the problem on his mind.[7] factual He dreamed of snakes writhing together and winding themselves like the serpents of the caduceus. It was 'a not insignificant thought', as he later self-effacingly put it – and from that true hallucination the problem of DNA was solved.

To regard one state (normal consciousness) as real and our 'hallucinatory' world as unreal and without value may therefore be quite wrong. Such a distinction presupposes that there is even a separation between the two states; that one exists in fact while the other is in some way untrue or abnormal. Shamans see no such division, however.

The curanderos of the Andes believe, instead, that the information given to us by San Pedro and by other teacher plants (or in dreams, meditations, and visions) is as valid, or more so, than that received from ordinary perception and thought. Furthermore, such information is given to us precisely so it *can* be used in daily life, not ignored, denied, or regarded as lacking in merit or purpose. To deny our dreams, after all, is to dismiss a large part of our human experience.

For San Pedro shamans, the visions and insights gained from the plant are there to inform our everyday behaviour in the 'real world' so we can make changes, heal, or do what is necessary to improve and enhance our lives. The changes we make as a consequence of our visions mean that we become new people, closer, in Miguel's words, to our real essence as 'true human beings'.

In turn, these life changes mean that we start from a new perspective the next time we drink San Pedro and so the process of spiritual and worldly advancement continues. This is not only natural and inevitable; it is to be welcomed and honoured as an enrichment of our condition and a part of our evolution.

Archaeological and anthropological evidence points to the same unified view of life and healing on the part of more ancient curanderos and to their perception of reality as a combination of the material and immaterial, so that one informs the other.

Furst writes, for example, that the shamanic worldview does not include the notion of duality or opposing forces which split the world into two, the sacred and the profane.[8] Instead, there is no purely physical world and no absolute and self-contained otherworld that is wholly of the spirit. On the contrary, the curandero, in his healing rituals, seeks to find unity and balance in the interactions between all the forces of the world through a vision that can inform – and transform – his patient's life, leading to an improvement in his existence.

This view of the world is flexible enough to incorporate even seemingly competing or contradictory elements, so that a person might find as a result of his visions, for example, that he is right *and* wrong, good *and* bad, blessed *and* cursed all at the same time. A new understanding of reality can then become part of his life through his acceptance of this unity and his behaviour (and the outcomes that stem from it) can change as a result of the information San Pedro has given him.

Huxley captures something of this unity between the worlds of ordinary and non-ordinary reality when he reflects on his own experiences that:

> If we could sniff or swallow something that would, for five or six hours each day, abolish our solitude as individuals, atone us with our fellows in a glowing exaltation of affection, and make life in all its aspects seem not only worth living, but divinely beautiful and significant, and if this heavenly, world-transfiguring drug were of such a kind that we could wake up next morning with a clear head and an undamaged constitution – then, it seems to me, all our problems (and not merely the one small problem of discovering a novel pleasure) would be wholly solved and earth would become a paradise.

There is a sense from this of how life could become better and more satisfying as a result of the emotional and psychological changes that arise from the visionary experience and how the increased love and understanding that plants like San Pedro empower us to feel for our fellow beings could lead to a new Utopia as we take our lives in a different and more positive direction because of all that our teachers have shown us.

There is also another sense, however, in which the visionary world interconnects and co-exists with the physical world: that they are already – absolutely and literally – no different from each other; that our visions are real in themselves and we do not even need, necessarily, therefore, to act upon them or *make* them real because they have a will, a vector, and a volition of their own.

'Visions' and 'reality' do not just *influence* each other; there are occasions when they *are* each other – to the extent that a prayer, a yearning or the receipt of a visionary blessing can itself change the nature of physical reality.

The experience of Donna, my ayahuasca and San Pedro companion, is one example of this, although I have encountered many similar situations during my work with teacher plants. She writes of her ceremonies that:

One vision involved my daughter. She was diagnosed with polycystic ovaries when she was 15 and has them quite severely. She is a real 'Earth Mother' and, from a baby, has been the most nurturing baby-mad child herself and her ambition was always to be a mum. The problem with polycystic ovaries is one of fertility, however, and when her condition was diagnosed we were told that she might find it impossible to conceive.

In Peru I asked ayahuasca if she would become a mum and had the clearest vision, like watching a film, of me and her boyfriend in a delivery room and her giving birth to my grandchild. I came from that vision crying with joy.

My experience with San Pedro confirmed everything I had been shown. The boundaries between where I end and the world around me begins became blurred, and two weeks later, after I got home to England, I received a call from my daughter, who was in shock because she had just found out she was pregnant, even though she was on the pill and apparently had fertility issues!

Ayahuasca and San Pedro were too powerful for those small problems! My grandchild is due on 7th July. I had the vision and knew all this before my daughter even discovered her pregnancy.[10]

Donna's summation of her San Pedro experience in Chapter 2 –

where she felt herself dissolving into 'the Breath of Life; Infinite and Eternal Love', and deciding thereafter to act differently in the world, with greater 'integrity', 'honour', and by 'accepting life's path rather than trying to dictate it' – is similar in some ways to Huxley's in that 'a heavenly, world-transfiguring drug' was able to transform her view of the world. Her visions created – as Huxley suggests – a new emotional response to the world that, in turn, has led to her behaving differently within it, so that the reality of her life has changed.

But that cannot be all that was going on for Donna, or the only gift she received from the plants. For, how do we explain her daughter's pregnancy, for example, which was seen first in a vision and then became a *'true* hallucination', even though a medical condition and contraceptive precautions would seem to make it impossible?

The odds against coincidence must be profound. The contraceptive pill is itself 98% effective against pregnancy – and that is without a physical condition that would require medical intervention and many hopeful prayers to correct.

Telepathy, then? Was Donna somehow able to 'tune in' to her daughter several thousand miles away and receive, through some subtle awareness, a sense of her pregnancy? This would be remarkable in itself but, unfortunately, this explanation doesn't really work either since her daughter didn't even know she was pregnant when Donna had her vision of it.

A related idea is that the pregnancy resulted from Donna's unconscious, yet obviously powerful, prayers or wishful thinking: that she somehow *intended*, through an act of will, that the pregnancy should happen, as a sort of gift to her daughter. But then, why was she not able to manifest such outcomes before her experiences with these plants?

In fact, Donna was not the only expert at manifestation on our plant medicine trip; if that is the explanation we are choosing for what took place. Another participant, Ben, wanted to set up a charity to help people in the developing nations and needed £4,000 (about $8,000) fairly immediately to fund it. It was money he didn't have and while he was in Peru he had left his solicitor in charge of selling his London apartment so he could raise the capital he needed.

Before our first plant ceremony Ben had the *intention* that his apartment would sell quickly and money would flow effortlessly to him. In fact, however, when he emailed his solicitor a few days later he found that it hadn't sold at all.

She did mention in passing though that, seemingly quite by chance, she had discovered a mysterious sum of money in Ben's account that neither of them knew was there. It was exactly £4,000; precisely the amount he needed. Looking at the date and time of her email and allowing for the time difference between London and Peru, it also appeared that she had uncovered this money on the night of our ceremony, just as Ben had made his prayers for it.

Reflecting on these events, I am reminded of words used by Miguel:

Paradise is *in* the plant, but we do not use San Pedro to escape there and turn our backs on this world. Instead, by absorbing its spirit, we *make* a Paradise on Earth.

I believe now that he meant it literally: our visions *are* our reality, even if science cannot explain to us why or how.

To differentiate plants like San Pedro, that provide the user with a visionary experience that may also include real-life outcomes like those above, from the hallucinogens like LSD which had become so popular for recreational use in the 1960s and 70s, the term 'entheogen' was coined by a group of ethnobotanists including Richard Evans Schultes and R Gordon Wasson. Both men were plant pioneers themselves, who were particularly known for their work with ayahuasca and 'magic' mushrooms.

Schultes and his colleagues felt that 'hallucinogen' was a belittling and inappropriate term, partly due to its use by psychiatrists and medical doctors to describe states of delirium and insanity. The word 'psychedelic', in more popular use at the time, did not seem to them a much better alternative because of its similarity to words like psychosis, which, again, implied that visionary or mystical states were a form of madness.

'In a strict sense,' they wrote, 'only those vision-producing drugs that can be shown to have figured in shamanic or religious rites would be designated entheogens.'

The inclusion of the word 'drugs' in their definition is unfortunate, because it has connotations of its own, of course: 'to be drugged' and therefore out of control or powerless. Perhaps 'substances' would have been a better choice. But still, the description as a whole is useful as it moves us out of the arena of recreational drug use and attaches a sacred value to a discrete and particular group of mind- and state-altering substances.

The literal meaning of the word entheogen is 'that which causes God to be within an individual', or which 'creates the divine within us'. Perhaps 'that which *reveals* the divine, or which causes us to remember our own divinity' would, again, have been better still, and certainly truer to the experience of San Pedro. These nuances, however, are less important than the fact that a definition was now available that set sacred plants apart from mainstream drugs.

Its emphasis on ritual and religious use (or what we might call sacred purpose) also made a distinction between shamanism and science, the former focusing on the divine and potentially life-changing aspects of such plants; the latter concentrating on reductionist logic and procedures which often missed – both physically and spiritually – the ways in which sacred plants actually worked.

Physically, for example, as well as its mescaline content, San

Pedro contains a range of compounds that have effects in their own right.[11] By concentrating only on mescaline, however, scientists may tend to miss or devalue their contribution to the experience as a whole.

Some of these compounds are sympathomimetics, for example: substances that mimic the effects of adrenalin and noradrenaline, the so-called 'fight or flight' chemicals that are released naturally by our bodies to prepare us for action when reality shifts and we feel uncertain or anxious. Perhaps it is these as much as mescaline, in fact, that give rise to our sense of awe and the awareness that we are in the presence of something mysterious and more powerful than ourselves, which are common feelings under the influence of San Pedro?

A further consideration is that, while nothing is usually added to the San Pedro that is drunk in ceremonies, there are occasions when it might be, such as when healings are conducted by the curandero for participants who have suffered a magical attack from a sorcerer.

In these circumstances, other plants – or, indeed, other ingredients – might be included in the brew, and these may have effects of their own. Such additives might include, for example, healing herbs and flowers, purgatives like tobacco, psychoactives like misha and datura (used by shamans, according to Furst, as 'a drastic form of shock therapy'), or powdered bones, cemetery dust, and traces of soil from sacred sites and archaeological ruins.[12] In ceremonies like Juan Navarro's, furthermore, while the San Pedro remains pure, other plants and medicines are administered separately during the same ritual, such as the singado (tobacco and alcohol) and contrachisa (which includes other cactus parts that do not contain mescaline) and it is reasonable to suppose that these may also have an effect on the San Pedro experience, even though they are not mixed with the brew, since they are ingested during the same timeframe. Their effects, however (if they exist), have not been studied, the available research concentrating, again, on the mescaline content.

Working with a single extract and concluding that the part is equal to the whole may be one of the biggest errors made by scientists who are genuinely trying to understand the effects of mescaline – although it is all too common in plant medicine research.

Spiritually, there has been no place for the soul in science or medicine since Descartes delivered his famous sermon that 'nature can be conquered by measurement' (a message, incidentally, that was given to him by an angel – a *spiritual being* – although this is conveniently overlooked by science).[13]

Scientific research, therefore – with measurement as its operating principle and goal – *must*, by definition, discount the spiritual (as well as the emotional, individual, and psychological) experience of anyone who has ever taken San Pedro, mescaline, or peyote, since spirit – and personal experience – cannot be effectively measured but is subjective and anecdotal only.

What scientists really measure in their laboratories, consequently, is a notion they have of 'what is really going on' at a structural or chemical level. The reality of thousands of people who have used plants for spiritual, emotional or physical healing for thousands of years is, more or less, ignored.

The philosopher Karl Popper wrote that the first principle of the scientific method should be 'falsifiability'. To qualify as science, that is, every experiment and every law that scientists arrive at must be capable of being disproved but hold up under scrutiny so that consistent results are always produced despite this.

Not many of science's discoveries truly fall into this category and therefore come closer to scientific opinion than scientific fact. It is highly unlikely, for example, that an injection of mescaline sulphate in a lab will produce the same quality of personal experience as a San Pedro ceremony in the Andes (and, in fact, research within the latter environment has not even been conducted, as far as I am aware) – and yet science presumes it so.

It seems to me, therefore, that the experiences of individuals who have taken part in genuine, real-life and not lab-based, healing events and opened themselves to San Pedro are preferable on every level to the conclusions of scientific observers about the supposed workings of the rods and cones in our eyes and a brain they don't yet understand. Even so, scientists continue to discount the spirit – and the validity of spiritual experience – in a way that sometimes smacks of arrogance.

Their position is not unlike that of Peru's famous son and mescaline explorer, Carlos Castaneda, when he first met his shamanic teacher, don Juan Matus.[14]

> I told him that I was interested in obtaining information about medicinal plants, Although in truth I was almost totally ignorant about peyote, I found myself pretending that I knew a great deal, and even suggesting that it might be to his advantage to talk with me.

Once he had met Mescalito, the spirit of the plant, under the tutelage of don Juan, however, Castaneda quickly realised how little he actually knew about anything.

Another early account of mescaline exploration comes from the British medical doctor and author, Havelock Ellis, and appeared in *The Contemporary Review* of January 1898, under the heading *Mescal: A New Artificial Paradise*.

Although it is presented as scientific enquiry, it hints once again at a deeper truth to be found beneath and beyond the scientist's fascination with purely visual phenomena, for, just as Castaneda discovered with don Juan, what begins as an objective exercise can sometimes become a subjective and emotional experience.

Ellis writes that 'The first symptom observed [upon taking mescaline]... was a certain consciousness of energy and intellectual power', suggesting an actual change in body and spirit, and in thought patterns and thinking, not something that could be dismissed as a 'hallucination' at all.

This was followed by 'kaleidoscopic, symmetrical images ... a vast field of golden jewels, studded with red and green stones, ever changing. At the same time the air around me seemed to be flushed with vague perfume – *producing with the visions a delicious effect – and all discomfort had vanished'*. (My italics.)

If the sentence above suggests a healing element to the visionary experience, Ellis's next observation perhaps hints at an emerging spiritual relationship to the world around him, where some other aspect or quality is apparent in objects that are otherwise familiar and ordinary:

'[My] visions... were extremely definite, but yet always novel; *they were constantly approaching, and yet constantly eluding, the semblance of known things.'* (My italics.)

This is the *presque vu* experience described by Klüver. It is a sensation well-known to those who have drunk San Pedro: that there is a unique personality, quality or essence that exists beneath the forms that things take; or, more prosaically, that there is more to reality than we know. It is, rather, as if the spirit or energy within things and within and between people is revealed to us and we understand that their identity – and our own – is more fluid than we have been led to believe; it is only their spiritual essence that remains a constant. 'Who are you?' becomes one of the most important questions we can then ask of ourselves and others, and of all other forms around us.

Tracie, a participant who drank San Pedro with me in 2008, says something similar in an account she gives of her experience:

I was able to perceive a more subtle web of energy. It was during the day and I was out in the countryside where the energy of the mountains seemed a bit slower.

When I rejoined my fellow travellers I could observe how

our energies interact and how connected we are to each other and to the physical world. We are constantly sharing portions of our energy fields. With every encounter, we exchange information and energy, and we come away changed just a little bit.

This realization made me aware of my influence on others and theirs on me, and I became careful with my interactions. I became conscious of speaking only the truth and of keeping my intentions pure.

I was also aware of the energy that other people brought into the garden and how it affected everyone. One friend came in enthused by the mountains and his enthusiasm sent ripples of excitement through the group.

Ellis gave mescaline to an artist friend who, it may be assumed, also underwent a healing on a physical and spiritual level. His experience, in fact, with its references to bodily changes and of cramping, 'paroxysms' and 'tinglings', is not unlike my own.

The first paroxysms... would come on with tinglings in the lower limbs, and with the sensation of a nauseous and suffocating gas mounting up into my head. Two or three times this was accompanied by a colour vision of the gas bursting into flame as it passed up my throat.

To me, this seems consistent with my sensation that San Pedro was 'checking me out' and scanning my body for weaknesses. In the example above, these illnesses and imperfections are then released through a vision of gas and flame. This is a form of healing then, a spirit extraction, as shamans might call it, and not just an idle hallucination. Its outcome is recorded in another passage from Ellis:

My body lost all substantiality. With the suddenness of a

neuralgic pang, the back of my head seemed to open and emit streams of bright colour; this was immediately followed by the feeling as of a draft blowing like a gale through the hair in the same region.

This sensation of 'breaking open the head', to use the words of Daniel Pinchbeck,[15] is consistent with the visionary plant experience and with the shamanic extraction of illness; it is a 'true hallucination', where healing takes place through the removal of pain, experienced as streams of colours, and the entrance into the body of a new energy, like a gale that blows away the cobwebs of our former limiting beliefs and leaves us with healthier and more empowering ideas about who we are and our place in the world.

'Henceforth,' says Ellis's participant, 'I should be more or less conscious of the interdependence of body and brain.'

Ellis concludes that:

Mescal intoxication thus differs from the other artificial paradises which drugs procure. Under the influence of alcohol, for instance, as in normal dreaming, the intellect is impaired, although there may be a consciousness of unusual brilliance; hasheesh, again, produces an uncontrollable tendency to movement and bathes its victim in a sea of emotion.

The mescal drinker [meanwhile] remains calm and collected amid the sensory turmoil around him; his judgment is as clear as in the normal state; he falls into no oriental condition of vague and voluptuous reverie...

Further, unlike the other chief substances to which it may be compared, mescal does not wholly carry us away from the actual world, or plunge us into oblivion; a large part of its charm lies in the halo of beauty which it casts around the simplest and commonest things.

This latter statement is, to me, central to the mescaline or San Pedro experience, as I have said before.[16] Whereas ayahuasca sweeps us away from ordinary reality and into the spirit world, San Pedro brings us closer to *this* world and exposes its beauty to us. As may become apparent in the next few chapters, it is this experience of beauty (in the world and in ourselves) that may, in fact, be the most profoundly healing and life-changing gift that San Pedro offers.

Ellis's final observation is this: that 'the rite of mescal is not only an unforgettable delight, but an educational influence of no mean value'. It is one with which not many people who have shared the hummingbird medicine would disagree.

Chapter 6

The Outsider Woman
The Perspective and Experiences of the Healer

The spirit of San Pedro takes one wherever it wants...
One can see many things according to the illness, or where a person
has been magically harmed one sees who it was that did the job. One
sees what type of dano [harm] one has and where it was made
Mario Polia[1]

Cusco, in southern Peru, offers some of the world's most beautiful and breathtaking scenery – so much so that the Conquistador Francisco Pizarro described it in a letter to King Charles V as so beautiful and with such fine buildings that 'it would even be remarkable in Spain'.

The oldest city in the western hemisphere, and a frequent stopping-off point for tourists and seekers on their way to the Sacred Valley, the Inca Trail and the mysterious mountain citadel of Machu Picchu, it was built by Pachacuti as the capital of the Incan Empire. According to legend, its city walls, and the mountains (some more than 6,000 metres high) that surround it, were incorporated into his design and the entire project, when seen from the air, takes the form of a giant puma, one of the guardian animals sacred to Andean culture and beliefs. Even this protective ally could not save the city from Pizarro, however, and it fell to Spanish hands in 1533.

The San Blas area was, in Incan times, one of Cusco's most important districts, inhabited by Quechua nobility. Nowadays, it is better known as the artists' quarter and is famous for its narrow and winding streets that rise steeply from the central square, the Plaza de Armas, and for its craft shops, galleries, and markets selling hand-woven textiles, paintings, pottery and other items made by local artisans.

The Church of San Blas is its central feature. Dating to 1544, it was built on the site of a much earlier sanctuary devoted to the god of thunder, lightning and thunderbolt. Inside it is the Pulpit of Saint Blaise, a filigree statuette carved from cedar and adorned with bronze, which is regarded as one of the jewels of colonial art. The artist who made it is not known but it was most likely funded by Bishop Manuel Mollinedo y Angulo, which dates it to the end of the 17th century.

Just at the back of the church, tucked away in a side street, is a building that was once a home for Franciscan monks but is now a guesthouse run by La Gringa: 'The Outsider Woman'; Miguel's teacher, the sorceress who had saved his life.

I was staying at this guesthouse for the second time, having visited it the year before, again seemingly at random, because I knew nothing of Miguel or La Gringa then. I had booked a room there then solely on the recommendation of a traveller I had met by chance in (of all places) the middle of the jungle a thousand miles from Cusco, during the retreat I had held there when I told the story of the hummingbird. Now I wanted to meet La Gringa and had asked the guesthouse staff to organise an introduction.

I was surprised to discover that she was not an ancient Peruvian woman with a withered face, wrapped in a dark *bruja's* shawl,[2] like so many of the old ladies who line the streets of San Blas selling their arts and crafts, or posing with their quaint toothless grins for photographs available to tourists for a sol or two each, and as I imagined a sorceress would be. Instead, she was a youthful-looking woman in her early fifties, with clear blue eyes and blonde hair. Even more surprising, she was not Peruvian at all.

Lesley Myburgh (her given name) was born in the small

South African town of Benoni. Growing up during the days of apartheid was painful and confusing for her and she became, from an early age, a lobbyist for equal rights.

Apart from that, however, her childhood and teenage years were as normal and unremarkable as they were for most white women from a relatively privileged background. She went to boarding school in Natal before studying art at Johannesburg College, and then found jobs as a window dresser and interior designer before opening two successful boutiques in Johannesburg. She married at twenty and gave birth to three children: Shanon, and her twin sons, Simon and Mark.

Like many people at that time she had an interest in spirituality and studied the Kabala and other esoteric disciplines, but had no special calling to shamanism. The subject of Peru always seemed to come up for her, however, and so, following the fates, in 1991, she decided to visit the country 'to see if it was all true' She says:

> From the moment I arrived I was completely overawed at the emotion I was experiencing. I felt like I had finally arrived home.
>
> That journey changed my life and I had incredible experiences with the land and the light, although I never drank San Pedro or ayahuasca on that journey. But, still, I knew from the moment I arrived that I would one day live in Peru.

To move closer to her ambitions, she began taking groups three times a year, from South Africa to Peru, so they could experience the magic of the land as well. This also enabled her to spend weeks in the country each year so she could learn more about the traditions that fascinated her.

It was on one of these trips, in 1993, that she met the man who was to become her shamanic teacher. It was an experience that made such an impact on her that soon after it she moved permanently to Peru.

I met him in a church in Pisac, I was with a group from South Africa and he was guiding another group. His name was Ruben Orellana. He was – and still is – a well-known and respected academic; an anthropologist and archaeologist who has studied the mystical aspects of several Andean sites, uncovering the true usage of many temples in Peru.

He is a consultant to The National Institute of Culture and was Head of Archaeology at Machu Picchu, where he discovered 44 new sites surrounding the city. But he is also a shaman and has a healing centre in the Sacred Valley. If anyone is qualified to understand and explain the use of San Pedro, as well as the pre- and post-colonial rituals that accompany it, it is Ruben.

He made me work very hard with the plants. The first few years, I drank San Pedro with him every week, sometimes two or more times a week. I am very grateful for this now as it helped me to clear many years and lifetimes of negative emotions, but it was not easy at the time.

La Gringa continued her apprenticeship with Ruben for four years, commuting between Peru and South Africa. Then, in 1997, she divorced. It was the same year that her sons turned 18 and they were able to move to Cusco together. It was also the year that Ruben asked her to become his assistant. 'I have been his student ever since and I hope I will always be able to learn from him,' she says.

The community in Cusco gave her the name La Gringa. It is an affectionate term, often given to women who are not indigenous to the area but who live there because of their love for the country. It means 'a foreign woman; someone not native to the area'. But it is also a term used for witches and means 'outsider' in a different sense: one who does not subscribe to the norm but follows the old ways of healing and power. This latter connotation is underlined by the name that Ruben gave her and which she adopted for herself in connection with her medicine work: Woman That Flies.

La Gringa, at Ruben's suggestion, and following his ritual guidelines, began to work on her own with San Pedro in 2001, ten years after her first journey to Peru, taken almost on a whim or, perhaps, guided by the whispers of spirit. Who can say, after all, what really leads us to the places where we finally arrive?

I wish I knew how many San Pedro sessions I have guided since then [she says]. But it must be hundreds if not thousands. I have three full guest books at my casa, signed by people who have drunk the plant with me.

Every time it is a different experience, but I have been blessed through them all to watch so many people being cured of all sorts of illnesses just by drinking this sacred plant.

Some of these cures have been of an emotional nature, but there have been physical healings as well – and, in fact, they are no different, for every illness is psychosomatic: of the mind and the soul as well as the body.

The miracles I have seen include recovery from childhood abuse, rape, paranoia and depression – what we [Westerners] would call emotional problems. But there have also been healings of cancer, diabetes, pneumonia, and many other physical conditions too, often at the same time, so I make no distinction between 'mind' and 'body' – and nor does San Pedro. What is clear is that it is a great healer. That is the important thing.

Intrigued by what she had to say, I returned with her to her home in the mountains and to her garden at the Temple of the Moon where I had first drunk San Pedro with Miguel. There, on a bright August day, I filmed an interview with her.

As we spoke, a few feet away from us, watched over by Miguel and others, ten people I had brought with me to Peru on a Cactus of Vision journey drank La Gringa's medicine as I had done. Some of their accounts follow in the next chapter.

The interview below is more or less exactly as it was given that day. La Gringa's answers to my questions show not only the healing potential of San Pedro but cast light on the ceremonies and traditions which surround it, and their evolution in the modern world.

For those who work as healers, what La Gringa has learned from San Pedro is also of interest because it suggests where illness may come from and how it may be cured – even by those who do not work with the plant themselves.

Can you tell me a little more about how you came to be involved in shamanism and what your early experiences were?

I first came to Peru in the '90s and had many amazing experiences before I even tried San Pedro. On one trip, for example, I was with my friend when we heard that her mother had died that day in South Africa. We were in Cusco and it was impossible for my friend to get home, so I took her to a church so she could say goodbye to her mother in prayer. There were a few of us on this trip and we made a circle of healing around her and began to pray: normal stuff, like the Lord's Prayer; nothing too esoteric.

In the middle of this, there was a loud knock at the door and I remember thinking how inconsiderate it was for people to disturb us at this time. Then the doors flew open – and they were big, heavy church doors – and there was no one there; just a ball of light that burst into the room and flooded through us. It hit us all in our stomachs, then flowed out of us and hung in the air over my friend for several minutes before it left the church again. It was like it had a will of its own.

My friend felt, of course, that it was the spirit of her mother come to say goodbye to her but I thought it was more than that. I was transfixed, like I had been touched by God. We cried about it for a year, every time we remembered what had happened. It was just so beautiful.

That experience changed my life. Before it, I had very low self-esteem and never thought I amounted to much but afterwards I knew there was nothing small about me – or any of us – because some power had touched me and through it I understood that we are all precious to God and children of the light.

When I got back to South Africa I became an evangelist! I wanted to tell everyone the great secret I had learned: that we are all special and filled with potential and glory. But no one wanted to hear it. They just thought I was nuts.

I couldn't understand their reactions at first because I was giving them the greatest news ever told. I felt rejected, too, because it seemed to me that, in a way, I was also giving them the best part of me.

Then I realised that it is not always good to share stories like this. The challenge to people's reality is too much for them to bear and it scares them. It wastes our energy too, and what we know to be true can also start to be lost in us when the people we love regard us as fools for believing such things.

I also sensed, however, that it didn't really matter if others believed me or not because we are all changed by experiences like these anyway. We *act* differently as a consequence of what we have felt, and so other people get the message through us – whether they want to or not! – just by the way we make new choices in life. We tell the same story, but in actions rather than words.

How long after that did you start working with San Pedro?

I drank it first when I returned to Peru a year later. My experiences then confirmed all I had learned before and taught me that the light I had seen was real. During my visions, out in the mountains, for example, I saw a stairway of light on a nearby hill and, assuming that it was a hallucination – a trick of my mind – but believing it must at least contain information or have some symbolic purpose for me, I called my shaman over to help me interpret its meaning.

'There is nothing to explain,' he shrugged. 'It is a stairway of light.'

'You mean you see it too?' I asked.

'Of course,' he said. 'Take a photograph if you don't believe it is there.'

I thought he was crazy. How could I photograph a hallucination, something that was just in my head? But I didn't want to be disrespectful so I took the picture anyway.

Later I got it developed, and there it was: a stairway of light, just as I'd seen it, although it had never been there in the mountains before and you will probably not see it there now. I called my shaman again and he came over to look at the picture, although he didn't seem all that surprised by it.

'That's what I've been trying to tell you!' he said. 'These things are not just in your mind. They are real. They exist. San Pedro shows you what is already there to be seen!'[3]

And that was a vision? Yet it was also real?

Exactly. It simply doesn't make sense! But now I just accept it. I have worked with San Pedro long enough to have seen all sorts of things that we would call miracles or impossibilities.

San Pedro shows us reality, but it also changes what we think of as real. I now understand our power, and that people have the ability to manifest anything if they choose. They just have to believe they can. And San Pedro teaches us this.

That wasn't the only 'miracle' I saw that day, however. My shaman at the time (not Ruben) was a gentle man and I felt so peaceful and protected as I lay on my back in the sun that when I opened my eyes and saw two small children looking down at me, they were so beautiful I thought they were angels. I was so in awe of them that it took me a few seconds to realise they were real and that they were crying and asking for help.

They said their father was sick at home and they had no

mother so they didn't know what to do. They were frightened that he was dying.

I went to their house with my shaman and when I saw the man I thought he was dying too. In fact, he looked so bad I thought he might even be dead already. The shaman, however, walked calmly over to him and started to blow on the top of his head through some coca leaves he had with him. He then used a feather, running it over the sick man's head and body; and then he said a prayer.

As soon as that was done the man opened his eyes and sat up, then started to vomit like he'd never stop. Immediately he looked better. The shaman said he'd be fine after that and when we left the house he was already out of bed and taking care of his children.

That was my first experience of a shamanic healing and all that the curandero had used was a feather and some leaves and, of course, the knowledge given to him by San Pedro. After that I knew that I wanted to work more with this remarkable plant.

Did you only work with San Pedro or with other plants as well?

I drank ayahuasca too, but only about a year after that experience in the mountains, and after many other ceremonies with San Pedro. My shaman insisted that I wasn't ready to drink ayahuasca before that, and I saw why as soon as I did. My soul left my body completely and I became part of eternity. If I'd drunk it before I had strengthened myself with San Pedro I'm sure it would never have come back.

Ayahuasca works on the spirit and you die every time you drink it. That is why it is called the vine of souls or the vine of death. It takes us to many different worlds, none of them truly our own; the one that we were born to and experience each day.

San Pedro is different. It teaches us how to live in *this world*, the one that we know, but in balance and harmony and to see it with new eyes. That is why my shaman wanted me to drink San Pedro first: because only when we know how to live in our own world should we begin to travel to others.

San Pedro is also grounding. It is *of* the Earth and the body. It teaches us about the true nature of the world and what reality really is. And it shows us that we must live in the moment – *this moment* – because the future is an illusion, and it is pointless to waste our time and energies, as so many people do, on things that may never happen.

It teaches us that the past is a fiction too, and that instead of dwelling on it and putting our efforts into retelling and reliving our past mistakes, we should learn from it and let them go. Only then can we be healed and get well; by realising that *this* moment is all we have.

Did you notice other differences between San Pedro and ayahuasca? Some shamans say, for example, that San Pedro has a masculine spirit while ayahuasca is feminine, and that San Pedro is 'straight like an arrow' while ayahuasca 'coils like a snake'. Did you experience any of that?

To me it is the exact opposite: San Pedro is the female spirit and ayahuasca is the male. But that is also just a cliché or a sexual stereotype, of course, because, after all, they are both really plants and not 'men' or 'women' at all. So let me explain it this way instead: for me, San Pedro has a gentle energy and is filled with lightness and joy, whereas ayahuasca has harder teachings to impart. That is what I mean by 'male' and 'female'. But ayahuasca can also disguise itself as female so we receive the strong lessons and guidance we need in a way that is not intimidating.

Ayahuasca can take us 'out there' and challenge our deepest-held ideas and beliefs, as can San Pedro, but the cactus is always nurturing and safe, and always concerned with beauty. It tells us that we are part of everything, that you are my brothers and sisters, and that nature in its true form is beautiful. It wakes us up and teaches us to be conscious of the Earth because we are nature too. And these are gentle gifts.

Before San Pedro I used to walk through the world and not notice it. Now I notice everything and I have new respect for the Earth.

How did you come to be with your present teacher, Ruben?

I met him a few years after my training began, in a church in the Sacred Valley, quite by chance. He invited me to drink San Pedro and he was just amazing. I learned so much from him right from the start. He is a very famous anthropologist as well as a shaman so he knows how things work from both a historical and spiritual perspective.

I have apprenticed with him for many years and, when I came to live here full-time, he asked me to be his assistant in exchange for further training. His fame and expertise means he is much in demand worldwide, so of course I said yes! It meant I could learn more about San Pedro, get the healing I also needed, and assist his work for others around the world. What a gift!

His training was very hard though. He was not like my first teachers, who were much gentler. He made me drink San Pedro twice a week for several years. Sometimes I would beg him not to have to drink it! I'd sob and say I was too sick to drink, because I just couldn't face another session or what it was showing me about myself. But he would just say, 'Good! You're sick! That – and the fact that you can't face the healing you need – is exactly *why* you need to drink it! Get your coat and let's go!'

At the time it was agony, but now I know he was right and drinking all that San Pedro was the best thing that could happen to me. I saw all the bad things in my life in a completely new light and was able to let go of them all. I think I cleared whole lifetimes of crap in those years! And I learned a lot about San Pedro and healing too.

I still work with Ruben, and I hope I always will. He has softened a little too, now, and no longer demands that I drink every week.

From what you've told me of him before, I'd say he's what I've been

calling an 'old school shaman', with lots of ritual as part of his
ceremonies – the singado and contrachisa, etc. Did he teach you that
too? And what did you make of it?

Oh yes. But I never felt comfortable with those rituals, and
one day San Pedro spoke to me and told me I should work differently, especially as I was now healing many Westerners who
didn't really understand those rituals anyway. I discussed it with
Ruben and he agreed that I shouldn't do them if that's what San
Pedro wanted.

Having gained his permission to work differently, I then had
no idea *how* to, of course, or what my ceremonies would look
like! I had just trusted what the plant had told me. But San Pedro
guided me and said I should keep things simple. So now I say a
prayer to open the ceremony and then, as much as possible, I
step back and allow San Pedro to do its work without me getting
in its way.

I do sometimes still use tobacco in ceremonies but not the
singado, which Ruben uses a lot, I just use tobacco smoke. It is
good to blow the smoke over people if they are going through a
tough time or have stuck energy somewhere within them. The
smoke frees it up and every time I have used it people have been
helped towards a spiritual breakthrough, so I see the benefits in
it.

I also use agua florida[4] to balance people's energies. Mostly I
ask them to sniff it from the bottle or from their hands, and it
helps to ground them, but sometimes I spray it over them if they
are really stuck or floating away.

And, of course, I also use the mesa, although mine is simpler
than many others. In Peru, shamans work with many different
layouts of mesa but when you have your own you learn to use it
in a way that suits you. It is a living thing so you develop a
relationship with it. San Pedro teaches you how to use it too.[5]
Learning the formal layout of the mesa – as Ruben taught it to
me, with the three areas of light, neutral, and dark, and the artes

to be used upon it, etc.[6] – is a good thing, but it is not *everything*. You must always do what is right for you and what helps other people and communicates healing most clearly to them.

The objects at the centre of my mesa are shells and stones which have meaning and power for me. I arrange them in a straight line, like a spinal cord with the stones as the vertebrae. This is consistent with the notion in Peru that spiritual energy is held in the small of the back and, as we advance on our paths and the plant spirits teach us, it begins to rise up the spine to the head, where it resides when we become fully conscious, in a similar way to the kundalini.

In the Andes we have three sacred animals: the serpent, puma, and condor, and you will sometimes see statues of all three, one on top of the other. The serpent represents our unconscious potential or divine energy, which remains dormant until it is activated and empowered through plants like San Pedro. This is held in the small of our backs.

The puma represents the centre of the spine and the body. In Peru, the puma is the great protector that guards our precious awakened energy as it makes its journey to conscious awareness.

The condor is the self that is fully awake and, like the bird itself, can soar above the world.

So, these statues are also a symbol for the divine energy and power that flows through us and brings us into new consciousness. The mesa I use is like that.[7]

You don't use chonta[8] or holy waters in your ceremonies either. You have simplified these aspects too?

I learned the use of those things from Ruben, but again they made little sense to me and eventually they just got in the way of my experience. Some shamans use chonta and swords as protections, for example, or to change the energies of patients and heal them. But I have always known that San Pedro protects me and my participants anyway, and that there *is* no greater protection than the plant!

I also know that it is a more powerful healer than a sword or a staff! So why do I need to hit participants with sticks or bathe them in water – and interrupt their healings by doing so?

Ruben and San Pedro are both happy with the way I work, and that is all that really matters. Ruben sees my approach to ceremonies as a form of evolution, in fact, which gives people the healing they need through the rituals needed for our times.

But it is also a *de*volution because so many rituals and ritual objects have been artificially added to our ceremonies through the influence of the Spanish Catholics. Before they came to Peru, Andeans believed in Inti, the God of the Sun, and Pachamama, the Earth, so their San Pedro rituals were simpler and needed fewer symbols, appeasements to God, or ways to keep 'evil' at bay. The idea of guilt and a God who needed appeasing arrived, more or less, with the Catholics and it was the Spanish who made our ancestors change their rituals or be killed. Before this, they were more natural and flowing.

So what we are doing may be an evolution, as Ruben calls it, but it is also a rediscovery of what was always done. It is as if we have evolved backwards rather than forwards in time!

Is your decision to hold ceremonies in the day instead of at night part of this 'backwards evolution' too?

Ruben holds his ceremonies at night and this is how he taught me, but as I grew in my understanding of San Pedro, night time ceremonies – for practical as well as spiritual reasons – became another thing that did not really work.

Perhaps it is to do with the Spanish again and their Catholic notions of guilt and 'suffering for our sins' that most San Pedro ceremonies are held at night! Because I always found it so cold and uncomfortable that I could never really relax enough to receive the healing of San Pedro. I mentioned this to Ruben and he understood exactly what I meant, so he began to hold ceremonies for me during the day. Then I really noticed the difference! In daylight is where all of my breakthroughs have come.

For one thing, you can look around you and see the beauty of the world, and notice how connected you are to everything: that you are beautiful and part of a beautiful creation. You can't do that in darkness.

What people should understand is that San Pedro is not a hallucinogen like ayahuasca, so they will not see images and pictures, and there is no point, therefore, in lying in the dark waiting for something to happen. San Pedro's teaching is *visionary* instead, in the revelations it brings about the natural world and our place in it, and in daylight you can see that more clearly.

That is why we hold our ceremonies in sunlight: because San Pedro wants it that way and that is how it was always done.

How do you prepare your San Pedro?

Ruben taught me a very complicated way, but again we have changed things in time. He peels and cuts the cactus then boils it for eight hours, which is how most shamans do it, but he also adds alcohol and sometimes other ingredients too.

At first I thought his brew was very strong – and for me, of course, it was. But then San Pedro taught me another way, so now I cook it for twenty hours and it is much stronger than Ruben's. Cooking it for longer also means that people are less likely to vomit when they drink it.

Other San Pedro feels weak to me now and rarely brings the same visions. Ruben says you don't really need visions for the healing to take place and he has a point, of course. But I still think they are important, because, as well as the healing, people need to know they *have* been healed. When the visions come they can feel it, then they understand it is real and they pay attention to what they are shown... about how to protect themselves and stay well, or their place in the world and the beauty of their lives. Without the visions they can't know this.

There are some other things to consider when preparing San

Pedro as well. I usually only work with cactuses that have seven or nine ribs because they produce the most gentle and beautiful brews. Those with six or eight are not so strong, while elevens and thirteens can be very intense but also sometimes dark. I never use either of these with my patients.

Those with four ribs we only ever use for exorcisms, and the patient and healer must both drink. You don't ever want to try a San Pedro like this. It is horrible and the visions take you to Hell.[9] While the cactus is cooking we often sing songs to it or offer our prayers that it will produce good healings. Every time we stir it we offer a new prayer, so maybe twenty prayers go into each bottle. It should never boil and the temperature must stay constant, so it is a lot of hard work.

Sometimes the spirit of San Pedro shows up while we are cooking it, in patterns on the surface of the water which tell us who will be coming to drink it and why. I have seen patterns in the form of ovaries, for example, complete in every detail; or hearts enclosed by circles. Then the next day a woman has arrived for help with a fertility problem and brought with her a man whose heart was closed to her dreams. In this way, San Pedro can show us what people need before they even arrive.

As we do the cooking, we are completely *in* San Pedro as well, for all of those twenty hours; so it infuses our dreams and becomes a part of us too, and we often dream of the people who will be coming to us for healing.

What healings have you seen San Pedro perform in ceremonies?

One that means a lot to me was for a woman from South Africa, my home country, who had always been closed to San Pedro and would never try it before the events of her life made it totally necessary. So her story also shows, in a way, that you don't even need to believe in the plant for it to heal you – although it is better if you do.

The woman's husband had died a few years ago. He was a big strong man but the disease he had suffered from meant he eventually wasted away to nothing. It took him a year to die while she nursed him through it. At the end of his life he was just skin and bones and she was emotionally and physically drained.

Then, just three months later, her son was murdered: stoned to death and left to die. He was just 26; a beautiful boy.

The woman was shattered, of course. She became lifeless, like the walking dead. Soon afterwards she had a stroke which paralysed her left arm and, from the shock of all she had been through, she developed diabetes as well.

I kept asking her to drink San Pedro but she was adamant that she wouldn't. She agreed to stay with me for a few weeks on a sort of 'spiritual holiday' and healing retreat, though. I was content with that because I knew that the energies of the land would begin to heal her, just as they had for me when I first came here, even if she never drank San Pedro.

Sure enough, one night she broke down in my arms and sobbed for hours. Then, when she came round she asked if she could drink San Pedro. I made her repeat it four times to be sure that I'd heard her right!

I gave her the tiniest amount possible, but it was just perfect for her, as San Pedro always is, and then she lay in my arms and cried her heart out for another five hours.

That is a good expression for what happened actually, because I had drunk San Pedro too and, through the eyes of its spirit, I saw strands of energy coming from her heart and circling her chest and arm like a tourniquet. I began pulling them from her and throwing them away.

The next morning there was a miracle. Her arm, which had been totally paralysed, had regained all of its movement. When she returned to South Africa she saw a specialist who tested her diabetes as well and that had gone too. Now she has no problems at all.

I asked her about her San Pedro experience later and she said that as she went through it she felt a lot of pain in her heart, which is where I had also seen the energy of grief that was binding her. As well as curing her physical problems, then, San Pedro showed her *why* she had them: because of the emotional distress she had been unable to let go of before that.

What I have learned from this is that illness is never a 'thing' that is in us; it is not 'diabetes' or 'a stroke'. It is a *belief* we carry: that we must mourn for those we have lost, for example – or for ourselves – through a pain or disability that makes our suffering visible. Illness is a thought-form; a negative pattern we hold on to and reproduce. San Pedro not only heals us but shows us this thought-form too. Then, the next time it arises, we know it and can make a conscious decision to think and act differently.

The problem you've described sounds psychosomatic: where the mind or emotions control the body and lead to illness. It's a term that has lost much of its power in the West today, but I've heard you say before that all diseases are psychosomatic. Can you elaborate?

The Andean view, more or less, it that *every* disease – even very direct and physical problems – comes from our minds and souls; or, rather, from the configuration of energy or spirit that makes up who we are. There is no such thing as a purely 'physical' illness.

Another woman came to me after she was diagnosed with cancer, for example, and had been receiving chemotherapy. She looked so ill that I took her in and she spent the next seven days with me. She was practically bed-ridden and vomiting constantly. At the end of this most unpleasant period she realised that her doctors were not helping her and she decided to work with the plants instead.

She phoned her doctor to tell him and to cancel her other appointments – and he was extremely negative and angry. He told her she couldn't do that, that she was stupid, and she would die because of her decision – which is not only arrogance but a curse, incidentally. Some of the medical profession are good at that: cursing their patients to die if they don't do what they're told and give away their healing and decision-making powers to their doctor.

Anyway, this woman stuck by her guns and now, through San Pedro, she is healed. It showed her *why* she had cancer – which no medical doctor can do – and told her she had a choice: in blunt terms that she could die or change her mind and live if she wanted.

I know that sounds just too easy, but our lives often are as simple as that: a matter of choice and belief. She *decided* not to have cancer any more because, once she had seen herself through San Pedro's eyes, she understood that life was just too precious to let go of.

I have also worked with women who have been sexually abused, often as young girls, and who are carrying the energy of that in their bodies, and usually a sense of guilt or shame as well, as if it was somehow their fault. This energy is also a thought-form and it is making them ill and, often, suicidal.

They need to drink San Pedro three times. The first is terrible, even for me to watch. They just lie in a foetal position and scream. The second time they are more relaxed but there is still a lot of crying. I usually drink San Pedro with them so I can connect to what they are going through and the plant can teach me what they need to heal.

The third time they drink everything changes and it is an experience of total joy. Afterwards they are so different that not even their friends recognise them. San Pedro shows them another way, a new belief about themselves, and helps them reconnect with the love and beauty of life which has been lacking for so long in their own.

That sounds like soul retrieval but instead of the shaman performing it, the intelligence of the plant does it for them?

That's right. It is soul retrieval or, rather, *life* retrieval. We hold our negative beliefs about ourselves as tensions in our bodies and, if we don't eventually release them, they become hardened and manifest as physical or emotional problems. At the same time, our good energies are blocked so that the fullness of our souls is not expressed and parts of us remain buried. San Pedro removes our negative beliefs so the positive can then shine through.

So it is a form of soul retrieval, but one where we return ourselves *from* ourselves.

Can you say more about negative thought-forms and how they affect us?

In the Andes, shamans talk about 'good ideas' and 'bad ideas' and these are, in a way, what I mean by thought-forms. When someone says, for example, that you have good ideas, they don't mean you are a creative genius! They mean you have good or spiritual thoughts, or that you are at one with the truth and goodness of the world. If you have bad ideas, it means that you are in some way out of accordance or resonance with the way things actually are.

Sometimes they talk about a 'good' or 'bad' wind instead.[10] These 'winds' are an accumulation of thoughts or energies which are attracted to each other and share a common affinity. The good energies of many people having positive and uplifting thoughts can create a good wind, for example, but, by the same token, negative thoughts can band together to make a bad wind. In both cases, they are a sentient force that circulates in the world.

Thoughts like these have physical effects. I recently took a horse ride with a friend, for example, to visit the Q'ero of the high Andes[11] and, some way into our journey, miles from anywhere and from medical help, my friend swooned and fell from her horse. She lay on the ground shaking and not of this world at all.

Luckily, we had a shaman with us who knew what had affected her and, taking out his coca leaves, he placed them on her and blew through them into her crown. She stopped shaking straightaway and then began to come round.

When I asked him what had happened and what he had done to help her, he said she had fallen prey to 'a bad wind'. She had been hit by a thought-form which had, in a way, possessed her. He had blown a different energy into her to remove it and fill her with light, and this was what had cured her.

But, imagine: if stray thoughts can do this much damage, how much stronger are our own thoughts? Our beliefs about ourselves and our powers and weaknesses or diseases are not random, after all; they are personal to us and may have been with us for years. So it is *literally* true that our thoughts can kill or cure us.

Of course, however, there are never really any 'good' or 'bad' thoughts at all, because good and bad are human concepts, after all, and because, if we choose to learn from them, all experiences are eventually healing.

I once had a boyfriend, for example, who I felt treated me badly so I spent most of my time crying. When I left him and drank San Pedro, however, it showed me that he had been one of my greatest teachers. Through him, I now know how it feels to experience emotional pain, so I can help others who are in relationships like this and cannot move on and feel love. And, of course, I learned more about myself and my needs as well, so, in a way, I must thank my ex-lover and teacher!

The important thing is this: our thoughts create reality, so we must be careful what we think. San Pedro helps us to do that by showing us what is ultimately real and worth caring about at all.

You mentioned exorcism earlier, and possession, when you talked about the woman who fell from her horse. Can you say more about this?

It is easy to see it in people when other entities possess them. They shape shift and become someone different right in front of you. They also do things that are out of character or not healthy for themselves and others.

Some shamans here in Peru say that the spirits are rising now and looking for new lives to take, so possessions will become more frequent. The changes taking place on Earth have roused them: 2008 and 2009 will be years of high activity and this will increase as we approach 2012.

They are angry souls who will even take life in a flower but a human body is even more of a prize for them, so we must learn to recognise their presence and how to protect ourselves from them.

What advice can you give for this protection?

One method is to hold stones in your hand and breathe into them when you feel other entities close. Often, the stones will not drop from your hands, even if you try to shake them loose, until these spirits have passed.

Another [method] is to sit quietly among rocks and mountains. Then you can take sustenance from the land so it grounds you and no other spirit can enter. These methods are natural, because all we really need do is reconnect with the Earth so it can heal and teach us.

Is exorcism something you've personally been involved with?

Well, yes. It is natural that I would, but I am not happy about it. Ruben always told me to steer clear of it. 'It is ugly and something you don't ever want to experience,' he said. He told me to call him and he would handle it if anyone ever came to me needing an exorcism.

Nevertheless, I did experience it once, though not through deliberate choice, in the spirit possession of an ex-heroin addict. He had done a lot of work on himself and was clear of the drug, but there was one demon that still possessed him.

He originally came to me for a healing, not exorcism, so we drank San Pedro together and, during the ceremony, I put my hands on him. Immediately, I felt electricity rush through me. Then, just when I thought the pain would be too great, something happened that I had never experienced before: I felt the spirit of the Virgin enter me and look out through my eyes at the patient. She began to speak through me, offering prayers and protections.

It went on for a long time like this and I realised I couldn't move. I began to get strange thoughts too and to speak in a strange voice. I asked my assistant for tobacco and agua florida, and noticed as I spoke that my voice sounded almost inhuman.

When the tobacco arrived I asked for it to be blown around me and then I felt better, but still not back to myself. The patient was cured, but I was freezing and shaking.

I called another shaman to help me and he knew right away what had happened: the entity had passed from my patient to me and, without the protection of the Virgin, I might have suffered even more greatly.

The shaman removed the entity using special methods and herbs, then gave me stones to hold, just as I said before. He also told me that I had acted naïvely and before I did anything like that again I must protect myself completely and surround myself with light. I learnt a lot from that.

Is there anyone you wouldn't hold a ceremony for, especially after something like that?

I once thought so. A few years ago some young people came to me who were travelling South America and asked for a ceremony to be performed. When I told them what it involved, they said not to worry; they'd taken a lot of drugs before and had heard about San Pedro, so they wanted to try a 'new drug experience'.

I must admit that I judged them in a bad light for trivialising San Pedro and seeing it as just another 'drug trip' – which it is not. It is a powerful spiritual medicine.

It was San Pedro that told me to relax. It reminded me that it can handle things for itself and make its own decisions about who could drink it, and to remember that I was the guide and not the healer. So after that I didn't judge and I gave them San Pedro.

Afterwards, they came to speak to me about their 'drug

experience' and told me their encounter with San Pedro had been the most humbling of their lives. San Pedro had told them straight, they said, that 'I am *not* LSD! I AM SAN PEDRO! Learn from that!' They did, and it changed their lives. They no longer take drugs and have stopped looking for trivial adventures.

So now I am humble as well, because I know that San Pedro will always give people what they *need* – even if it is not what they thought they *wanted* or expected to *get*.

I like the expression you use, in fact, that with plant spirit medicine you should have *intentions* but not *expectations*. That seems a good approach. But, in any case, I trust San Pedro and I know it will act with integrity towards everyone, so now I no longer discriminate.

There is a diet that goes with San Pedro, of course, just as there is with ayahuasca. But with San Pedro it is easier. Can you say something about it?

All teacher plants require some ritual precautions prior to and during the ceremony. This is what we call 'the diet'. It refers not just to restrictions around food and drink, as the name might suggest, but to other behaviours as well, so we approach the plant with pure intent. So, when we talk about the 'diet', it is really more like the ancient Greek understanding of a *dieta*: a change in lifestyle, not just in what we eat.

Ayahuasca demands preparation some days before, including food and behavioural taboos, sexual abstinence, fasting, and meditation. San Pedro does not ask for such major changes. Nevertheless, for a day before it is drunk, food and drink should be as bland as possible and contain no alcohol, meat, oils or fats, spices, citrus fruits or juices, and there should be no sex.

For about twelve hours before the ceremony, there should be no food at all. This means a day of fasting if you are drinking San Pedro at night or no food from about 10pm on the night before if you are drinking it the next day.

For a few hours before the ritual, it is also good to find the time for a period of quiet reflection so you can think about what you would like to heal or learn about yourself.

That is really all the diet requires, although there are some specific conditions where a consultation with your shaman and medical doctor is recommended well in advance of drinking San Pedro. These include problems with the colon, high blood pressure, heart conditions, diabetes, or mental illness. None of these will necessarily prevent you from drinking since the condition itself may be the very thing you want San Pedro to cure, but your shaman and doctor must know.[12] A general rule with plant work is: the purer your body and spirit, the more powerful the medicine and its teachings. The diet helps with this.

One final question: I've heard it said that the 'processes' involved in ceremonies contribute to San Pedro and its effects: that the personality of the shaman may be important[13], or that she acts as a sort of hypnotherapist and offers healing suggestions to her patient, while the ritual includes practices like meditation that are also relaxing and healing. The implication is that these processes are as important – or more so – than the medicine itself. What do you think of that?

I sometimes get asked things like this, mostly by scientists and academics. They want to know what the 'make up' of San Pedro is, what its 'active ingredients' are, and 'how it works'. I tell them I don't know and I don't care, because for me it is not the 'mescaline content' or its 'properties' that are most important. San Pedro is a healing *spirit* that produces miracles that I have seen with my own two eyes.

So I really *don't* know or care how San Pedro works. I can't 'explain' a miracle any more than they can! But I know this: if you *needed* a miracle because your life was in that much pain, and if – by the grace of God and San Pedro – you got one, you wouldn't care *how* it worked either!

Part of the disease itself, it seems to me, is the need to 'know' and to explain the world in terms of its 'mechanisms', when its nuts-and-bolts really don't matter at all. It is the *beauty* of the world that should attract, engage, and inspire us! When we drink San Pedro that is one of the first things we learn – and then our questions become irrelevant anyway. So the real answer, for those who want to know the hows and whys of San Pedro, is simple: drink it and you will see!

But for those who 'really need to know'…?

As I've said, this 'need to know' is not really a *need* at all, but a desire, a belief system, or a view of the world in itself: we *think* we need to understand or be able to explain everything away. This desire and this thinking is, in many ways, the disease itself. It is indoctrination by society and, since it contributes to the illness itself, I am sympathetic to those who suffer from it. But, really, there is not much more I can say.

We were talking earlier about ayahuasca and San Pedro and whether they have male or female spirits and this, again, is an urge we have to categorise and 'understand', instead of embracing the mystery. In all the years that I have drunk San Pedro, it has never shown me a particular personality or spirit[14], for example, but I *know* that it has one and it embodies me when I drink.

People who see me in ceremony say that I change physically and become first a little girl and then, at the end of the day, an old woman filled with wisdom and light. There is a lifetime's evolution, growth, and development in a single day with San Pedro – from innocence to knowledge – and what happens internally, to my soul, is reflected in the outer world and shows on my face. So, for me, *that* is how San Pedro works: it gives us a lifetime of insights and information in the course of a single day. We receive knowledge in place of ignorance, strength in place of weakness, and it makes us responsible grown-ups instead of children. If there is a 'process' involved it is this, and it is visible to others as well.

As for the other things you mention – 'personality', 'hypnosis' and 'meditation' – I don't know, and I really *don't* care. I never 'suggest' anything to participants, as you know from your experience of drinking San Pedro with me. I say very little, in fact, at the start of the ceremony or throughout it; I step back and do not intrude, so the plant can speak for itself. I find it hard to believe, therefore, that my personality has much to do with anything, since I am not really present.

Now, you ask me, when people drink, do they enter a meditative state? I would say so, wouldn't you? Look around you at these people here: quiet, contemplative, and lost – or, more likely, *found* – to the world. But I wouldn't call it meditation or hypnosis, would you? I'd say they were in a state of healing and grace instead – just as they always were, in fact, beneath the blanket of the world that has settled over them.

But once again, who really cares? The 'what' of San Pedro is that it heals lives. Let us leave the whys and the hows to the academics, for whom such things seem to matter.

Chapter 7

The Journeys of Others
The Perspectives and Experiences
of the Healed:
The Accounts of San Pedro Drinkers

There are two ways to live:
As if nothing is a miracle or as if everything is a miracle
Albert Einstein

'Miracle cures' and the list of healings La Gringa had mentioned sounded impressive, even though experiences like these are common among those who have drunk San Pedro. I had received an instant cure to a physical illness myself, and the plant – just as La Gringa said – had also shown me *why* I'd had this problem in the first place: because of the beliefs about myself and a 'Godless' and disempowered world that I was holding on to. Once I knew what these beliefs were, I could change things and begin to let them go.

But I also know that for scientists and cynics, or those who have never worked with San Pedro, there is a lot to accept in those words. We are not so open to 'miracles' these days.

So I asked La Gringa to put me in touch with some of the people who had drunk the medicine with her, so I could hear the accounts of their healings firsthand. She gave me three names: Kane, Jamie, and Michael.

I also gathered accounts from some of the ten people who had returned with me to the Temple of the Moon to drink San Pedro with La Gringa and me. Finally, I 'came across' a few other people on my travels, too, who had also drunk San Pedro with La

Gringa or others, and I collected their stories too.

In total, I include twelve accounts of San Pedro healings in this chapter. They range from the 'entirely physical', such as David's recovery from cancer, to the 'purely emotional', such as Simon's reconnection with his grief and anger at the loss of his sister and his ability to move through it to find resolution and peace.[1]

Twelve accounts is probably not a statistically significant number in the whole scheme of things, and my approach to their collection was not 'scientific' either. No one was wired up to monitoring equipment, for example, as Strassman did with his volunteers for his study of DMT[2]; no temperature readings were taken, no blood samples collected, and no other physical analyses were made.

Rather, people underwent their own experiences and, a day or two later (in the case of my own participants, anyway), I asked those who wanted to, to reflect on what had happened and, in their own time and in their own words, to send me their reports. In terms of objectivity, therefore, it is important to stress that nobody knew in advance of taking San Pedro that they would be asked to recount their experiences later (or at all), or that there was even a 'study' taking place, so no expectations were set up.

In terms of the 'set and setting'[3], the context was, of course, ceremonial, and the people present had come as participants on a healing journey to Peru so they were aware that there *was* a healing purpose to the ritual itself.

Nonetheless, nobody told them that they *must* undergo a healing, or what form it must take. They were simply invited to attend the ceremony and, without elaborate explanation, given San Pedro to drink. Then La Gringa and I retired from the ceremonial circle to allow the participants space while we watched over them from a short distance away.

Most of the reports I got back were received within a month or two of the ceremony. With those individuals whose names La Gringa had given me, however, there was often a much longer period for them to reflect, as some had drunk San Pedro with her up to a year or so before.

What took place during this reflection time, and the insights and developments that San Pedro provoked, is interesting in itself when compared, for example, to Strassman's research. What he found was that, while the effects of intravenously-given DMT were explosive and dramatic within the first few minutes of injection, ultimately there were few, if any, long-term benefits for his volunteers. The impact faded rapidly with time.

He writes, in fact, that:

As the years passed, I began feeling a peculiar anxiety about listening to volunteers' accounts of their first high-dose DMT session. It was as if I didn't want to hear them. These psychotherapeutic, near-death, and mystical sessions repeatedly reminded me of their ineffectiveness in effecting any real change. I wanted to say, 'That's very interesting, but now what? To what purpose?'

His conclusion was 'the deep and undeniable realisation that DMT was not inherently therapeutic'.

We might, I suppose, expect a similar outcome with San Pedro: that those who have gone through a 'life-changing experience' would, over time, settle back into the routines of the mundane world and make few, if any, actual changes to their lives. This does not seem to be the case, however. Rather, as the accounts of my participants (most provided weeks or even years after the experience) tend to show, the spiritual effects of San Pedro linger, and almost compel people to take action so they put their realisations to use.

Some of the participants I am in touch with today, for example (now more than a year after their ceremony at the Temple of the Moon), have, relatively-speaking,[4] made extraordinary changes to their lives. They have left unsatisfactory relationships, moved house or even country, given up unfulfilling jobs, changed careers or returned to college, patched up differences with their parents and others, and so on; all of it, they tell me, as a result of what San Pedro showed them. Some have returned with me to Peru again so they can repeat their experience and 'top up' on their healing or renew their intent to make changes and become different people. And no less than three of my original ten participants (i.e. 30%) have either moved – or are seriously contemplating a permanent move – to Peru so they can be closer to San Pedro, which they now regard as their 'spiritual teacher', and to the healing it offers them. These are their stories.

Kane: My greatest lesson was to forgive and love myself

Kane had just come from Iquitos and the jungle, where he had drunk ayahuasca, when he met La Gringa and drank San Pedro with her. It was his first time with the plant. 'My journey to Peru was intended as a healing mission,' he says.

I had chronic heartbreak that didn't subside, even after two years. I knew that something in my life wasn't right but what I didn't know was that this was just the tip of the iceberg. The heartbreak was only a symptom of a much larger, deeper, problem that surfaced after I visited Peru.

I drank San Pedro in the mountains with Miguel. There wasn't much ritual but I did observe the dietary guidelines over the previous days. At the time I drank it I was also still being worked on by ayahuasca, and I think this also influenced my San Pedro experience.

San Pedro brings so much clarity and is gentler than ayahuasca. I was given answers loud and clear. I got the healing I was after. I brought resolution to my broken heart.

My San Pedro journey became very dark at times and I was shown how, for the past two years or longer, I've been really cruel in the way I treated myself after my break-up, and that the evil I was experiencing was none other that myself – or a part of me that had been abused and was buried. This angry, violent, destructive part had been sitting in the background my whole life but I was not aware of it. My greatest lesson was to forgive and love myself.

At the time I didn't understand that but now I can see that all the horrific shit I'd been going through was not caused by outside sources but by myself, or this injured part of myself.

Over time [following my San Pedro experience] I have learned how to love this part [but at first] I was fighting it, like it was an enemy, because I didn't understand its nature; I just had this evil voice inside of my head. In the end I learned that the more I fought it, the more insane my life became. Although I experienced fear, grief and sadness during my journey, I didn't see it as negative. It was definitely a powerful healing experience and I could understand and process the teachings easier than those of ayahuasca.

I met Mother Earth and suddenly realised that I've been standing on her my entire life. I felt ashamed and stupid for not knowing that she's always right there beneath me. But I also felt like I was forgiven, as any mother would do for her child. I'd say that, yes, there is an intelligence to San Pedro and it is closely tied in with the Earth.

My San Pedro journey lasted about 24 hours in all. I got zero sleep. I spent a lot of time lying on a mattress or sitting in the sunshine with my shirt off but I did manage to go for walks with Miguel in the mountains and into the Temple of the Moon.

The experience I had will *never* leave me! San Pedro answers your questions clearly, and without confusion or the need for interpretation. I understood what had happened with my relationship and I was finally able to let go.

I would definitely try it again. Without a doubt. But this time to increase my awareness and communication with Pachamama [Mother Earth], to assist and to heal her.

Jamie: There is no suffering, only the pursuit of truth

'There is no proper way to begin this story and no possible way of ending it,' writes Jamie, a young American woman with a poetic style, who sent me her account by email. She was one of La Gringa's contacts and had drunk San Pedro with her about a year previously, suggesting that her realisations and new sense of truth and connection to love had not disappeared with time but had, if anything, grown stronger and more intense. 'I know now that the truth is love, always has been, and always will be,' she writes.

High in the Andes, alone with endless peak upon peak bathed in alternating showers of shadow and light, I sat with San Pedro. The only way to tell this story is to try and share with you some of what was shared with me...

In moments I found myself overcome with tears of sheer joy and gratitude... for my parents and all my ancestors for bringing me into this world, for giving me this beautiful opportunity to be here under this sky, with these birds and this dog and those gently swaying trees...

For all of you, every single one along the way, for making my life so beautiful and for delivering me into this present where I have arrived in full knowledge and love of myself...

For God, who has brought me into this gorgeous moment of gift and privilege...

For Pachamama, who always holds me in her familiar arms, no matter where I go...

For the magic my body can make, right now from my fingertips, from the crown of my head, from my toes, my feet, my knees, everything radiating, everything alive, transmitting, feeling, being, knowing the ultimate truth and reality of love. On high hillsides carpeted in green, alone with the slow passing of men, women, or children tending herds of grazing animals, I was shown a sacred temple deep in the earth[5] where the hands of lives before ours diligently, delicately, carved and smoothed the stone to reveal the bodies of jaguars, snakes, condors, and llama.

Steps leading into the heart of this earthen temple reveal a slab stone table with a natural crack in the earth above it through which the light of the full moon would fall while, inside, medicine men would offer up the body of a llama to give thanks for the continued fertility of their people and the land which sustained their life.

I know now that the truth is love, always has been, and always will be [and] I recognize the resolve asked of me: never compromise yourself to another; never compromise that inner core of fire and strength and self-knowing. Keep in sight yourself. Love and embrace; fully engage; give and receive; learn and grow... *this* is falling in love. Give yourself entirely. In truest love, there is no holding back. Know your path, your calling. Know what it is you must do and in whose service you must never falter.

This is the ultimate realization of love: there is no suffering; there is only, ever, the pursuit of truth.

The world will heal and be saved. It will know and live in love. Make it so in everything you do, in every act of good conscience. Make it so in every thought you think, in every bit of magic you invoke and gift to the world in heart and deed. Make it so wherever you are and whoever you are with; give yourself entirely. Make life a celebration with them.

In returning home, remember to greet each beloved with humblest thanks and appreciations in every encounter. Never take for granted the love that is before you.

This is how it feels to be in balance, as a human who is part of the larger race of humans, a simple creature like any other on this planet. This is how it feels, with the quiet mountainsides, the green grass, the song of the wind, the gray of ceremonial stone. This is how it feels to be one among a family of bird and flower and dog and other people in their own quiet moments of search and wonder, each of us belonging, each of us home. Before we learned to build skyscrapers and movie theaters and internet cafes, we sat here in the presence of these intelligently crafted stones and warmed ourselves by a fire held in their care. Hundreds of years suddenly doesn't feel like all that long ago.

Michael: What we most desire will come true

'One action can change your entire life,' writes Michael, *whose San Pedro experiences were so astounding and liberating that he intends to write a book on them himself. 'For me, that action was knocking on the door of Casa de la Gringa.'* [The guesthouse in Cusco owned by La Gringa].

Michael's experience centres on what he understands to be a 'past life recall' where he was persecuted by soldiers for his spiritual beliefs, and protected by his parents, who gave their lives for him.

Of course, it is possible to interpret this in psychological terms as well, in which case we would probably conclude that his experience of persecution is something he is dealing with in this lifetime, along with dissatisfaction at his relationship with overly-protective parents.

Perhaps – again, psychologically-speaking – we might even say that Michael's experience represented a rebirth of kinds. Certainly, one of its most significant moments was his sense of 'travelling along a pink-stemmed road that was spiralling down', which sounds like a birth canal, except that, in his case, he is reborn through a flower – through the powers of nature, that is.

However you choose to look at this, the outcome speaks for itself and includes new confidence, a new direction in life, and a better under-standing of – and greater love for – himself and his family.

As I worked my way through Cusco's narrow cobblestoned streets, I saw an ad welcoming people to take part in a San Pedro ceremony high up in the hills. I felt a tinge of nervous energy as I stood there reading about the sacred plant which has been used in shamanic ceremonies for centuries. I wondered if this was a sign to try it. I had so many fundamental questions about the direction of my life – my fears, my profession, my love life…

I looked up and caught the eye of a man who had stopped at

the top of the hill and turned back towards me. We glanced at each other for a split second then he made a left onto another street. He had a knowing look on his face, like he had something to tell me, so I followed him down the road. We zigzagged a couple more times and I saw him enter a building up ahead. I walked up and stood in front of a massive, locked door. I was transfixed, not knowing why I was there or feeling the way I did. I eventually looked up and realized it was a hostel. It sounded familiar – Casa de la Gringa. I rang the doorbell, a guy named Marcel answered, and I walked in.

The owner of the hostel held San Pedro ceremonies at her house in the hills of Cusco and I told myself this couldn't possibly be a coincidence. I sat down and was drawn to a large collection of testimonials from people who had previously stayed at the casa, many of whom had participated in these ceremonies. I engulfed myself in these people's testimonies and was amazed at how San Pedro had changed so many lives. One after the other had poured out their souls. How could drinking a plant do all of this?

I made up my mind to just do it. Little did I know that my experience with San Pedro would present some of the most difficult physical and mental challenges of my life. It would also *change* my life.

For two days I prepared my body for the ceremony – no alcohol, no meat, and no sugars the day before. I woke up on Friday ready to take San Pedro. There was also a French couple there who were going to participate in the ceremony with me. The woman seemed a bit nervous but, surprisingly, I was calm.

We took a taxi to [La Gringa's] house. Miguel drove up with us. We wound up on a steep dirt road lined with old brick houses that sat along the edge of the hill. The landscape was beautiful... green and lush... high up in the hills where the locals conducted their daily lives.

We entered and were invited to sit down in her garden under

a little tent. We plopped down on a bunch of mattresses on the grass and were asked to wait a few minutes while they prepared the San Pedro.

It was as you'd expect – a green colour with a lumpy consistency. They told us that it pretty much tasted how it looked. Before drinking, we each went around telling each other a little bit about ourselves, what our intentions were for the ceremony, and what we wanted to learn from the experience. I started off and told everyone that I wanted to overcome a fear of risk-taking which manifested itself in various aspects of my life – travel, work, relationships, etc. Why did I have the fear of stepping outside my comfort zone? What was holding me back?

The French couple introduced themselves, talked about their intentions, and when we had all finished, La Gringa said a prayer for San Pedro to bring us clarity in a way that was unique to each of us. With that we drank the San Pedro.

I didn't feel anything for the first thirty minutes and was beginning to think that nothing would happen. Maybe it was all a hoax. Or maybe I wasn't open and receptive enough to it. Thirty minutes later I started to feel more light-headed and my legs became weak and tingly.

As time went on I became restless and felt like I was trapped. Miguel noticed my state of mind and asked if I wanted to go for a walk near the Temple of the Moon. At first I said no as I was starting to have trouble walking. But a feeling of claustrophobia overwhelmed me, so I got up and went outside with him.

We walked up to a point overlooking the valley near the Temple of the Moon. I began to feel more and more uncomfortable and had a combination of sensations – fidgeting, shortness of breath, and jolts of energy shooting violently through my body. I was suddenly overwhelmed by a deep feeling of sadness and had to put my head down to deal with the onslaught of emotions. I closed my eyes, and then I experienced what I later realized was a past life.

I began to see the image of a circular stadium. Everything was covered in red, the colour of blood. I felt surrounded by people and soldiers, and closed in. I desperately wanted to leave but I was trapped. There was so much evil that surrounded me, yet there was one source of light standing by me: my parents (from this lifetime) were protecting me from the soldiers and the people who wanted to harm us. I had the feeling that we were living in the Roman Empire, and there were people like me who were being killed. Were we early Christians?

I was just a baby, maybe two or three years old. My parents sensed that we were all about to be killed and they sacrificed their lives to save mine. They died instantly and I was suddenly alone in the world to fend for myself, feed myself, take care of myself. In an instant I became an orphan to the world. Then the vision disappeared.

I lifted my head and began to cry harder than I had ever cried. I felt the pain of being alone, of not having a parent to feed me, shelter me, guide me through life. I felt the pain of my parents, knowing that they would never see me grow up or have the chance to be the parents they wanted. I cried for the sacrifice they made. I felt the pain of the world and so many children and families who had experienced the same fate.

In my broken Spanish I explained to Miguel what had happened. He put his hand on my shoulder and comforted me. Everything will be okay, he said. 'Tranquillo, my friend, tranquillo.'

After a few more minutes, the purpose of my past life recall became clear. I understood my relationship with my parents like never before. I understood the reason they had always been so afraid for my safety. When I was growing up I had received a great deal of love and attention from them but at times it felt overwhelming and, to a certain extent, suffocating. Any time I had done something out of the ordinary they worried. I now understood where their worry stemmed from, and my frustration towards them turned to love and compassion.

I realized that the best thing I could do was remind them that I was fine and safe wherever I was and not resent that I had to do this but honor them for it. I stopped crying and Miguel and I walked back to the garden. I looked at my watch and only two hours had gone by. What could possibly be next?

I was emotionally and physically drained and laid down on the mattress to rest. I was shivering, but not cold. My heart was racing and I was twitching every ten seconds from the sharp jolts of energy racing through my body. I began to get a little nervous. I'd never felt these sensations before and couldn't seem to control them.

La Gringa came to check on me and said everything was fine. She told me it was normal and there was a reason that this was happening to me in this way. 'The plant speaks to people in different ways,' she said. She suggested that I go talk to the flowers in the garden and ask them what I needed to know in my life. It was a strange request but I figured that things couldn't get much stranger, so I stumbled over to the flowers and asked them what my purpose was in life.

They immediately began to open their leaves, as if they were speaking directly to me. I remember thinking how strange that was, that a plant was actually talking to me. I started to feel like I was entering the flower and traveling along a pink-stemmed road that was spiralling down. As I moved through this organic space it sounded like a thick liquid or goo would sound if you poured it slowly into a glass. But it was so beautiful here. I was *in* a flower!

Everything turned green, the colour of the stem... I was entering the stem and the roots of the flower. After a few more minutes I became part of the earth itself and had a feeling of complete peace. I had become one with everything around me and started to feel like I was leaving my body. This made me nervous again and my peaceful state was suddenly accompanied by paranoia.

La Gringa came over to check on me again. I tried to formulate the words to describe the experience in the flower but nothing came out. Then I noticed a strange thing with her face. It kept morphing into other faces until it felt like I'd seen the entire face of the world flash before my eyes. I told her this and she said that San Pedro was trying to explain that we are all one; all part of the same source. There was nothing to fear since we are all part of God.

Her face changed again. One minute it was absolutely beautiful – youthful, strong, compassionate, and caring; the face of an angel. The next she looked like a demon, with veins popping out of her head and a frightening, evil look in her eye. I realized that these changes were a direct and immediate result of my thoughts. When I had positive and loving thoughts she looked beautiful. When they were negative or fearful she looked evil. My thoughts were controlling my external environment.

I told her what was happening and she said that's what happens in life: our thoughts are *things* and create our reality in the physical world. For the first time in my life I understood what people had been saying all these years (the books, the lectures, the world philosophies and religions): 'Ask and you shall receive.' *Our thoughts create reality.*

Instead of being at peace with this I began to panic. My heart started racing, and I suddenly couldn't breathe! Was I dying? I started to cry and asked for all of this to stop. I didn't want to feel this pain any more or experience these thoughts. I wanted to live!

Five minutes later I felt the urge to vomit. I ran to the side of the garden and purged. La Gringa came over again and told me that it wasn't the San Pedro I had released but all of the negative emotions and fears I'd been carrying my entire life. Over the next hour I purged even more and each time I felt much lighter, liberated from my past worries and the restrictions I had put on myself. I was no longer paranoid… [and] felt safe…

I lay down and looked at the garden. It was absolutely beautiful and the colours were radiant. I realized that my thoughts were controlling the appearance of the garden. When I had positive thoughts, the entire garden was beautiful. When I had fearful or negative thoughts, everything withered and turned grey. The appearance of the garden was constantly changing before me.

It dawned on me again that this is what my mind is like on a daily basis – [and that] what we most desire (positive or negative) will actually come true. We have the power to create our own heaven or hell with every passing thought. I was overwhelmed with the sense of possibility...

After a few minutes Robert came up, introduced himself and sat down next to me. He had been hanging out the entire day in the garden but we never spoke until now. He asked if I wanted to go outside again and walk around the Temple of the Moon. I jumped at the chance.

We left the garden, walked to the base of the Temple and sat down. The day was fading. It was about 5.30pm and the setting sun illuminated the landscape. The colours of the mountains, the trees, the grass, were all a vivid green.

Something was changing in me. I had an intense desire to climb to the top of the Temple and a feeling that there would be a sign waiting for me there. I looked at the mountains and the valley to my left and felt their presence. They were alive; breathing just like me.

I felt that the mountain wanted me to speak to it. The first thing that came out of my mouth was 'Hi mountain, please smile.' The mountain formed a smile with the rocks and grass on the side of its hill. It literally smiled back at me! I was stunned, but given everything else that had happened that day, I accepted it and smiled back. I asked myself, if I could get a mountain to smile, what could I do next?

I asked the sky if I could move the clouds into the distance and create a sunny day above Cusco. The sky agreed and I began to move the clouds, pushing them away to the outer edges of town. It was incredible, yet it felt so natural.

I noticed that the more positive thoughts I had and the more confident I was the more the sun came out and the clouds dispersed. As I reflected on this, it was clear that I was receiving the same message again: *I create the reality I want.* This time I understood it in my soul. I felt so alive, so full of courage and energy.

The next day I felt like a new person – energized, aware, calm. Over the next few weeks I was transformed. Anything seemed possible. I was ready to create what I most desired.

Some months later I headed back to Cusco and felt called to try San Pedro again. I had learned a lot from my past experience but I still felt something was unresolved. This time I had a specific question: 'What do I need to do to find the right person in my life?'

I had some of the same physical reactions – nausea, a racing heart, little jolts of energy flowing through my body – but I started to recognize that when I got these intense electrical charges, it was San Pedro trying to speak to me. I was no longer afraid of the minor convulsions but welcomed them. This was a huge revelation for me, and I became grateful instead of fearful.

I suddenly saw the vision of the stem of a flower [with] a face rotating around [it]. At first it was my face but [then] it became that of a woman. Eventually our faces would blend as it finished its rotation, so we became one and the same, yet still distinct individuals. When we blended I felt we were enhanced in some way and even more complete.

I often had feelings of claustrophobia when women got too close to me. This vision addressed that fear head on. I realized that it was a good thing if we merged; [that] I wasn't losing myself because there was nothing really to lose – I was part of this other life force to begin with and together we were so much more alive and complete. I asked if there was anything I needed to do to attract 'her' into my life, and received a simple and direct answer: 'Just love yourself.'

I am now in the process of changing my life and I feel a sense of liberation and excitement like never before.

Simon: The little things are often the biggest

'I have been on what I would call a shamanic path since 2001 but I had never taken hallucinogenics before my trip to Peru,' writes Simon, a businessman from Gibraltar in his late 30s who accompanied me on both my Magical Earth ayahuasca journey to the Amazon and my San Pedro journey to the Andes.

I was used to many extraordinary experiences in meditation but nothing, and no amount of reading, could have prepared me for what I was to experience during my two weeks in the rainforest with ayahuasca. I had woefully underestimated the strength of the brew during our last ceremony and realised just how much I had also underestimated the power and wisdom of the plants, and how much I was 'in my head' about all of this.

Because of these experiences, I decided to drink the bare minimum of San Pedro, with the intention of simply asking for a gentle healing. I drank just half a glass compared to everyone else who drank a whole one.

As it took effect, I was shown incidents from my teenage years. Revisiting them now was making me chuckle but I also purged into the grass, realising that my depression in my twenties and thirties had acted as a mask, making me forget so many good times growing up.

In my twenties I didn't really have a girlfriend, not until I was 29; only a few one-night-stands and a brief fling, and this had got me down. San Pedro showed me, though, that even in these small relationships there were delicious moments which were worth savouring and remembering.

I knew I really wanted to purge my depression away – and the mask that had made me forget the good times – but I was conscious of not disturbing others and the big purge never came. Instead, I found myself sat by the most wonderful red, yellow, and orange plant. It wasn't looking particularly different to how it would if I was not on San Pedro but what I realised was that I was (finally) so 'out of my head' and in the present moment that I was able to notice it in a way I never normally would, being so wrapped up in my thoughts. I saw detail I had never seen before and realised just how beautiful it was. In this, San Pedro gave me one of the most important insights of all: *The little things are often the biggest.*

I went for a slow walk around the flower bed, photographing each flower in detail. I remember thinking that I would never be able to really explain my mental state but maybe these photos, taken from each and every angle, sometimes not even looking at the screen, just trusting San Pedro with the shot, might somehow capture my feelings and the experience of San Pedro.

When I finally sat down again I knew I really had to purge this time. Miguel came over then, right on cue, and told me that if I drank water the purge would be effortless. I followed his advice and sipped water from a bottle. I felt it surge in my intestines and then, with a single cough, I released a stream of water. Within it there was a terrific amount of negative energy and it felt so much better to be rid of that crap.

I went for a walk then on my own to the Temple of the Moon. I looked at the trees and it was as if someone had turned up the contrast and sharpness in my brain. I was seeing everything: the way the trees danced in the breeze, the power of the rocks; I was aware of it all. So this is how it is to be fully present. I felt supreme.

I looked up at the clouds and saw them as 'lines of energy' – I don't really know how to describe what I saw any better, or what I was feeling, but I could see knowledge and images in them and I surrendered myself to the blissful state I was in.

They started to morph and were soon producing the most spectacular patterns. Almost in slow motion, different clouds in different colours were forming above me and I could see how the wind and atmosphere shaped them. Again, I was so present that I could take in every aspect of the shifting clouds and felt in such total harmony with them that I was not sure if I was creating these patterns or if the clouds were doing it just for me. I had the sense that in surrendering to them and watching their patterns in the sky, my heart was also opening and San Pedro was working on me at a very deep level, even altering my DNA. I have no idea if that is true, but it is how I felt that day.

Things were now calming down for me. I had been laughing and giggling to myself all day but I now felt able to rejoin our group and sat with everyone else in our circle, all of us loved-up, having had one of the most amazing experiences and healings of our journey so far.

Before my second San Pedro ceremony I thought for a while about what my intention should be. I felt that there was still more healing to be done and that I should ask for that. I guess I could have drunk a whole glass of San Pedro had I wanted to, but I felt that the dose was almost immaterial, so a half-glass would again be fine for me. I sat on the mattresses waiting for it to take effect, alongside Donna and Kathryn [two other participants].

Miranda, my older sister by two years, had died in 2001 of an aneurism. She was three months pregnant at the time and, after a day or two of tests, had been declared brain dead. She had died in Ireland and, due to the abortion laws there and her unique medical circumstances, her life support machine could not be turned off. The situation had been a world first, I think, and, as I thought about it again now, I realised that San Pedro had this in mind for me as a healing.

It began to show me that the situation was larger than simply coping with the desperate grief I had felt at the loss of my only sister because she was also the one person I felt had never judged me. Instead, she had always been there for me during my troubled times in my twenties.

The year before she died I had also split up with a girlfriend and even eight years later I was still having dreams about her. I had not moved on and had suffered greatly at the split, always thinking that it had been my worst decision to split from her. If only I had had more wisdom and been able to talk things through with her to work out our differences.

What I now understood as a result of San Pedro was that I *had* to experience this intensely upsetting set of circumstances. It could not have been any other way [because] I had been so 'in my head', in such a comatose state myself, that only this would knock me on to my spiritual path.

I felt sad and grieved but although I felt like crying, for some reason, I wasn't able to. I remember opening my eyes at one point and found that I was lying alongside a lovely shrine set into a recess in a small garden wall. On it were Christian images and, with the Mother Mary there, I was reminded of how I had been affected by the Catholic Church and had such strong disagreements with their attitudes towards my sister and her unborn child when the doctors had administered ever-stronger doses of adrenaline and other chemicals which they knew would probably kill her foetus, but which they were required to do in order to 'protect' it from abortion.

I looked over at Donna then, lying before the shrine in bliss, and it seemed to me that she *was*, somehow, my sister. San Pedro showed me through this how much I had travelled along my path and how, even though I had experienced such a dreadful split from my girlfriend and been treated so terribly by her and the man who had taken her from me, I could still send them love and learn from the experience. It felt like a sign of my growth and progression.

San Pedro also reminded me of my journey since Miranda's death and of all the amazing women who had come into my life since then; friends who had been there for me, offering their guidance and gifts. 'You have lost your sister but look at all the sisters who have now come into your life,' San Pedro said.

I knew there was one final purge to come and felt its energy like a multi-coloured ball inside of me. San Pedro told me to imagine it drawing the last drops of crappy energy out from my every cell and it came up through me and I coughed it out, more gently than I was expecting.

I collapsed onto the mattress again, and now San Pedro was telling me that it was play time! I laughed out loud. I was so relaxed and blissed-out that I almost couldn't handle it and had to laugh to ease the tension! Slowly I began to sit up and went out of the garden to explore again.

It was a wonderful walk and this time I ventured further, enjoying the scenery from every possible angle. At the Temple of the Moon, I gave thanks to my ancestors, my family, friends and for Miranda, with whom I felt much more connected. San Pedro had guided me gently through what could have been a traumatic healing experience.

We left the ceremony and the garden at around 5pm. Back at our casa, I was still processing a lot of emotion and had a chat with Ross about it. I saw then that the emotions I felt were not 'good' or 'bad' but simply 'what was', and I was able to let go of them and just 'go with the flow'.

I had a sense of completion then – and now – that I had managed to heal all I was meant to on that journey. I am sure there is more to do and that if I diet the plants in future the experience will be even more intense. But I will also be ready for it; more relaxed, more surrendered, and more willing to go to where San Pedro takes me. For now, though, I am ever-grateful for the insights, healing, and revelations it shared with me.[6]

Tracie: The world is an exceptionally beautiful place
Tracie, another participant on both my ayahuasca and San Pedro

journeys, is a drug and addictions counsellor from Norfolk Island, near New Zealand. She has also experienced addictions herself and, while she does not address either of these issues directly, her accounts are interesting from both perspectives because of what they imply about the connections between us and the flows of energy that make us what we are.

From these discoveries about what is "really 'real'" (in her words), it is a short step to acknowledging that our beliefs do, indeed, create our realities and then applying this to the treatment of those who are suffering from addictive and depressive illnesses.

My journey began in the walled garden of a beautiful casa at the foot of the Temple of the Moon. I shared it with ten others and was privileged to witness their healing experiences as well.

The San Pedro tasted like chlorophyll and was a bit hard to swallow, due to the consistency more than the taste. It took about 40 minutes to take effect and reached its peak about four hours later. It began with a sort of aching or tingling feeling in my teeth and mouth, and with a slight headache that seemed to get worse after drinking.

We could do as we pleased after drinking, and I decided to go for a walk in the countryside. The scenery was spectacular; even more so with the heightened awareness of San Pedro. I could feel the energy of the place and made it to the top of a mountain, with a great view of the Inca ruins and the Andes rolling away into the distance. I had an overwhelming sense of belonging, not just to this area, but to the earth as a whole and the importance of every curve of the mountain range, every boulder, rock, stone, and blade of grass. The life-force of the mountains felt ancient and slow, while the life of the clouds seemed young and quickly-changing, but all of it part of the same incredible tableau, and all of equal importance.

I ventured down from the mountain, visiting trees and rocks, and taking a closer look at some of the sites I'd seen from afar. I rested on a large rock shaped like a seat and felt cradled by the mountain behind me and welcomed by the valley ahead. I had such a feeling of peace and acceptance that I was almost reluctant to head back to the garden.

When I did return I drank some water and relaxed in a hammock to observe my fellow travellers. We had been advised not to talk to each other too much or interfere in each others' journeys, so when I saw my friend on her knees, sobbing, I just watched until she came to the end of her crying – and then rose up with the broadest smile on her face, totally calm and released! Other people curled up into themselves while some took pleasure in the garden, photographing plants.

I guess about five hours in I started to get a bit restless, so I tried talking with one of the people who hadn't drunk San Pedro and found that I was in full control of my words and thoughts. I could have a normal conversation but I also found that I was choosing my words carefully, realizing the power of words and even thoughts – and that I didn't have enough vocabulary anyway to express exactly how I felt.

Through the eyes of San Pedro the world is an exceptionally beautiful place. Every living thing has its place and it is all of equal importance. As Ross later put it, with San Pedro you realise that 'we humans are no more important or beautiful than a mud brick – but we are no *less* important or beautiful either!'

I have come home with new eyes and can bring the beauty of the world to mind and into reality by just remembering my San Pedro experience.

Tracie: Further thoughts on my journey
This email was sent by Tracie a few weeks after her return to Norfolk Island. Her experience had stayed with her and she had developed a deepened understanding through her reflections upon it.

Some basic physics: everything in the physical domain is made up of energy and information. The formula $E=mc^2$ tells us that energy equals mass in different forms. Every solid object is made up of molecules, and molecules are made up of smaller units called atoms which are made of subatomic particles that have no solidity at all. They are, quite literally, packets of information and energy. Hence, nothing is really 'real'.

So how are invisible waves of energy and information perceived as solid objects? Well... events in the quantum domain occur at the speed of light and, at that speed our senses cannot process everything that contributes to our perceptual experience. Objects made up of different substances vibrate at their own frequencies. So the reason we don't see the world as a huge web of energy is that it is vibrating too fast.

Our senses, because they function so slowly, register only chunks of this energy and these clusters of information *become* every physical object in the visible universe.

During my seventh ayahuasca experience I was able to see this web of energy and the shadow of my physical body a long way away. Upon reflection, I think that the speed of my senses had come close to catching up with the speed of light. I was without a physical body for a good hour and, as it slowed, I was eventually able to stand up and even to negotiate my way to the bathroom.

One fellow traveller was quite distressed by what I now understand to be a similar experience. In his distress he was calling for someone to 'turn it [his visions] off' and lamenting that the floor had disappeared. I now believe that for him the floor *had* disappeared. I didn't attempt to move or stand for a long time either because I also felt that I had nothing to stand on (neither legs nor floor), and there was no real point in moving anyway.

The web of energy flickers in and out very quickly (at the speed of light, I guess), and leaves gaps in our existence...we are here and then not here, and then here again. I thoroughly enjoyed this experience but probably couldn't have withstood its intensity for too long.

This brings me to San Pedro. Reflecting on my experience I am drawn to the same conclusion: that it also speeds up the senses. I was able to perceive a more subtle web of energy in the countryside, where the energy of the mountains seemed a bit slower. When I rejoined my fellow travellers I could also observe how our energies interacted and how connected we are to each other and the physical world. We are constantly sharing portions of our energy fields.

With every encounter, we exchange information and energy, and we come away changed just a little bit. This realization made me aware of my influence on others and theirs on me, and I became careful with my interactions, conscious of speaking only the truth, and of keeping my intentions pure.

I was also aware of the energy that other people brought into the garden, and how it affected everyone. One friend came in enthused by the mountains and his enthusiasm sent ripples of excitement through the group, many of whom visited the mountain with him during our next San Pedro session.

I would like to experience both of these plants again with the intention of observing our energy fields and learning more about our ability to tap into this energy.

Cara: I no longer feel 'hardened'… Whatever needs to be healed in you will be

Cara describes herself as a 'once hardened American journalist'. She first visited Peru some years ago to interview La Gringa for a feature she was writing on the medicines of the Andes. She initially made contact by email but La Gringa ignored her, not sure if she (La Gringa) was the right person to speak on behalf of the plant, or where Cara, as a journalist, was coming from. In response to this silence, Cara, the 'hardened journalist', simply turned up on her doorstep, determined to get the story anyway.

La Gringa decided that if Cara really wanted to know about San Pedro, the best thing was for her to drink it. She did – and hasn't really returned home since. I am not sure if her article ever got written because, according to her, San Pedro changed the course of her life.

I met her in Cusco three years after she first drank the brew (although she has drunk it many times since), and, ironically, ended up interviewing her. During our conversation, she told me what San Pedro means to her.

My first time with San Pedro was to heal a relationship problem with my dad. Things had been difficult between us for years and it was affecting my relationships with other men, my relationship to love and intimacy in general, and especially my relationships with children. Because of what I had experienced, I was afraid of them and, although I might one day have wanted children of my own, I wouldn't allow any child near me. I felt dirty, as if they might get polluted by just being close to me. I didn't know it then but I was desperate, nearly dying, when San Pedro found me.

As soon as I drank it, I dissolved. I became the sky, the clouds, the flowers, and I saw the beauty in all things, including myself and my relationship with father. I realised, at some deeper level than we are ever usually aware of, that *everything* is exactly as it is meant to be.

I saw the connection between my father and myself more clearly and it now seemed obvious to me that we had made a contract between us before I was even born, so that everything that had happened between us was predestined and, ultimately, an act of love, sacrifice, and connection – on his part too.

I had a dream of a white flower opening up and embracing me. It pulled my face towards it and kissed me, and then we rested, head to head, as it were, and I knew that this was a blessing from my dad's soul to mine. It gave me a new understanding of what my relationship with my dad was really about, and it also changed something in me.

Within two weeks of drinking San Pedro, I had met the man who would become my husband and, within a few weeks of that,

I was pregnant. There's no bigger way to say that it healed my relationship problems because none of that would have been possible without it. Before this I was afraid to be near children, but San Pedro gave me my daughter.

Today I am still a journalist, but no longer hardened. I believe completely in the power of San Pedro and have drunk it many times since, always with positive results. Most recently I drank it again to heal some differences that have grown up between my husband and me. As a result of that experience, I can now recognise – and own – my 'stuff' in relationships and if I choose to heal them – which I do – I know that I can and what needs to be done.

I would never suggest to anyone that they drink San Pedro just as 'an experience' or to say that they've done it, because, from what I know of it, if you set out just to 'try' it, *it* will try you too!

But, if you approach it with the right heart and respect it as a teacher and healer, I would recommend San Pedro to everyone. Even if you don't know why you're drinking it and do it as an act of faith and an investment in your healing and future, whatever needs to be healed in you will be.

David: A new direction in life

David moved to Peru after his divorce, about ten years ago, and, shortly after that, found lumps in his body. Even though he was still in his 20s, he 'just sort of knew' they were cancerous. He visited a specialist in one of Peru's larger cities and a lump was removed for analysis. It turned out that it was, indeed, cancerous, and he was recommended for chemotherapy, with the proviso that he should expect only limited success.

I had no money to pay for treatment and, given the prognosis, there didn't seem much point in it anyway. I was very resistant to the idea of San Pedro as an alternative, though, because I didn't believe in 'miracles' or the powers of plants and spirits.

A friend of mine knew some shamans, however, and without

telling me, arranged a healing for me – a sort of 'prayer meeting' – at his house. I wasn't there but those who were drank San Pedro and sent me their wishes for better health.

I found out later that the energy was so strong at that ceremony that every electrical socket in the house blew when they sent me their prayers. The shaman told them it was a sign that the energy causing my cancer had also unblocked and my tumours were gone.

The next day I took a three-day bus ride to the hospital to see how much chemo I was going to need and how much the full course of treatment was supposed to cost. The consultant made some more tests, but he said the results were strange: there was a 'signature' of cancer in my platelets but the lumps in my body had completely vanished so there was no need for treatment any more, only to monitor my condition.

A few weeks later my friend confessed to the healing ritual and, against my better judgement, I agreed to take part in another ceremony and drink San Pedro with him.

Not long into it, I experienced a huge amount of pain in my body. It wasn't localised to where the cancer had been but felt like my heart was exploding or breaking in two. I stood up and started to vomit.

What I threw up I can only describe as unearthly. It looked like wafers or shards of glass that were rock hard and had bubbles of air trapped inside them. They were completely solid and transparent. I could pick them up and look through them. I asked the shaman what they were.

'They are the energy which was stuck inside you,' he said. 'They have been blocking your heart for years so you could not love life and were inclined towards death. Now they are out and you are completely free of cancer.'

I tried to stay sceptical, but it looks like he was right. I have been well for the last nine years and took another test just over a year ago which showed that I was still totally clear.

What went through my mind when I drank San Pedro and threw up those fragments of glass was my rage and sadness over my divorce, just before I noticed the lumps and was diagnosed. I don't know if emotions like that cause cancer but I am more open-minded now because, from that day forwards, I have never had another problem. I am also much happier than I was, more relaxed, and no longer angry. My health is good and I have a new direction in life.

So my attitude to San Pedro has changed, and although I still hardly ever drink it myself, I have recommended it to many others and they have had good results from it too.

I suppose, in conclusion, that I owe it to San Pedro to say this: that it showed me why I had cancer and gave me a choice –that I could die or change my mind. I guess I *decided* not to be angry or to have cancer any more because I realised how precious life is.

Marianne: Whatever song our hearts must sing

Marianne is a healer in South America. Now in her mid-50s, she has been working with San Pedro for many years, using it in ceremonies to help others. During this interview, conducted in Cusco in 2008, however, she told me about a personal experience which took place some years previously, when she was first training with her shaman and teacher.

I had only drunk San Pedro a few times when my shaman took me out into the mountains one day with another of his students. We both drank and then he said to us, 'Today you will experience all of the pain you have ever known in your lives during this single ceremony. It is important, because only by doing so can you know the pain of others and be able to heal them properly.' I remember thinking, *'Now* he tells us!'

I began walking in the hills, wondering what would come next. I crossed a river and found a cave that called me then sat down there to wait in the darkness.

As the San Pedro grew in me, I began to see the faces of all the people who, in my life, had hated me or said bad things about me. I experienced every negative feeling it is possible for a human being to have. I looked at those faces and thought what might happen to me 'if only looks could kill'. Then I realised that, of course, they can and do kill, and that I was lucky to be alive because of all the anger and pain in the world – and so was everyone else because of what they had experienced too. I understood the resilience of human beings then and the powers we have within us.

Eventually – after what seemed like many lifetimes – my shaman came to find me. He gave me more San Pedro and told me, 'Now you will experience all the love you have known in your life'. He left me alone again and I saw every face that has ever looked at me with kindness, and I understood the importance of love.

In my visions, I also saw a cord of light that ran from my belly to the belly of my husband. I was just getting divorced from him and as I looked at that cord I saw an axe descend on it and chop it into pieces so no connection remained between us at all.

It was dark by the time I made my way from the cave and, as I had no torch, I didn't know how to find my way back. But I trusted San Pedro and, along the way, the road was illuminated as the plants on each side of me lit up to make me a path of light, like beautiful stars which had fallen to Earth.

When I got home to my husband I knew for sure that our marriage was over. There was such ugliness between us, which was so different to the love I had been shown by San Pedro, and the possibilities for beauty in the world, that I knew there was no future for us.

I had felt this before but, like many people, I had chosen to overlook it for the sake of convenience and it had become a silent agreement between my husband and me that, although our relationship was not serving us, we would stick it out for an easy life.

Now this seemed dishonest and, even though my husband had not drunk San Pedro, he saw it too and began to confess to several affairs. Instead of being angry with him, however, I felt compassion for the insecurity he must have felt in order to go with other women, for the needs he could not control, and for his courage now in telling me these things – and I found it easy to forgive him.

We had been married for 25 years and, lawyers being what they are, the legal process could have turned our separation into a battleground but now we made sure that our divorce was entirely painless. After my day with San Pedro, experiencing all of the love and hate of the world, it felt right to both of us that we should aspire only to love.

It is choices like these that make the difference to our lives. San Pedro had prepared me and, through it, I had already lived my pains and disappointments so what did I have to prove by living them again now and hating my husband?

We are good friends now, in fact. He is happy in his world and I in mine. 'To each his own', 'live and let live', and 'forgive and forget'; these are some of the lessons San Pedro has taught me.

Before I was shown these things, I would probably never have said so, preferring to believe that my perspective and pains were more important than his or anyone else's. Or, like many married people for whom the spark of love has gone, I might have said that it is better to stay together and experience a familiar and joyless ache than face the uncertainty of a future alone.

But now I know better and I understand that *true* love is all that matters – in whatever form it takes and whatever song our hearts must sing.

Kyle: It started on Ebay...

Kyle is an American musician in his 20s and one of the ten participants present on my Cactus of Vision journey. 'Even though I'd never been to South America or drunk San Pedro before,' he said during this journey, 'my soul needed this trip so badly that I sold my car to pay for it.'

It seems that his instincts were right and, after it ended, he wrote to tell me it was 'exactly what I needed – and what I imagine many people need. In Cusco, so much of my life, so much of everything I've ever known, was given the space and brilliance to be brought together. The results were deep.'

Kyle's band is successful and he has albums out and a full life on the road. After drinking San Pedro, however, he also realised that something was missing. The cactus has now become his teacher and he has continued his studies with it. He also plans to return to Peru to drink San Pedro again and possibly even to move there. The following account, however, does not concern his time in Peru but another encounter with San Pedro subsequent to it.

A deepened understanding of cosmic laws and forces, and of how these translate into ethics, values, and meanings – the 'what-should-bes' of human life and right-living – is common for many people after experiences with teacher plants.

Benny Shanon, in his study of ayahuasca, The Antipodes of the Mind[7] *reports, for instance, that there is frequently an 'appreciation that values – in particular, love and justice – are not confined to the province of human life but apply to existence at large and to the forces or beings that govern the universe'. These powers, and the values that derive from our awareness of them, are perceived by those who have worked with sacred plants as bigger than us and having to do with 'harmony and balances between cosmic forces'.*

There is definitely an element of this in Kyle's report (as there is in many of those above), which he sent to me three weeks or so after our journey to Peru had ended. The humorous style in which it is written should not be allowed to detract, therefore, from its content or from the lessons learned.

I'd like to share with you my recent San Pedro experience. This isn't particularly regarding my experiences in Cusco, as lovely as they were, but a ceremony I took part in a few days ago. Because of it, I came to be carrying a 100lb dog statue a mile and half in the still of night and it all started on eBay.

It turns out that there is a very nice and punctual fellow there who cultivates and sells potted San Pedro. So it was mail-order, sent packaged right to my door (who said we don't live in a free world?), and, with a little research, chopping, freezing, boiling, straining, and a whole lot of praying later, I had before me a beautifully thick, snotty brew in a plastic bottle.

Along with my offerings and invocations, I started the ceremony with some typical Western residue of the 'What if I take too much?' and 'Can I poison myself?' nonsense that we're fed by our so-called experts. I ended it knowing that not only is [San Pedro use] safe and healthy but it has been predetermined by the stars since before anything happened at all.

That knowledge came, of course, after the nausea, vomiting, rage, envy, and fear – the usual detox before the party. But even those moments are ecstatic to me now; honourable and poetic even – to say the least.

It's amazing and impossible to describe what comes next. Seeing in the texture of a wall, for instance, how your purpose, your beauty, and your talents are seamlessly one with the tantric pulsings, the pure life-force of all of creation, is a little hard to describe. But it's true. Just as it's true to me now that the wall I stared at for hours is no different and no smaller than the deepest yearnings of the cosmos. Just as it's true that it's entirely possible to glimpse the finer workings of the creative spirit and the rise and fall of man in the slow movement of a finger on skin.

So, during my revelatory laughter, sitting there at the entrance to my room (which is a side entrance via the backyard), I noticed this dog statue perched next to me: a sizable solid stone statue that I had stolen from people down the street one night a few years ago when I was drunk with some friends.

Now it seemed to be eyeing me. And then I was spoken to. Whether it was archangels, my long-lost conscience, or some amoebic astral creature, I don't know; nor do I really care. But I realized in that moment that, since I am intrinsically a part of everything, whatever I do in the world also happens to me; that my individual body is a microcosm for the world at large; a world that I create.

Hence, stealing this big stone dog, which I had been using to keep my door closed at night (my door knob is broken so I attach a cord to the dog's neck and tie the other end to the door to keep it closed) had automatically resulted in people trying to steal things from me – like my time, my attention, and my power.

It's also kind of funny that I had literally been using this dog to keep my door closed at night. That which I stole has been keeping my own door closed. Beautiful.

So then I found myself carrying this stolen 100lb beast – which was really my own curse – back to its rightful owners, even though it had been missing from their lives for about three years. I left it right in the place I took it from and the look on their faces when they saw it again must have been priceless.

Since then – lo and behold! - my mom has stopped calling to hassle me for money and my old acquaintances – the ones who took up so much of my power and time – have also eased up, like clockwork.

I used to have a cyst on my vocal cords from so much singing as well, and I realized the day after drinking San Pedro and taking back the dog that it is no longer there. The doctors said it needed surgical removal.

So, all in all, then – a victory.

Suzie: I wanted to fuck the Earth

Suzie's story arises from one of those 'chance events' that now seem synonymous to me with San Pedro. She is actually my neighbour, a professional yoga teacher and massage therapist in her 40s who lives right across the road from me and who I have stopped to chat with in the street from time to time for the last several years. During one of these chats a few weeks ago I noticed that she had a suitcase in her hand

and asked her where she was going. 'To Spain, to drink San Pedro,' she said.

Before that moment I had never known that she had an interest in teacher plants and, while she knew that I was a writer and that I visited South America often, she knew little about my work, nothing about my experiences with San Pedro, or that I was working on this book. Sensing the influence of the hummingbird, I told her nothing else about my writing project at the time, but when she returned I made sure to ask if she would produce a report for me on her thoughts and feelings regarding San Pedro.

What follows is what she sent (bizarrely, in this world of technological 'miracles', emailing it to me from literally across the road that separates her house from mine). It is interesting in what it reveals, and for comparison purposes, since Suzie (along with Marianne) is one of the few people in this study who did not drink San Pedro with La Gringa and I, so any commonalities might therefore be presumed to reveal something intrinsic about the plant and not the nature of the ceremony or the personalities – the 'set and setting' – involved.

I was one of a group of twenty people staying in a beautiful bohemian farmhouse in Catalonia, about two hours drive from Barcelona. The views of the surrounding land were amazing, with hills, woods and a snow-capped range of mountains in the distance.

We had just completed two days of ayahuasca ceremonies with an Argentinean ayahuascero trained by the Shipibo Indians. The San Pedro ceremony that followed was to be the culmination of our three-day stay.

The huge six-foot cactus was first sectioned and we were shown how to strip off the outer layer, almost like a sheet of plastic, away from the inner skin (which is the ingested part). The cactus was then boiled for several hours.

We had intended to start the ceremony as the sun rose but, as it was so cold and misty, we delayed for some hours until the sun came out. We walked silently and with empty stomachs then to a

7th century ruined chapel in the woods about a mile away, where the ceremony was to be held.

I drank a small glass of the pale green, slightly bitter juice then waited for an hour or so before walking with our shaman to a place in the woods where he said I should stay. He left me there and the San Pedro started to take effect. Everything around me became very still and quiet and slow, and my mind seemed almost to stop.

I realised just how many voices – like a chattering crowd of drunken monkeys – are usually in my head, and the relief of inner silence was blissful. Colours became more intense as well, and I could see everything around me with intricate detail, as though I was looking through a magnifying glass.

I crouched on the floor of the forest, running my hands over the earth, examining leaves and making sculptures from them and the stones and berries. I joyfully created two mask-like faces and felt so happy and free, and innocent and child-like.

Perhaps an hour passed as the San Pedro became more intense and I walked slowly to a lovely place with a fantastic view over hills and mountains. But strangely, I was still only really interested in the floor of the forest, searching out stones that glowed and pulsed with life and subtle layers of colour. I felt incredibly warm and sensual and had the urge to take off my clothes and roll on the ground, delighting in the feel of my body.

I stood up for a while and started to move and dance and do a sort of made-up type of tai chi. My body was strong and sexual and I felt like I wanted to fuck the earth. It was so cold, however, that I was wearing seven layers of clothes! But I still felt perfectly comfortable.

Insects, which are not usually my favourite things, seemed so sweet and happy and to almost have a sense of humour. They moved so purposefully and intelligently. I realized in their happy communal noise that I spend a lot of time alone and there is always a background sense of uneasiness for me; a sort of inner static, of always waiting for the next thing, never just *being* in perfect happiness and ease. I felt uncomfortable with that but I also knew now, though, that everything was just as it should be; that there is never anything wrong, and that nature and the Earth is in the perfect bliss of the moment. Hours passed in this state of communion and oneness with the Earth.

After some time, I started to feel sleepy and found it hard to sit upright. Rags of music drifted from unknown distances and I heard the sound of a drum coming closer. Our shaman arrived, his eyes and face shining with love and goodwill. He handed me a glass of ayahuasca and it was the best-tasting thing ever – probably the only time I've ever enjoyed the taste!

It grew dark and bitterly cold then and I sat in the woods and wondered if the others at our ceremony had forgotten about me. I could feel my old mind patterns beginning to take hold and realised that I had no idea where I was or how to get back to the house or the chapel, and I struggled a bit with feelings of fear and abandonment – my old patterns again. I could hear singing and felt left out and lonely but observed myself very clearly and laughed at myself for it, not allowing my usual feelings to take hold.

At last the shaman came back and led me to the chapel, all the time less than five minutes away! There, we sang some more and then closed the ceremony.

Walking back to the house in the pitch dark, but not having any fear of falling or tripping, I felt happy and comfortable and awestruck, and very connected to the others around me.

Reflecting now, nearly a month later, on the question 'How has San Pedro affected my life?' I can say that I feel and see so much more in nature. I deeply appreciate the beauty of trees and plants and can perceive their energy and depth where before it was flatter. My vision seems to be less three-dimensional and I see layers, especially in the ground.

My massage work has definitely got deeper too, in that I am

much more aware of people's emotions and can usually sense very accurate information about them simply from touch and even just by being in their presence, so it's made me more 'psychic', although I don't really like to use that word. This is a bit of a double-edged sword, however, as sometimes it's hard to close down as well and I feel like I have no skin but am always more awake and present.

I find it harder now, too, to reconcile my awe at the beauty of what *really is* with the hell of the world and the chaos of my mind and emotions. It's difficult to express, but I hope that's clear.

Donna: 'Just be'

The following interview was conducted with Donna, another Cactus of Vision participant, at her request, while she was under the influence of San Pedro during one of our ceremonies.

It is notably difficult to express yourself or put into words your sensations and experiences with teacher plants while you are still in direct contact with them (some even struggle to find words weeks or months later, as Tracie and Suzie have commented). Like most visionary or revelatory accounts, therefore, it is either brilliant and makes absolute sense or it is nonsense, depending on how you look at it.

I include it here, however, because it seems, in some simple way, to sum up the experiences of everyone whose reports have also appeared.

Ross (RH): Donna, this is a big question, but it's what you asked for! From your perspective right now, what do you understand by 'the meaning of life'?

Donna Waugh (DW): *Laughing.* Just be. That's all. You don't need to do much else; just be.

RH: What does that mean exactly? Is there a method to it?

DW: Yes, reach out to others. Forget what you've been told about the world and all the measures of so-called success that society throws at us. There is more to life than that! There is no separation and you are never alone. We are all connected and what happens to me therefore happens to you. If I don't reach out to you, we are all poorer for my inaction and all of us therefore suffer because I never acted and you never received – so we all remain unchanged. And what is the point of life without change or human experience?

RH: So what happens if we don't reach out or make changes?

DW: We get sick. All sickness – in ourselves and in society – comes from feeling alone. When we feel loved, we're powerful, and nothing in the world can harm us, but the moment we feel alone we lose that power and get sick.

RH: So separation causes illness?

DW: Loneliness. The sensation that love is missing. That's why we get ill.

RH: So what's the secret to good health?

DW: Stop being afraid. There is no *point* in fear. The world does not mean us any harm, so there's nothing to be afraid of. It is beautiful and we are beautiful too. All we have to do is make a choice to believe that and live it.

RH: What would this sense of fearless look like? How should we behave?

DW: It looks like God and *that's* how we should behave. God wants us to live *in His image,* so however you conceive of God, you are here as an ambassador for that and for His will on Earth. So why *would* you make yourself small or shy away from power? You represent something greater than that, after all. What *right* do we have, really, to hide away or to speak about the world and ourselves in words other than awe and beauty? Why would we throw God's gifts back at Him like that and what right do any of us have to do so?

RH: From where you are right now, do you have a sense of God? What does He look like to you?

DW: Look in the mirror!

RH: So I am God?

DW: Of course! We all are. Why did you ever think different?

When did you stop *knowing* that?

RH: I see. Thank you. Speaking now for San Pedro, do you have a final message?

DW: It's the same message: just be. Find your truth and live it with dignity. Speak it and help others to find and speak it too. But more than that – just be. That's really all you need to know.

Conclusions

In Benny Shanon's book, which I mentioned earlier,[8] the author distils the essence of more than 130 personal ayahuasca journeys, along with data from others who have drunk the brew in various settings. All told, about 2,500 ayahuasca sessions are covered, a figure that moves us considerably towards an understanding of the nature of this plant, its visionary effects, and the information it has to impart.

By comparison, the dozen accounts I have included, most of them conducted in one ceremonial context and with one shaman (La Gringa) and a single journey facilitator (myself) pale into insignificance, are open to bias, and, I well imagine, have little statistical validity.

But, still, these criticisms aside, it is interesting to see what common factors emerge from these accounts, so that we can at least begin to answer the question, 'What do people see and experience during their encounters with San Pedro?' These, then, are the results of asking that question.

Truth versus Fear

The issue of what we might call 'truth versus fear' came up in one way or another in at least eight participant accounts (i.e. for 66%, or two-thirds of our sample).[9] It appears to be a property of San Pedro that it empowers us to address our fears (or requires us to do so), almost as a form of initiation, so we emerge with a greater sense of courage and understanding, feeling healed and more in touch with what is 'real' for us.

Although I have not included my own experience in the figures above, fear (in my case, of being alone in the world and abandoned by God) was certainly a factor in my first journey with Miguel, for example. By dealing with it I was not only able to heal a physical problem but realised new truths about the human condition, the mechanisms of sickness and good health, and about how I should act in the world.

Michael's fears were different and manifested as 'feelings of claustrophobia when women got too close to me'. His vision 'addressed that fear head on' and also enabled him to arrive at a new truth: 'that it was a good thing if we [men and women] merged... I wasn't losing myself because there was nothing really to lose.'

Because of her childhood experiences, Cara was afraid of intimacy and especially of connections with children. What she realised during her journey, however, is that 'everything is exactly as it is meant to be'. As a result of this, she was able to move beyond fear to find love and, ultimately, 'San Pedro gave me my daughter'.

Marianne makes a distinction, in the account of her marital difficulties, between staying together through duty and fear, and acting from 'true love'. In order to arrive at this understanding, she, too, had to experience suffering and terror, in the form of all the hate and negativity (as well as all the love) she had ever known.

Suzie, meanwhile, alone in the woods, was left to work through her fear of abandonment. With the aid of San Pedro she was able to do so; she 'observed myself very clearly and laughed at myself for it'. Eventually, she realised that it was not really fear she was experiencing at all, but 'My old patterns again', and from that she was able to move on and conclude that 'everything was just as it should be... there is never anything wrong, and that nature and the Earth is in the perfect bliss of the moment'.

Suzie's case also reveals what appears to be another quality of

San Pedro: that while it may show us our fears or events from our lives which are challenging and uncomfortable, it never gives us more than we can handle. In fact, it offers us protection along the way. Hence, Suzie, while feeling alone and abandoned, was able to actually laugh at it.

Kane also experienced a vision where he was shown a part of himself that had been 'abused and was buried... [An] angry, violent, destructive part'. And yet, like Suzie, 'Although I experienced fear, grief, and sadness during my journey, I didn't see it as negative.'

Through encounters like these, in Jamie's words, we come to realise that there *is* 'no suffering' – apart from that which we create for ourselves – but 'only, ever, the pursuit of truth'.

Having sensed this, we understand something else too: the need to be cautious with our thoughts, words and actions, because of the effects they have on us and the way that they change reality. As Tracie remarks: 'I became careful with my interactions, conscious of speaking only the truth and of keeping my intentions pure.'

Finally, there is Donna's account, where she speaks from the position or perspective of San Pedro itself. In many ways, this sums up the need to move beyond fear and find a better truth for ourselves: 'Stop being afraid. There is no *point* in fear. The world does not mean us any harm, so there's nothing to be afraid of... All we have to do is make a choice to believe that and live it... Find your truth and live it with dignity.' And what would this new sense of fearlessness look like? 'It looks like God and *that's* how we should behave.'

The Importance of Love

People who emerge from their exploration of fear also come to sense the importance of love, and to feel greater love for themselves and others. This was true for at least 50% of those who provided reports.

Kane, for example, says that his greatest lesson was to learn to love himself and to appreciate the Earth for the love and care that it gave him. Jamie's realisation was that 'the truth *is* love, always has been, and always will be', and that it is important to 'Give yourself entirely' to its pursuit and 'Never take for granted the love that is before you'.

Michael's journey enabled him to reconcile his differences with his parents and, rather than resent them for the protection they gave him, to understand where their worry stemmed from, so his 'frustration towards them turned to love and compassion'.

Simon had experienced 'a dreadful split' from his girlfriend and 'been treated so terribly by her and the man who had taken her from me' that it had coloured his perspective of relationships for years and led to his depression. As a result of San Pedro, however, he was able to 'send them love and learn from the experience'.

Marianne, too, came to understand 'the importance of love', while Donna goes further, commenting that 'The sensation that love is missing' is the cause of all illness. 'When we feel loved, we're powerful, and nothing in the world can harm us.'

Finally, although Cara's experience is not included in these figures because she did not explicitly mention love as a part of it, one could actually conclude that her entire journey was an exploration of loving relationships and its outcome was love as well, in the form of her marriage and the birth of her child.

To Forgive is Divine

Allied to love in many cases is forgiveness; 17% of participants mentioned this specifically in their accounts and it is implied by many others (such as Marianne's forgiveness of her husband and his affairs, and Michael's re-evaluation of his relationship with his parents).

Among those who mentioned forgiveness directly are Kane, who learned to forgive himself, and Simon, who sent love to the girlfriend who had hurt him and also found peace with the doctors who he believed to have treated his sister badly.

Healing Relationships

Not surprisingly, in view of the above, relationship issues (including the relationship to oneself) occur in 92% of accounts. For Jamie, Cara and Michael it is their relationships to their parents (and, in some cases, to their ancestors more widely). For David and Marianne, husbands and wives were a feature. For Kane and Suzie, their relationships with themselves and the outside world were important; Kane in understanding and coming to terms with a hidden part of himself and Suzie in challenging her feelings of abandonment.

For Simon, the issue concerned his sister, his girlfriend and, to an extent, women in general. The resolution brought by San Pedro was to remind him of 'my journey since Miranda's death and of all the amazing women who had come into my life since then... "You have lost your sister but look at all the sisters who have now come into your life," San Pedro said'.

Other journeys concerned relationships of a more spiritual or 'cosmic' nature. Both Tracie and Donna commented on the connections between us all, for example, and between human beings and the planet as a whole. 'I had an overwhelming sense of belonging... to the earth,' says Tracie. 'Every living thing has its place and it is all of equal importance... When I rejoined my fellow travellers I could also observe how our energies interacted and how connected we are to each other and the physical world.'

To an extent, Kyle's experience is like this too. While returning the stolen statue, he acknowledges – and is, in fact, driven to action by – his insight that 'I am intrinsically a part of everything, whatever I do in the world also happens to me; that my individual body is a microcosm for the world at large' and that, consequently, 'stealing... had automatically resulted in people trying to steal things from me – like my time, my attention, and my power'.

Reality is what we Make of it

Kyle's story brings us to another of San Pedro's teachings: the understanding that 'reality' is not something that inheres in the world but is created by us as a consequence of how we view it, and by our thoughts, ideas, actions and words.

About 58% of people mentioned this. Kyle is one of them, of course, commenting that the world is one 'that I create'. Michael is another. 'Our thoughts are *things* and create our reality in the physical world,' he writes. 'We have the power to create our own heaven or hell with every passing thought.'

Jamie and Kane (whose changed view of reality enabled them to speak with the mountains and clouds) are others, as is Simon (who was also 'not sure' if he was creating patterns in the clouds or if they 'were doing it just for me'). Tracie also realised 'the power of words and even thoughts' to create reality and that nothing, therefore, is 'really real' unless we make it so.

The Beauty of Nature and the Nature of Beauty

Most people, 67% in fact, mentioned that they felt more greatly and intimately connected to nature as a result of drinking San Pedro. Suzie, who wanted to 'fuck the Earth', and who says, a month on, that she can still 'feel and see so much more in nature' is probably the most dramatic example but many others also reported a more profound appreciation of nature and the living world, and of their place within it.

Kane, who says that he 'met Mother Earth' on his journey, expressed a desire to try San Pedro again, 'this time to increase my awareness and communication with Pachamama, to assist and to heal her'.

Jamie comments that, for her, everything came 'alive, transmitting, feeling, being, knowing'. Her words, in fact, are reminiscent of Huxley's when he writes of his mescaline experience that it was one of 'Being-Awareness-Bliss – for the first time I understood, not on the verbal level, not by inchoate hints or at a distance, but precisely and completely what those prodigious syllables referred to. And then I remembered a passage I had read in one of Suzuki's essays: 'What is the Dharma-Body of the Buddha?' (The Dharma-Body of the Buddha is another way of saying Mind, Suchness, the Void, the Godhead)... the master answers 'The hedge at the bottom of the garden.' Through her encounter with San Pedro and the new world it opened up to her, Jamie achieved her own moment of enlightened insight and came to understand as well that nature embodies God (and *vice versa*) and that the human being is 'a simple creature like any other on this planet', no more and no less magnificent than a hedge, a tree or a carving in stone.

For Michael, 'The landscape was beautiful... I became part of the earth itself and had a feeling of complete peace... I looked at the mountains and the valley to my left and felt their presence. They were alive; breathing just like me.'

Simon found himself 'sat by the most wonderful red, yellow, and orange plant... I saw detail I had never seen before and realised just how beautiful it was... I looked at the trees and it was as if someone had turned up the contrast and sharpness in my brain.'

During her visionary walk in the mountains, Marianne noticed that 'The road was illuminated as the plants on each side of me lit up to make me a path of light, like beautiful stars which had fallen to Earth', while Cara *'became* the sky, the clouds, the flowers, and I saw the beauty in all things.'

Perhaps the final word in this section should go to Tracie, however: 'Through the eyes of San Pedro the world is an exceptionally beautiful place. Every living thing has its place and it is all of equal importance... I have come home with new eyes and can bring the beauty of the world to mind and into reality by just remembering my San Pedro experience.'

Although our accounts are not included in the figures above, the sensation of becoming the wind, inherently a part of nature, and of 'breathing with the mountains', was also common to the experiences of Donna and myself, of course. Were we to include these too, then the percentage of people experiencing this heightened sense of, and communion with, the natural world would increase to 83%.

God in the Landscape

Finally, there is a sense, particularly in connection with nature, that the world is ensouled and enchanted; that God exists and that the true order of the universe is love.

On Donna's first journey, mentioned earlier in this book, she experienced a union with the divine and became 'Infinite and Eternal Love'. She mentions God again in her interview, and comments on His purpose that 'God wants us to live *in His image*... you are here as an ambassador for that and for His will on Earth.' My own encounter, too, led to an experience of the nature of God and my place in His universe, which was not dissimilar to Donna's.

In total (not including my account or Donna's first experience of San Pedro) 42% of people mention God or His/Her representation as 'Pachamama' or 'Mother Earth' in their reports. Kane, as we have already seen, says that he 'met Mother Earth'. Jamie felt that she had to give thanks to God, 'who has brought me into this gorgeous moment of gift and privilege.' Michael understood that 'we are all part of God.' And Kyle realised that it is even possible 'to glimpse the finer workings of the creative spirit and the rise and fall of man in the slow movement of a finger on skin.'

Many of these realisations are consistent with those that arise from ayahuasca experiences too. Shanon remarks, for example, that 'Universally, Ayahuasca makes people reflect about their lives and leads them to what they feel is an enhanced psychological understanding of themselves.' It 'also induces reflections having to do with other people' and enables us to 'gain deeper understanding' of them.[10]

Reality, too, is often 'conceived as constituted by one, non-material substance which is identified as Cosmic Consciousness.' This is accompanied by a sense of 'a force that is the ground of all Being and that gives nourishment and sustenance to everything. Often this force is characterised as embodying love.' It is what I have described here as 'God'.

What seems to distinguish San Pedro from ayahuasca, however, is its immediacy and presence. Many participants who had experienced both plants remarked, for example, that San Pedro does not take us 'out of ourselves', as ayahuasca does. Rather, it is as if the plant possesses the body and compels us to see the world 'through the eyes of San Pedro', in Tracie's words.

By doing so, it also removes us from our 'heads' and the confusions of the rational and analytical mind, so that we are more present, of the moment, and in our bodies, as participants like Simon discovered. What it then reveals to us from this vantage point is the power and beauty of the world, the majesty of life, the soul-connections between us, and the knowledge that 'We, too, are That': aspects of God and a vibrant, living nature.

I put these findings to La Gringa and asked her to comment:

San Pedro can achieve healings like these because it is a master teacher. It helps us grow, learn and awaken and it assists us in reaching higher states of consciousness. Through it, we learn the truth of life and reality: that our health and our sense of purpose and balance is simply a choice we make; that we have a destiny; and we are more powerful than we think.

San Pedro reconnects us to the Earth and helps us realise that there is no separation between us – you, me, the soil, the sky. We are one. It's one thing to read that, of course, but to actually *experience* it is the most beautiful gift we can receive.

And so San Pedro teaches us to live in harmony, and that

compassion and understanding are the qualities of all true human beings. Through this, it shows us how to love, respect and honour all things. It shows us, too, that we are children of the light – precious and special – and to see that light within us.

Each person's experience of San Pedro is unique, as we are all unique, and drinking it is therefore a personal journey of healing and your discovery of yourself and the universe. But there is one thing which is always true: The day you meet San Pedro is one you will never forget. It is a day that can change your life forever... and always for the better.

Where Are They Now?

Does San Pedro really change lives 'forever' and, if so, is it 'always' for the better? I have said before in this book that there does seem to be something about the experience which 'lingers' and, more so than Strassman's DMT studies (perhaps more so even than with ayahuasca), for example, leads to life changes and benefits that are, if not permanent, then certainly long-lasting.

Just before this book went to print, I caught up with some (though not all) of the people whose accounts feature here to see where their lives had taken them. I also made contact with a few of the other participants who made up the group of ten who drank San Pedro with La Gringa and I that day, but who did not provide reports. It is now more than a year since their experiences. What has happened since then and what changes, if any, have they made as a consequence of San Pedro?

Kane and Jamie I know less about. I did exchange emails with Kane while writing this book and he was positive and upbeat about his life and relationships. This, he put down to San Pedro. He was also looking to 'settle down', although he had not ruled out plans to visit Peru and drink San Pedro again.

Michael, as I said in my introduction to his account, was so taken by his experience and what he was able to learn and heal in himself that he is writing a book on San Pedro too. His life continues to be good and he is enthusiastic about the future.

Simon has given up his job as an online business manager and moved back to the UK from Gibraltar so he can return to school. He is now taking an environmental MSc degree course at Schumaker College so he can learn more about 'the spirit of the Earth'. After that he plans to change careers and do something more 'worthwhile'. In the meantime, he is writing his thesis on San Pedro and the impact of teacher plants on 'Gaia consciousness'.

Tracie has divorced and moved away from Norfolk Island. She plans to return to Peru and live there. Soon after our ceremonies with San Pedro ended she did, in fact, make an offer for a piece of land in the Sacred Valley, where she wanted to set up a healing centre, with a special interest in the rehabilitation and treatment of drug and alcohol addictions, working with San Pedro to do so. That purchase fell through, but she still intends to follow her dream and, by the time this book is out, she will be living in Cusco.

Cara, the 'no longer hardened journalist' continues to live in America but visits Peru once or twice a year to drink San Pedro and occasionally help La Gringa at ceremonies, supporting other participants' experiences. Her approach to her relationships remains positive and she is happy. She believes strongly in the power of San Pedro to effect healing and change.

David has now been clear of cancer for ten years. He is happily remarried, has children, and continues to live and work in Peru.

Not so much has changed for Marianne. She works as a healer in Peru and her faith in San Pedro has never faltered.

Kyle returned to America after his San Pedro experiences and now works with the plant on his own. He is, however, going back to Peru, and hopes to live there full-time as soon as his finances and music commitments allow.

The 'lure of Peru' continues to exert its influence on others, too. Kathryn (another of my participants, who did not supply a report) wrote to me a week or two after she got back to New Zealand, following her ceremonies with San Pedro, that 'I still feel changed; not coming down from the high of our trip and its mind and heart-opening experiences at all. It was a wonderful highlight to my life and the lessons are becoming ever-clearer as I share them with friends. I was stretched way beyond where I thought I could go – and I enjoyed it!' Some months on, she is now back in Peru for an extended three-month stay during which she plans to work with San Pedro again. 'The girl who said "never again!" wants to do it again!' she commented.

Alec, too (who also did not supply a report), has decided, like Tracie and Kyle, to relocate. He stayed on in Peru after our programme ended, as a result of what San Pedro had shown him. 'I missed my flight back and decided not to book another', he told me by email. 'I am staying in the mountains, loving life, and I plan to stay here for another month... or two... or three!' He did so, in fact, attending other San Pedro ceremonies, and only returned to America some months later. During his stay, he sold his house and plans to buy a new one in Peru.

Suzie, too, has been bitten by the travel bug and is hoping to see more of the world. She is aware of her 'issues' around abandonment and continues to laugh at herself for them. Her commitment is to a more outgoing and adventurous future.

Donna has left her job and her home in England and, with a similar ambition to Tracie, has opened a retreat centre in Spain, where she also plans to work with San Pedro to help others to heal.

Of the thirteen people mentioned here, then, I know something about twelve of them and where their lives have gone following their work with San Pedro. Of these twelve, all of them have, in one way or another, made changes and feel positive and hopeful for their futures. That is 92% of our sample (and I suspect the figure would have been 100% if I had received information from our missing participant).

Relocations (5), books (2, including this one), and healing centres (2), from a sample of thirteen; these are not insignificant developments. On the balance of this evidence, at least, it appears that La Gringa is correct: San Pedro changes lives and usually for the better.

Fig 1. Participants on the author's Magical Earth journey to the Amazon, where this story begins, awaiting floral baths as a preliminary cleansing before ayahuasca ceremonies.

Fig 2. Kirsty, a jungle participant paddling in the red river, where the story of the hummingbird was told. Healing and toning tannins from the leaves that fall into the river upstream turn the water red.

Fig 3 (left). Preparing ayahuasca: Simon, a participant breaks up the vine, which must be shredded and added to other plant ingredients before it is boiled for several hours to release its visionary qualities. Simon's San Pedro account also features in this book. Fig 4 (middle). A Shipibo shaman oversees ayahuasca preparation by Mark, another participant, who also journeyed with me to Cusco to discover San Pedro's hummingbird medicine. The patterns on the shaman's tunic represent the nature of the spiritual universe as it is revealed by ayahuasca. Fig 5. (right). Shamans tend the ayahuasca as it cooks, adding the other ingredients necessary to produce the visionary brew.

Fig 6. Mandy, another Magical Earth participant, blows her prayers and intentions into the ayahuasca as it cooks.

Fig 7. San Pedro participants in Cusco with the author (in the white shirt). In the back row, left and second from left, are Donna and Tracie, and in the front row, second from left and on the right are Simon and Kyle, whose healing San Pedro journeys are told in this book. The image behind the group is a painting of San Pedro cactuses.

Fig 8. San Pedro shrine, featuring spiritual and Catholic imagery, healing symbols, and three bottles of the San Pedro brew. Fig 7 (right). A close-up of the mesa with objects of power and significance including stones, shells, and crystals, laid out, as Lesley described it, in a representation of the spine: the channel for spiritual energy. In the foreground is a San Pedro cactus. The normal dose per individual is about this size: a length of cactus measured from elbow to wrist.

Fig 9. The beginning of a San Pedro ceremony. Participants make themselves comfortable as the cactus starts to take effect. The dog, Loba, was a stray and uncomfortable with human contact until she drank San Pedro by accident when it spilled onto the grass during an earlier ceremony. Now she attends all rituals and enjoys the company of all participants.

Fig 10. Four hours into the ceremony. Participants Alec and Donna feel the loving effects of San Pedro. A month after his experience Alec wrote that "The lessons keep coming and life gets better and better!" He had decided to stay on in Peru as a result of what San Pedro had shown him. "I missed my flight back and decided not to book another. I am staying in the mountains, loving life. I plan to stay here for another month... or two... or three... and I look forward to when we meet again... hopefully in my new home in Peru!"

Fig 11. The stairway of light: A San Pedro 'vision' captured on film.

Chapter 8

'Every illness is Psychosomatic' The Mind-Body Connection: The Perspective of Western Psychology in Relation to San Pedro Healing

The cure of the part should not be attempted without treatment of the whole. No attempt should be made to cure the body without the Soul... the great error of our day is that physicians separate the heart from the mind and the mind from the body
Socrates, Philosopher and Healer

Although it is a common belief among Andean healers, I was still intrigued by La Gringa's idea that *all* diseases are psychosomatic and there is no real difference between our physical and emotional or spiritual states.

I was certainly open to the idea, and had experienced something like this during my own San Pedro healing: the awareness that the sickness I felt in my body – the headache, pains, and breathlessness that I had put down to altitude – actually began in my mind, with a belief that in Cusco I would naturally get ill.

Many of my participants and interviewees had said as much in their accounts too – most dramatically, David, I suppose, who had managed to cure his cancer through a change in attitude and belief. And I had heard about a range of other healings from La Gringa– from grief to diabetes and paralysis – all of which had one thing in common: they arose from a change in spirit or mental perspective on the part of the sufferers.

In effect, they had all, with San Pedro's help, healed

themselves by 'changing their minds', so I knew there was some truth in La Gringa's words. But, I still wondered, could *every* illness arise from the mind and soul? If so, how?

I'd heard shamans from other traditions and in many other cultures say similar things as well: that illness is a choice; and, these days, even many Western doctors conceded that emotional and mental factors can and do play a part in the onset and development of physical problems. Stress is an example, where an emotional reaction to social conditions can lead to symptoms including high blood pressure, strokes, heart attacks, and so on.

As recently as the 1980s, however, when I was taking my psychology degree, we lived in less enlightened times. In those days, psychosomatic illnesses were generally dismissed by doctors and psychiatrists as 'hysterical conditions': paranoid beliefs on the part of patients that they were suffering or in pain when the doctor (who knew better than they did) was quite certain they were not. The doctor's logic was that since there was no bodily *cause* to this illness, only a bodily *effect*, the patient must be deluded or making it up.

This was the legacy of Descartes again, and his obsession with measurement to the detriment of actual *understanding*. A broken arm could be understood, for example, because its cause and its cure were obvious. A stress-related heart attack, however, was far more intangible and worrying, not only because of its greater severity, but because it implied an acceptance on the part of the doctor that emotional problems could cause physical illness. From there, an uncomfortable path lay ahead where science might also have to consider notions such as the soul or other 'invisible forces' – feelings and social factors – that couldn't be sized-up, calculated, or recorded by medical instruments.

Perhaps we've evolved beyond that now but there is still a fair amount of cynicism among medical professionals about the validity of psychosomatic illnesses and their status as 'real' conditions, and many doctors would still dismiss La Gringa's ideas of the causes of illness.

And yet, there is really nothing which should be controversial, even to Western doctors, about the notion of psychosomatic or mind-body illnesses. According to Richard Gregory in *The Oxford Companion to the Mind*,[1] diseases are psychosomatic, and real enough, if just two conditions apply:

(i) Symptoms are accompanied by demonstrable physiological disturbances of function [i.e. there is a physical problem of some form or another], and
(ii) The illness as a whole can be interpreted as a manifestation or function of the patient's personality, conflicts, life history, etc.

Given a straightforward and non-emotive definition like that, it seems apparent that most (if not all) diseases would fall under this category since personality, living conditions, social history, and so on, inevitably play a part in how we experience the world and the illnesses that we may therefore be prone to.

Gregory continues that:

There tends to be a remarkable consistency in the psychosomatic disease, which tends to recur in a stereotyped form. The pattern is peculiar to each patient and more or less fixed... [as in] the asthma-eczema syndrome.[2]

From time to time [however] there may be a 'syndrome-shift'. Thus a patient who has had several attacks of atopic dermatitis develops bronchial asthma, or perhaps, later in life, rheumatoid arthritis. A sufferer over many years from migraine develops ulcerative colitis, or a patient who has had a recurrent peptic ulcer develops essential hypertension.

This also supports the Andean view that the body is not a discrete and self-contained system but that we are made up of, and respond to, emotional, psychological, and social factors as well as physical processes, because if physiology alone was to blame for every illness, we would perhaps not expect to see such a 'syndrome-shift', but a common and consistent form of disease.

If at the root of every illness there is a spiritual imbalance, however, as Andean healers believe, then that would account for this shift. The imbalance would express itself, that is, in a disturbance to the human being as a whole. The disease might then *appear* as an emotional, mental, or physical problem (or all three), following, in a sense, the 'path of least resistance' so that 'spiritual toxins' exit the body as quickly as possible and with the least possible damage overall as the system returns to balance.

In this sense, what we call illness is actually part of the healing *process* and, according to Puma, one of Peru's more famous curanderos who, with Joan Parisi Wilcox, produced the book *Masters of the Living Energy*, about the healers of the Andes,[3] sickness is never 'just a disease' but a message from our souls about how we are living and how we may need to change to bring ourselves back into a good and harmonious relationship with the world.

Puma (Fredy Quispe Singona) was born in Chinchero, Peru and, at the age of six, was struck by lightning, which is a sure sign in the Andes of being chosen as a shaman. He began training from that moment with his grandfather, a curandero, in the traditional ways of healing. Puma now works with the groups I take to Peru, offering coca leaf readings, ceremonies, and spiritual cleansings. I spoke with him recently about the nature of illness.

Where there is imbalance in our lives, it is the job of the soul to tell us, [he said.] Sometimes it does this through illness. It starts small, with a whisper from the spirit, but if we don't hear it, it will raise its voice until it becomes a roar. This is how people get sick and what we mean by 'the progression' of a disease: what begins as a cold becomes a heart attack – because we are not listening!

If we pay attention, however, we make the changes our souls are asking for; we rest, we heal, we look again at our lives, and then the cold goes away and the heart attack never comes. In this way, our illnesses can often be friends.

Concepts like this – that illness is a message from our souls – can seem unusual to us but, in fact, a number of Western psychologists have made similar connections and described what we might call the spiritual – or certainly, non-physical – triggers for disease. One of them is Stan Gooch.[4]

Some hysterical [i.e. psychosomatic] sufferers break out in a skin rash or boils whenever (say) they have to visit their mothers, or have asthma attacks when they approach the district where they grew up... A mental problem can in fact be converted into virtually any form of physical symptom or illness – and so can be a very serious position indeed.

Psychosomatic symptoms can also be transmitted to others, just as if a virus was being passed on. The common expression for this in the West is 'mass hysteria' or 'medically unexplained epidemic illness'. In the Andes, such outbreaks would more likely be regarded as a type of spiritual contagion where a wholly non-physical cause (such as sorcery or hexing) nonetheless produces a consistent form of illness for several people at once.

What is interesting here are not the differences between the Western and Andean theories of disease, but their similarity: both regard the mind and the power of belief as the most important factor in illnesses like these. As the healer, Eduardo Calderon, once said: 'The mind is what makes one fly [or fall]... What works is the mind. Sorcery, hexing, and curing are there. Without this, there is nothing.'[5]

According to Simon Wessely, director of the King's Centre for Military Health Research in London, mass hysteria is a phenomenon that has been documented since medieval times. The reasons given for such epidemics tend to reflect society's beliefs at the time. In the Western world in the past, he writes, 'witchcraft or demonic possession were often [also] blamed... In today's industrialised world [however], environmental contamination is more likely to be invoked.' The fact is, though, that nobody really knows what causes outbreaks of illness like this, although the mind is, again, a vital factor.

In fact, says Wessely, the most effective way to cure such epidemics is to explain to the sufferer 'the rumour or suggestion behind them'; to tell them 'it's all in your mind', in other words. Then 'the symptoms vanish within days.'[6] His solution begins, in a way, to sound like La Gringa's or Puma's: that by showing people their beliefs – the non-physical origin of their disease – they can deal with the cause and not just the condition. From this more empowered position, they can then let go of their problems.

It is not always that easy, though, to 'explain' things away to a sufferer, as Wessely suggests, or to persuade them that their *real* problem which is causing *real* diabetes, *real* cancer or *real* paralysis is the result of 'rumour and suggestion'.

What may happen instead in such circumstances is that a conflict is set up, in fact, between the patient (who knows he is sick) and the doctor (who is disputing this obvious fact) to the extent that medical opinion becomes worthless to the sufferer, who may also not trust the doctor to provide a cure for him either, since he won't even acknowledge the reality of his disease.

Where San Pedro treatments may therefore win out is that the patient, through the guidance of the plant, is able to see the origin of his *own* illness, without judgements or interpretations by others, and learn from it how to heal himself.

This was my experience when San Pedro taught me to breathe

that first time I drank La Gringa's brew: the realisation that, yes, the illness *was* in my mind (which did not make its impact any less real) and that the way to cure it, therefore, was to *change* my mind. Nobody else could have told me this, though; I had to discover it for myself.

Once I understood this, it was, again, the matador-spirit of San Pedro (not a counsellor, therapist, or other external 'expert'), who showed me how I would heal. This spirit exemplified for me – and also helped me to develop – a 'fighting spirit' against disease. Like Michael, whose account features in the previous chapter, I realised that reality was open to *my* interpretation and I could choose illness and despair or beauty, power and dignity.

By deciding on the latter, the outcome (for both Michael and I) was a new and more positive mental and spiritual attitude; a state of mind, in fact, which has been shown by Western researchers to be effective in combating even serious physical problems.

The psychologist, Richard Gross, for example,[7] writes about a study of women who had been diagnosed with breast cancer and undergone mastectomy. Those who reacted by showing 'a fighting spirit', in Gross's words, were significantly more likely to be free of cancer five years later than those who accepted their fates or felt powerless and unhappy after their operations.

Another study quoted by Gross found that our attitudes and moods are even linked to the number of antibodies we have: the specialised immune proteins that help the body fight disease. '[The] higher the level of positive mood,' he writes, 'the higher the level of [beneficial] antibodies.' Put succinctly: illness is indeed a choice that we make.

David Myers, in *Social Psychology*, refers to similar studies:[8]

Several... have confirmed that a pessimistic style of explaining bad events (saying, 'It's my responsibility, it's going to last, and it's going to undermine everything') makes illness more likely. Even cancer patients appear more likely to survive if their attitude is hopeful and determined.

One study of cancer patients showed, for example, that those who participated in morale-boosting weekly support groups survived on average for 37 months: 'double the 19-month average survival time among the non-participants.'

Support factors like these play a part in San Pedro ceremonies as well. Bonnie Glass-Coffin refers to the community aspects of these healing rituals, for example, when she writes about her active participation, as a patient, in healing the others present so that everyone helped and supported each other:[9]

I participated, like all the others present, as she [the shaman, Isabel] directed... When not taking their turn before the *mesa*, each patient joined the chorus of those who vigorously cleansed the one before the *mesa* and shook out the illness according to Isabel's direction... Then, we all shared in orally spraying the *mesa* to end the ceremony.

Many of the people I spoke to also mentioned a change in perspective as a result of taking part in their ceremony, where the world became better, brighter, and more beautiful – worth their being a part of – and they understood the connections they had to each other and to the Earth. The ceremony (and San Pedro) created a supportive and healing environment where they felt loved and held, and which, in most cases, gave them a new outlook on life. As a consequence, their moods, morale, and spirits were elevated, their understanding deepened, and their ability to control their circumstances was enhanced.

These factors – control, predictability, and understanding – are also ones that have been shown by psychological studies to substantially reduce the effects of stress on the body and the physical symptoms that can arise from it.

The San Pedro experience, then, is empowering in itself, because, no matter how desperate the condition he is seeking healing for, or how loose or temporal the community he joins, the patient understands, simply by being present, that he is not alone and can take comfort from those around him. This, in itself, may provide some relief from the stress of his illness or, at least, a sort of social support by which he can better cope with it. It is always powerful, psychologically-speaking, to know that our problems are shared – or, at least, that others have problems too – and gives a sense of combined strength and new resources to cope with them.

The ceremonies that go with San Pedro, furthermore, have the *intention* of healing. The patient enters a ritual context, a set and setting, where the shaman and the spirits she works with surround him with positive purpose and an atmosphere designed to produce a change in belief that, no matter what the problem, a hopeful outcome is possible. From this perspective, 'miracles' – in La Gringa's words – may indeed result. Or, as the psychologist David Myers puts it: 'Beliefs can boost biology'.

La Gringa was dismissive when I asked her about hypnosis and meditation and their possible contribution to the San Pedro experience:

> I never 'suggest' anything to participants. I step back so the plant can speak for itself... [Participants] are not 'hypnotised' but become a part of all that is – just as they always were beneath the blanket of the world that has settled over them.

I put the question to her for good reason though, because others have looked at meditation, suggestion, and hypnosis to try to understand more deeply the mind-body connection referred to by psychologists like Myers, and which La Gringa herself had mentioned. Their findings may have some bearing on the 'whys and hows' of San Pedro healings.

Dr Schneider, of the centre for natural medicine at the Maharishi University in America, for example, has spoken about a long-term study into the effects of meditation, which offers evidence that it is able, in itself, to reduce death rates by nearly a quarter.

> The study found that in older people with mild high blood pressure, those practising transcendental meditation had a 23% lower risk of death from all causes... The transcendental meditation group [also] had 30% fewer deaths from heart disease and 49% fewer from cancer... Previous research has found that transcendental meditation can lower stress hormone levels and blood pressure.[10]

During San Pedro ceremonies, some – at least – of the elements of meditation are present. This is especially true in those ceremonies run by Miguel and La Gringa, where the participant is encouraged to simply relax and concentrate on his spiritual experience, with little interference from the shamans.

But even in the more involved, stylised, and ritualistic events led by curanderos like Juan Navarro, there is still an emphasis on being *present*, leaving the outside world behind, and investing oneself fully in a healing action so that the mind becomes focused on health and well-being.

In this way, San Pedro ceremonies may themselves provide a form of extensive meditation, lasting for ten hours or more, which is geared throughout towards physical transcendence and spiritual reconnection. This deep and prolonged trance-state might produce similar effects to those described by Schneider; an outcome enhanced by being in the presence of like-minded souls.

Where these beneficial effects may lead is suggested by other studies that have shown that people have the power to create events in their minds which can manifest in reality. Given the right context and support, people can actually heal themselves by simply thinking themselves well.

Stan Gooch[11] writes of one such study where a boy born with a progressive skin disease was cured as a result of hypnotic suggestion. It was, says Gooch, 'Probably the most daunting and famous case of hypnosis on record.'

> The condition, *ichthyosiform erythrodermia complex*, is resistant to all forms of treatment. In it, a thick, black, horny layer covers most or all of the body, and this layer itself is covered with further warty excrescences. The skin, if such we can call it, is as hard as a fingernail. Any bending or flexing of any part of the body causes painful cracks, which ooze bloodstained serum. The condition also gives rise to an objectionable smell that others find intolerable.

On February 10, 1951, observed by specialists and later reported in the *British Medical Journal*, the boy was hypnotised and told that his arm would clear of the disease. Five days later, the scabrous outer layer softened and fell off to reveal normal skin beneath it. In later sessions the rest of his body was also healed.

The scientists who conducted this study assumed that some as yet unknown part of the brain must have been responsible for causing the disease, and for carrying out the suggestion that it stop. But what exactly is an 'as yet unknown part of the brain'? The implication of words like these is a non-objective one: that the brain is responsible for all of our life experiences and that scientists will one day discover its mechanisms. Until they do, however – assuming they ever can – might we not just as well call this 'mechanism' the soul or spirit or 'mind'?

Whatever words we choose, the outcomes of studies like these suggest, at the very least, that we all have an innate potential to overcome disease and be healthy, since we share the same brain structure (or, if you prefer, spirit). So, if one little boy can heal himself from such a 'daunting' disease, then we all can – no matter what our problems.

The power of the mind to affect the physical may also play a part in the onset and progression of disease, more-or-less as Puma explained it, and as other studies have shown. Subjects under hypnosis have developed spontaneous wounds and blisters, for example, when they are told that they have been touched with hot coals, even when they have not.

Dr R L Moody[12] believes that wounds like these are often associated with powerfully unhappy memories. He relates one case of a woman, for example, who, under hypnosis, described being beaten by her father when she was a child. As she did so 'whip marks appeared on her legs, buttocks, shoulders and hands. These were witnessed, photographed and reported by physicians, and had moreover to be dressed and treated.' The woman herself had been entirely unaware of these memories, but still they had acted upon her, even though they were suppressed or hidden away.

I was reminded, when I read this, of La Gringa's patient, whose painful memories of the deaths of her husband and son had produced her diabetes and paralysis, and who was cured when San Pedro led her through a full experience of them and provided her with a healthier alternative to holding on to her pain.

Freud mentions a similar case, in the celebrated treatment of 'Anna O'[13] who suffered paralysis of the extremities on the right side of her body, as well as disturbances of vision, hearing, and speech, and whose problems stemmed from her grief at her father's prolonged illness and eventual death, which she had felt powerless to prevent.

Anna, a young woman at the time, had put her own life on hold to care for her father and, one day while she was feeding him, the thought went through her mind, 'I wish he was already dead'. In that moment, as she reached over to give him food, her paralysis had begun.

As part of her treatment she also underwent hypnosis, during which she described 'profoundly melancholy phantasies... sometimes characterized by poetic beauty'. At the end of it she was completely healed and had full use of her body again.

If the power of belief can, under circumstances like these, cause illness or injury, it lends credence to the ideas of Andean healers that thought-forms, bad ideas, ill-winds, hexes, and curses can also create disease. For what is a thought-form or a curse, after all, but an absolute belief that someone or something else has power over us and that we can do nothing about it except suffer as a consequence?

The real challenge for the healer in situations like this is to change the patient's patterns of belief so that a cure can result. The San Pedro ceremony, the attentions of the shaman and the guidance of the plant provide the environment in which this change can take place.

What I have concluded from all this is that it is probably true to say that every illness has at least a psychosomatic component and arises first in the mind or, if you prefer, the soul; in any case, from a very personal part of our beings that is deeper than simply the physical.

Most people, of course, do not *choose* to be ill. Rather, as a species, we are easily conditioned and controlled by our habitual ways of thinking. We tend to stay within the boxes of our mindsets until someone or some other force lifts the lid on them and shows us a world outside and a different way of thinking and connecting to power.

Until then, we see no alternative to illness, even though our problems are, in a sense, all in our own minds, and a message from our spirits to pay greater attention to our lives and understand our ability to change them, so we can be well and in balance.

This 'wake-up call' is another gift of San Pedro. Through the new ways it shows us to comprehend the world, we can adapt and create health just as easily as sickness.

In fact, if you accept the view that our beliefs are easily programmed, as psychologists like Stanley Milgram may have shown us,[14] this is one area in which our affinity for conditioning may actually work in our favour because, by experiencing new teachers such as San Pedro, we are just as easily able to *re*-condition ourselves – away from illness and towards freedom from habitual thinking, through the motivation and support it offers us.

Will power, determination, self-reflection and a 'fighting spirit' contribute to our physical health. The door to these powers can be opened by many keys and one of them, most certainly, is San Pedro.

Chapter 9

'The Hummingbird Takes Us to God' The San Pedro Cosmology: The Perspective of Andean Healing and Curanderismo

The art of healing comes from nature, not from the physician.
Therefore the physician must start from nature, with an open mind
Philipus Aureolus Paracelsus

'The hummingbird is the stopper of time,' said don Eduardo.[1] 'And once time is stopped we can sneak between the hands of the clock to perform our healings – or any other miracles we wish. For you should know that all of these things take place outside of time.'

Don Eduardo is one of Cusco's natural healers, or curanderos. His practice, like so many others, is in a back room of his house: a plain white building with a rusting tin roof, no different to the other ramshackle dwellings that line his litter-strewn side street well off the tourist map.

I first met him in the early 2000s, during a stay in the city with a group of others who had come to drink San Pedro before taking the tourist route to Machu Picchu. Before our first ceremony, however, a painful infection had flared up in my leg. To cope with the rituals we had planned and to climb the sacred mountain, I knew I'd have to get it fixed.

'It is very grave,' said Eduardo, after taking a look at it. 'It is an energy - *mal puesto*[2]– which has been sent to create havoc. Do you know who might have done this?'

As a matter of fact, I did. I had not long returned from Haiti, where I had been leading another group of Westerners to take part in vodou ceremonies and healings, following the publication of my book, *Vodou Shaman*[3]. There is nothing wrong with vodou, per se, despite the prejudice that surrounds it in the West. The word, from the Fon language of Africa, simply means 'spirit', and it involves practices and the use of plant spirit medicines that you might find in any other shamanic culture on Earth. It was not the vodou that concerned me, then, but the fact that the *mambo* (priestess) we had been working with had turned out to be a crook who had done her best to part participants from their money without delivering much of what we had paid her for.

Ironically, in terms of the prejudices surrounding vodou, she was also a white woman, not a native of Haiti at all. But she had connections to indigenous healers and access to a *hounfor* (ceremonial area), and she was fluent in the Haitian language, so that is why we had chosen to work with her.

As things turned out, it couldn't have been a worse decision. She was a disruptive and hostile influence from the start, and had directed a lot of anger towards me in particular because I wouldn't let her get away with the scams she was trying to pull. Since returning from Haiti, I had continued to receive bad energy from her and her more fanatical followers had not just been sending 'spiritual' attacks but abusive emails and even death threats my way.

Eduardo nodded when I told him this. It sounded right to him.

He led me to his mesa, a long table on which he had assembled all sorts of herbs, shells, ritual items, artes, and bottles of brown, green, and yellow liquids. Others contained clear fluids which held graveyard dirt, flowers, whole tiny snakes, anaconda vertebrae, and the teeth and claws of jungle animals taken for their powers.

He crushed the pink shell of a crab onto a square of paper. This was interesting in itself for, although I hadn't told Eduardo this, the guardian spirit of the mambo who had caused so much trouble was La Siren: 'the siren' or mermaid. The use of the crab was therefore like turning her own deity against her, represented by one of the creatures of the ocean. Eduardo also added herbs and flowers to the paper, a sprinkling of grey-white powder, and folded it all into a bundle which he sprayed with agua florida and prayed animatedly over.

Then he held it up, set it alight – fire against water – and began to work the smoke over my leg and across my body, catching the intrusive energy he saw there and despatching it to a place where it could do no harm.

After some minutes of this, he led me to another part of the mesa and produced a bottle of greenish liquid which, plainly within it, held the body of a tiny hummingbird.

'You must drink this,' he said. 'You have been attacked by forces which have tried to drag you into their shadows. The hummingbird takes us to God and returns us to the light.'

Like anyone, I suppose, I was not delighted at the prospect of drinking the murky fluid surrounding a corpse, but I had come this far and I trusted the medicine, so I lifted the bottle and gulped down its contents.

It tasted surprisingly fine: like aguardiente, the fiery alcohol in which flowers and plants are often preserved by Andean healers, and also of honey and spice. There was a slightly earthy or meaty aftertaste, but even that was acceptable. I have drunk and eaten worse.

Eduardo then prayed for me, chanted words I did not understand into the top of my head, and 'flourished' me with perfumes which he sprayed around me: 'for triumph and for victory.' 'The poison will be gone by tomorrow,' he added – and it was.

The next day, there was no more infection, not even a trace of the blistering and inflammation that was obvious before, and my strength was back to normal.

I heard later that things did not go quite so well for the

mambo, however, who, in Eduardo's opinion, had caused my problems. First, her room in Haiti was burned to the ground in a mysterious arson attack. Several people then went online to expose her as a fraud. After that, it was rumoured that a warrant had been issued for her arrest as a result of some of her activities which had caused two of her initiates to be arrested themselves. This had led her to run, in the dead of night, back to her home in America, where her practice had continued to suffer and she had been forced to take a job as a janitor to make ends meet.

Coincidence? Perhaps. Perhaps not.

The hummingbird is a symbol, [Eduardo continued.] No, it is more than a symbol; it is a *power*, a hope or a blessing – for love, sweetness, and beauty: all of the attributes of God. And this is what you have taken into yourself.

It is the tiniest of birds and the only creature that can stop dead in mid-flight. It can hover, go forwards, backwards, up or down as it wills, and so it represents our choices in life and the many ways we may deal with them, for our lives are not just sequential; a movement from one place to another, like from A to B. We can travel in many different ways; from B to A or A to Z if we wish!

The hummingbird lives on nectar – the sweet things – and searches for sweetness in all it does. It is loved by the flowers because it spreads their sweetness too, and, from their pollen, new flowers grow.

It is the guardian of San Pedro because of the joy and light it brings. Like the condor, it is a spirit more than a creature, and the only animal that can look on the face of God. With hummingbird medicine you can also know God and, through this, understand and adapt to whatever circumstances confront you, so you always stay positive. Then you don't waste time looking backwards and wishing for what might have been, or forwards and wishing for things which may never come. Instead, you make the most of *what is*, because this moment is what we have and where our healing begins.

The Andean view of the universe and of God, from which its healing methods, like those of Eduardo, derive, is sometimes described as like a series of eggs nested one inside the other. The first of these 'eggs' – and the purest form of reality - is *Jatun*: 'the great force of life'. It is a dimension so mysterious and unmanifest that it can only really be known by God, and it is here that all of His plans for – and the true reality of – everything resides.

In this dimension everything that happens (or does not happen) to us – whether 'good' or 'bad' in our terms, and whether embraced and accepted by us or wholly and completely rejected – has a healing and evolutionary purpose.

This purpose may elude us completely because it is so beyond our understanding, but it nevertheless flows through all things as an energy which stands for what is ultimately right, even if it manifests as the unwelcome fates that befall us as individuals.

If we are wise, therefore, we accept our lives for what they are: expressions of the divine, and renounce our need to comprehend and control everything around us. By letting go, we find peace.

If we are not so wise, however, we may rail against God or the world in general, and refuse to accept anything but our own points of view. Such actions are futile, of course, since human beings are *not* God and we are therefore bound to fail if we try to do battle with a force so powerful that we cannot even comprehend it and which, in the whole scheme of things, has our best interests at heart in any case.

To be healthy, we must all finally abandon our fears and let go so that the plan of the universe can unfold and carry us with it. San Pedro is our ally in this because it allows us – even if it is fleeting and ever-so distant – to understand the will of God and remove ourselves from the fight.

Within the egg of Jatun is another, called *Wirococha*, which is described by some as a lake of memory and wisdom, similar to the collective unconscious imagined by Jung. It contains the spirit-essence or soul of every being on Earth and it is to this place, most commonly, that San Pedro takes us so we can draw from the knowledge and experiences of those who have walked our path before us: the ancestors, the 'soul of the world', and the spirit allies to be found there.

More subtly, within the Wirococha is another egg: *Pachamama*, the world as we perceive it. Pachamama is the most tangible of energies because it is the one we belong to, the one we recognise, and the one most manifest. It is soul in its bluntest form: physical reality and its spiritual or energetic shadow. This reality is the point at which we enter San Pedro ceremonies so we can be blasted free of form and enter the next level of being: the realms of Wirococha and Jatun, which is where our healing and the hummingbird will take us.

Andean healing practices are addressed first to Pachamama but in the hope that they will make their way, through the power of prayer and vision, to the ultimate realms of the intangible where true blessings are found.

In fact, however, since Andean healing does not really embrace the concepts of duality and separation, its philosophy of healing is even simpler than this, because a change at the individual level of Pachamama also changes, in some small way, the nature of Wirococha and Jatun. As our energies become clearer and more pure, that is, God is better able to recognise us; or, perhaps, we become more God-like ourselves, in a way similar to that proposed by the religious philosopher Teilhard de Chardin, where we evolve through the goodness of our actions until we merge once again with 'the Godhead'.

Within Pachamama, there are three levels, which broadly correspond to the shamanic cosmology of the 'three worlds' (upper, middle, and lower) that provide a means of understanding the universe for many traditional cultures.

In the Andes, they are known as *Ukupacha* (lower world), *Hanaqpacha* (upper, or divine, world), and *Kaypacha* (the middle world). The latter includes physical reality as we know it and its spiritual counterpart, so that every material thing has its energetic parallel or, as science now tells us, is made up of energy and has very little that is actually solid about it.

In Andean psychology these three realms are also planes or states of consciousness, in some ways similar to Freud's notion of the make-up of the psyche. The first, Ukupacha, in Freudian terms, would correspond to the Id, the place of primal experience and the shadow-self, where our instincts, intuitions, and fears hold sway. The second, Hanaqpacha, is the Super-ego, the moral or divine self which drives us to act in an ethical and compassionate way towards ourselves and the world we live in. The last, Kaypacha, is the Ego: the moderator between the two which enables us to make choices so we can operate effectively in the world.

During San Pedro ceremonies, within this model of understanding, the shaman and/or the spirit of the plant leads the patient from Kaypacha (Ego) – a situation that is not working for him because of his unbalanced interactions with the spiritual and material forces in his life – to Hanaqpacha (Super-ego): the transcendent plane where the human spirit meets the more universal forces and subtle energies that surround him. These energies can then be experienced, directed, and integrated so they play a more central role in his life and he can move from denser ego-led concerns to a lighter and more expansive way of being.

In order to reach this state, however, it is often necessary for the patient to descend first into the more shadowy world of Ukupacha (the Id), because it is only here that he can unveil and explore the hidden forces of his unconscious and see the beliefs, patterns, and complexes that are driving his behaviour and leading to unhealthy outcomes.

For me, the experience of this descent was the revelation of my belief that the world is a desert, and my certainty that I had been abandoned by God. I had never known this about myself before: that I harboured such a deep and fundamentally negative view of the world which had so coloured my life. But once I knew it, I could change it.

Kane also experienced a journey that was 'very dark at times. I was shown how for the past two years or longer I've been really cruel in the way I treated myself and I learnt that the evil I was experiencing was none other that myself, or a part of myself that had been abused and was buried.'

During Michael's descent into Ukupacha, 'everything was covered in red, the color of blood. I felt surrounded and closed in. There was so much evil. I became an orphan to the world.'

Cara felt 'dirty... polluted. I didn't know it but I was desperate, nearly dying.'

For David, 'what went through my mind when I drank San Pedro and threw up those fragments of glass was my rage and sadness over my divorce just before I noticed the lumps and was diagnosed.'

And Marianne had to experience 'every negative feeling it is possible for a human being to have' before she could find new light and understand that love is all that matters.

As I dealt with my revelations, I began to understand – first at a subtle level and then more physically and practically through the experience of healing – that I was creating my own illness and my fate as a response to the unconscious decisions I was making about 'how the world is.' My ascent began when San Pedro showed me a different way to respond: with dignity and power.

This, again, is similar to the realisations of others and may be part of the San Pedro experience itself. Thus, when Jamie emerged from her journey she also concluded that 'there is no suffering, only the pursuit of truth', and Michael discovered that 'what we most desire *will* come true... Over the next few weeks I was transformed.' Cara, too, realised that '*everything* is exactly as it was meant to be.'

For all of us, our San Pedro journeys had led us from the mundane world to a deeper understanding of our thoughts, beliefs, causes and effects, and, finally, to a new world which *was* touched by God. At the end of it we felt compassion for all beings because they were no different to us. We were all just trying to make sense of a world in which we had felt cast adrift.

As Huxley remarked: 'The way to the super-conscious is through the subconscious, and the way, or at least one of the ways, to the subconscious is through the chemistry of individual cells.'

A similar journey taken by a more conventional Western route might have meant years of psychotherapy or spiritual study to arrive at the same place and know that the pain, fear, anger, and sadness of the world all stemmed from a feeling of being alone and that our salvation therefore comes from opening our hearts and reaching out to the people and the spirit around us, because they are me; I am That.

This understanding of the human condition is fundamental to Andean shamanism, which is sometimes called 'the path of the heart' and is guided by the desire to find beauty in life moment-by-moment. The principles on which it is based are:

Munay: 'Doing the little things' with compassionate and loving intent so that every day is infused with a sense of beauty and when we close our eyes at night we rest in the peaceful knowledge that, as far as we were able and aware, we hurt no one by our actions, including ourselves.

Yachay: An informed wisdom which is greater and deeper than simple 'knowledge'. The former is provided by spirit, while the latter is a function of the more limited rational mind which is often led by ego, habit, and shadow. Yachay is one of the gifts of San Pedro which helps us understand the truths of our lives at a more soulful level and – if we choose – to live in beauty.

Llankay: Taking appropriate, wise and compassionate actions so we build a soul that is powerful and light. In this way we also become good ancestors and helpful spirits when we move on from this world to the next and the energy we leave behind is healing in itself – a 'good wind' – even if it is only a beautiful memory for our children and the knowledge that they were loved. Because of this the world becomes less fearful for them and for us all.

Kawsay: Respect for all life in the awareness that we are connected, one, and part of a whole, or, in the words of Henri Michaux, that we are all really just 'a passage in time.' Knowing this, we understand the fragility of our condition and the need for love because whatever we do in the world or to others, we also do to ourselves.

Ayni: Perhaps the best-known and most important of Andean principles, ayni is the way of reciprocity, a form of giving without the desire to receive in return but in the awareness, nonetheless, that we will be rewarded for our actions as the energy they create continues to circulate. Again, in the words of Michaux, it is the realisation that 'one is nothing but oneself' and, at the same time, everything: part of a shared fate. The Andean approach to healing which aims to activate these principles so they become real in one's life is *curanderismo*, from the Spanish word *curar*: to heal. It is a blend of traditions. Rooted first in Andean natural medicine, it also absorbed the influences of the Spanish and their approach to healing which was itself shaped by the Moors and, beyond that, by the Greek and Egyptian systems which influenced them.[4] According to curanderismo, disease is not just caused by physical processes but by social, psychological, emotional and spiritual factors too. Thus, 'there is a natural form of diabetes and a form caused by a supernatural agent, such as a *brujo* (witch or sorcerer). The same is true for alcoholism, cancer, and so on.' Curanderos therefore 'manipulate the supernatural world as well as the physical world' to effect their cures and 'On the spiritual level, illness can be caused, diagnosed, and cured by spiritual forces called *corrientes espirituales* (spiritual currents).'[5] *Bilis* (or 'rage') is one example of a disease which is both physical and spiritual in nature. It arises from emotional causes and is common in people who feel themselves wronged by another and so excluded from justice that they carry their anger like an energy within them which is strong enough to lead to stomach upsets or ulcers unless it is released. Their burning desire is for the wrongs they have suffered to be recompensed and while they are not a churning acidity is felt in their guts which is a like an impotent or repressed anger at wrongs that go unavenged.

Empacho and *pulsario* are similar conditions which also result from emotional causes. Both are blockages of energy at the top of the stomach which prevent its normal functions and cause digestive disorders. Shamans describe such conditions as a form of crystallised pain, sorrow or anger. They are more frequently diagnosed in women and may also be related to hormonal imbalances, with symptoms including restlessness, anxiety and irritability, but men can experience them too. When David threw up fragments of glass during the healing for his cancer he was also releasing empacho: crystals of sorrow and anger which had grown as a result of his divorce.

Illnesses in both sexes, and especially in children, can also arise from *mal aire*. This is literally 'bad air' although it refers more to a 'bad atmosphere' surrounding an individual or family. Children are particularly susceptible as they are more sensitive to moods and environments. It can result in colds, shaking and earaches, all of which may have a symbolic meaning as well as a physical presence (earache, for example, might manifest from a desire not to hear what is being said to, or around, the child). Problems arising from social factors include *envidia*: envy or jealousy, such as when a neighbour desires what is yours or resents you for your success. Instead of working to achieve the same results and benefits for themselves, however, they direct an unhealthy energy towards you and this becomes a form of spirit intrusion which works away at your soul. *Mal puesto* (hexing or cursing) and *mal ojo* (the evil eye: staring intently with the desire to harm) are related to envidia and can result in vomiting, diarrhoea, fever, insomnia and depression on the part of the person who receives the attack.

A more spiritual problem can also arise, known as *mal suerte* or *saladera*: bad luck, where the sufferer's energy becomes so low or they become so disheartened that they cannot achieve anything positive. A related condition, more common in the Amazon, is *daño* ('harm'), a magical illness which is often sent by a sorcerer working on behalf of a client and is therefore serious. Its symptoms include pain, fatigue, problems with breathing and, over time, the appearance of tumours or other diseases which take physical forms in the body. Daño must be treated magically to remove the spiritual poison or *virote* – the 'evil thorn' or dart – which has been sent to the sufferer, and return it to its source.

Susto is soul loss; a condition where we lose part of our spirit, or our energy becomes so blocked and depleted that we no longer have access to our full power or to aspects of ourselves that we need for our well-being and to get on with our lives. It may arise from shock, trauma, abuse, or injustice, and its symptoms can include nervous disorders, feelings of fear and panic, loss of appetite and energy, lack of trust in or engagement with the world, or a general malaise and decline, as if from a broken heart.

Jean-Pierre Chaumeil makes an interesting observation about illnesses like these in *Varieties of Amazonian Shamanism*.[6] In the jungle traditions of the ayahuasca shaman, he says, diseases are more often diagnosed as having been sent to the sufferer by a neighbour or sorcerer (as in cases of daño). The cure normally involves removing the problem and returning its energy with full force to whoever has sent it. In the modern urban setting, however, and in areas like the Andes where San Pedro is the medicine of choice, such approaches have become softened – or in Chaumeil's word, 'moralised' – so that the healer is more inclined to locate the source of suffering not wholly in the spirit world or with an external enemy, but within the patient himself.

This is congruent with the teachings of San Pedro: that we must face ourselves and our responsibilities so we find our salvation within, because that is where true healing lies. By doing so, we understand the connections between us and the imbalances which have led to our illnesses and we find that these often relate to some moral or social transgression on our parts as well which have caused our problems or at least contributed to them through a chain of events that gave rise to disease-causing energy. Thus, even if the illness has been deliberately wished on us by a rival, we as sufferers are not absolved of all responsibility but part of the web of interactions that led to it.

Mal puesto relates to a curse that has been directed at us by an enemy, for example, but the questions arise, even so: What have we done to draw attention to ourselves in this way? Why do we have enemies in the first place?

Mal aire is another example. It is commonly diagnosed as arising from a bad atmosphere in a home, so it is not an entirely spiritual problem but also relates to the social and psychological make-up of the people who live in that household, because if they were happy and powerful they would not attract such an intrusive force.

The onus is also on the patient, therefore, to identify and correct whatever he has been doing to weaken his spirit and put himself at risk. By taking responsibility for his illness, he gives himself the power to heal it.

It could be argued, in view of this, that Andean healing is more sophisticated than jungle medicine. It does not involve just one cause and effect, for example, or one action and counter-action, but necessitates a deeper examination of our psychology, including our morals and motivations, behaviour and under-lying beliefs. In this way, we come to understand the wider pattern of interactions and the subtle flows of energy that influence our lives, just as Kyle discovered after drinking San Pedro and making his odyssey to return the stolen statue. Once he had done so he found that his own life cleared up too and that people stopped stealing time and energy from him.

The San Pedro shaman, as well as a plant alchemist and a practitioner of traditional medicine, therefore also becomes a sort of psychologist, priest, confessor or therapist who can help us see our patterns of behaviour and how they fit into the wider universe.

Asked if she considers 'psychotherapy' like this to be a tool of the modern curandera, Doris Rivera Lentz, another of Cusco's 'La Gringas',[7] agrees that:

I need to use psychology in my work. I show the patient that he is not the victim of sorcery but is creating the problem in his mind. Bringing it out is the first part of becoming well again.

It is true that some people will take vengeance through black magic when they feel prejudiced or offended in some way. When people think they have power and feel superior, the ego can become very negative. The first thing I do [though] is to wake up the consciousness of the person who has been harmed and tell them that evil does not exist. 'You are inventing it', I tell them. Neither good nor bad exists... we create the good and the bad.

I recognise that the person may *feel* attacked [but] when someone falls ill it means they are weak and the curandera must speak positively and encourage them to shine light on it. Then they can create positive thoughts for themselves.

People get ill because they are not in equilibrium. Resentment, for example, causes cancer. Someone who is aggressive and violent is weakened in their heart, stomach, and solar plexus: the *ñawi* or *naira*[8] where emotional attitudes are held. In the Andes, people will frequently consider an aching stomach to have been caused by sorrow. People who do not have the freedom to express their feelings suffer from throat problems, and so on.

How does the San Pedro ceremony help them? I had wondered. What finally drives people to seek healing?

'Desperation [as in a spiritual crisis],' said Doris. It is this which will 'show the necessity of love. We need to work daily to balance ourselves, so the collective fear [of a lack of love] will not infect us. Even if those around you are overcome, *you* must maintain your centre. Individualism doesn't work and this [realisation] will unite us in a shared future... [We must] come back to a new kind of community consciousness.'

Don Eduardo had said much the same thing during my healing with him:

What matters is that people come back to equilibrium so they are more whole, more human and they remember who they are. People who are balanced know something of God. Huachuma[9] provides our answers because it leads us back to God and His community of souls.

That is where the hummingbird flies: to the surgery of God, where everything is put right and our courses in life are corrected. Curanderos heal; sometimes we even cure... But huachuma is the remedy![10]

The spiritual cosmology of the Andean healer, then, is one where invisible forces are born from unseen worlds which exist both within and without us. These forces, although immaterial, can affect us not only emotionally but physically and bring us good fortune or ill-health depending on our alignment to, and relationship with, them. The work of the curandero is to restore the patient to balance so he is in harmonious standing to these powers and not acting against them or allowing them to overwhelm him.

To create this necessary balance three things are important:

1. Convincing the patient that a cure *is* possible and enlisting his help to find it in the diagnosis and treatment which follows. This may require a confessional or psychotherapeutic approach on the part of the healer to discover what the patient has done to contribute to his own ill-health; a process which in curanderismo is known as *placitas*: 'a heart-to-heart, soul-to-soul discussion.' Once the patient's role is understood part of the cure may then be for him to make amends, in a practical way, to those he has offended, even if they have also done him harm. In this way, balance is at least restored between the patient and the cosmic forces which act upon him.

2. Persuading the patient that his mind, spirit and other resources are powerful and, with the help of the curandero, his greatest assets for dealing effectively with his problems; that 'One frightens oneself', or 'The mind makes one fly', as Calderon put it.

3. Enabling the patient to become more aware of the forces around him, his relationship and responsibility towards them, to others and to himself, so that continuing good health is assured.

San Pedro may be of help in all of these areas, but it has special significance in the latter for, as David Luke says in his Introduction, there is research to suggest that the mescaline cactus gives us access to areas of our brains which we do not ordinarily use but which, when activated, allow us to perceive the cosmic order and experience ourselves within it.

This research stems in the main from the theories of Henri Bergson, the 19th century philosopher who developed the 'concept of multiplicity'. This states that our moment-to-moment experience of the world is built or invented by us through our selection of specific information from the 'the immediate data of consciousness'[11]: the vast array of knowledge that is actually available to us and which Huxley called 'Mind at large'. This data is both internal and external and includes the memory of every experience we have ever had, along with the perception of everything that is happening anywhere and everywhere in the universe.

Most of this data is unimportant for our survival, however; some of it is 'useless' and contradictory, in fact, so it would simply overwhelm and confuse us if we had to try to make sense of it all. It may even be *detrimental* to our survival if every split-second, life-or-death decision (like how best to avoid an oncoming car) had to be made consciously while pondering the millions of options available to us.

Bergson believed therefore that the primary role of the brain, in the face of this multiplicity, is to act as a filter or gate for memory and sensory experience so we select what is useful from the range of data available according to the situations in which we find ourselves. In this way, we construct the world by rejecting some of its information content and embracing that which remains.

Literally, therefore, we are self-limiting beings and there are things, forces, and energies around us right now which we cannot or will not, under normal circumstances, perceive because our brains do not allow it. If these filters were bypassed, however, and 'the doors of perception' were opened, then we would be capable of remembering and experiencing *everything* from a richer, fuller and more 'cosmic' perspective.

This seems to be what my participants experienced. It is what Michael means when he talks of a 'past life recall' (i.e. the perception of his life from a more expanded point of view) and what Tracie is referring to when she says she felt 'an overwhelming sense of belonging to the Earth as a whole' so she was 'able to perceive a more subtle web of energy' which connected her to others.

It is also there in Marianne's experience of 'every negative feeling it is possible for a human being to have' and 'every face that has ever looked at me with kindness' and in Kyle's realisation that even the texture of a wall can reveal 'your purpose, your beauty and your talents... [all] seamlessly one with the tantric pulsings, the pure life-force of all of creation.' It also seems to me the best explanation for Donna's gift of vision and foresight that enabled her to see her daughter's pregnancy before even she was aware of it.

'About the physiological effects of mescalin we know a little', writes Huxley. 'Probably (for we are not yet certain) it interferes with the enzyme system that regulates cerebral functioning. By doing so it lowers the efficiency of the brain as an instrument for focusing mind on the problems of life on the surface of our planet. This lowering of what may be called the biological efficiency of the brain seems to permit entry into consciousness of other classes of mental events, which are normally excluded, because they possess no survival value... The man who comes back through the Door in the Wall will never be quite the same as the man who went out. He will be wiser but less cocksure, happier but less self-satisfied, humbler in acknowledging his ignorance yet better equipped to understand the relationship of words to things, of systematic reasoning to the unfathomable Mystery.' Dr Luke writes[12] that:

Recent research into the neurochemistry of psychedelics lends some support to [Bergson's and Huxley's] simple notion. For instance, Vollenweider and Geyer[13] propose that information processing in cortico-striato-thalamo-cortical (CSTC) feedback loops [in the brain] is disrupted by psychedelics via 5-HT (serotonin) receptor agonism (specifically 5-HT_{2A} receptors), thereby inhibiting the 'gating' of extraneous sensory stimuli and subsequently inhibiting the ability to attend selectively to salient environmental features.

In other words: plants like San Pedro do, indeed, expand our normal brain processes and widen our perception and experience of the world.

Furthermore, [he continues,] psychedelics are also thought to induce presynaptic release of glutamate from thalamic afferents, leading to a simultaneous overload of internal information in the cortex.

It is thought that these combined information overload effects are at least partly responsible for the 'hallucinogenic' experience with these drugs, which are known to induce greatly altered or amplified incoming sensory information. This disruption of the sensory gating function by psychedelics could also underpin the neurochemistry of ESP... elicited with any number of psychedelics such as mescaline.

That entheogens like mescaline and San Pedro have a central role to play in psi experiences[14] is supported, in Luke's words, by 'a wealth of collectively compelling anecdotal, anthropological, clinical, and survey reports, along with a body of preliminary experimental research... Mescaline is one substance in particular that, according to the historical, anthropological and anecdotal evidence, is known to induce psi experiences.

'Ever since the use of peyote was first documented in the mid-16th century by the personal physician of King Philip II of Spain, Dr Francisco Hernández, it has been reputed to have prophetic qualities. "It causes those devouring it to be able to foresee and to predict things..."[15]

'San Pedro has been used traditionally by the indigenous people of Peru, Bolivia, Chile and Ecuador for the same type of magico-religious practices, such as divination... a sixteenth century Spanish officer stationed in Cuzco, Peru, described how the natives "take the form they want and go through the air in a short time; and they see what is happening".[16]

'This literature is backed up by experiential reports from non-indigenous mescaline-users, like that of the French researchers who gave mescaline to six subjects, one of whom temporarily developed very detailed and accurate clairvoyant abilities.'[17]

After his mescaline experiences in 1951, Humphry Osmond also claimed to have successfully transmitted telepathic information to a fellow researcher, Duncan Blewett, who was also under the influence of mescaline, 'leading an independent observer to panic at the uncanny event.'[18]

Dr Luke concludes from the research so far that 'mescaline did indeed give rise to reports of telepathy and precognition among those using it', along with 'the perception of auras, the experience of encountering the plant's spirit, and a sense of unity.'

This sense of unity – expressed here as reunification with the self – is surely what Kane is describing when he says that 'My greatest lesson was to forgive and love myself', or Jamie when she is able to embrace a 'present where I have arrived in full knowledge and love of myself.'

On the evidence of this, the most profound gift of San Pedro may well be the expansion in awareness it gives us. Through it, we come to understand the 'bigger picture' of the universe, the flows of energy within it, and how we connect to them so we can learn, in Miguel's words, to become 'the true human' and find the balance and healing we need.

This is what don Eduardo meant when he referred to the

hummingbird as 'the stopper of time' which 'leads us to God': San Pedro as the force which disrupts our normal, limited perception of reality and gives us a wider and more holistic experience of the universe and the range of healing information it contains.

Chapter 10

"That God Quit a Long Time Ago"
Perspectives on God and San Pedro

Is man one of God's blunders? Or is God one of man's blunders?
Friedrich Nietzsche

'I said that I would introduce you to God, not that God would make sense to you!' said don Raphael, laughing.

Another San Pedro ceremony; this one different again. While I had experienced a new awareness during the ceremonies I had attended with Miguel and La Gringa, I had never felt myself remotely close to 'God' in, I suppose, a religious sense of the word, as I had taken don Eduardo's comments to imply. During my first ceremony with Miguel I had even found myself excluded from Paradise. Like Heinrich Klüver's concept of *presque vu*, the *feeling* of being welcomed into the presence of God had remained elusive and just out of reach.

This, I reasoned, must have something to do with me; with my notion of 'God' or my own relationship to 'unity' – and therefore to my sense of being in the world. That, at least, is what the Andean model of healing would imply: that the outer reflects the inner and distance from God meant distance from oneself.

I had decided to drink San Pedro again, therefore; this time with the intention of entering the Paradise I had felt myself outside of, in the hope of resolving – or, at least, understanding – my sense of wilful isolation. Don Raphael had accepted the challenge of guiding me through this.

Raphael was born in Piura, near the white beach of Cabo Blanco, famous for its marlin and said to be the inspiration for Hemingway's *The Old Man And The Sea*, with its world-weary fisherman and the adversary which becomes his worthy opponent and ultimately, perhaps, his saviour.

Piura is also known for its sacred lakes – Las Huaringas, in the Quechua language – where sky and water meet, which have been important in curanderismo since pre-Hispanic times because of their healing powers.

The legend of the lakes, another Andean fable, tells of a deaf mute who went into the mountains to look for El Dorado, the lost city of gold, where he hoped to find riches and a cure for his ailments. It is said that he found the hidden city and was, indeed, cured, but so touched by the beauty of his surroundings that he forgot his desire for gold or any wish to return home and now his spirit haunts the land, lost in awe and enchantment. It is a metaphor for the journey we all make to God.

Raphael began the ceremony by blowing *mapacho* smoke throughout the room, filling it with sweet aromatic clouds of the jungle tobacco which is so different and so much purer than the drug we know in the West.

It arrives at the markets in long tubes of highly condensed shredded leaves, each tube weighing several pounds, and is then broken up by the traders and hand-rolled, with no chemicals or additives, to make individual *cigaros* two or three times the thickness of a normal cigarette; a sort of white paper cigar which is bundled with others and sold in rolls of 50 or 100. You can buy them at Belen Market in Iquitos for a few soles, although they are less common in the Andes.

Mapachos can be smoked like normal cigarettes, but they rarely are. The shamans believe they contain good spirits and use them ceremonially instead to cleanse the energy of their patients and keep the things of the night at bay. There are few shamans who, during their healing rituals, do not constantly have a mapacho in their mouths to ensure that the environment they are working in is safe and pure.

Raphael then burned sticks of Palo Santo: incense used in the

Andes to freshen and sweeten ceremonial spaces. It has one of the most beautiful aromas, uplifting and soothing at the same time. The smouldering sticks are racked in piles or hand-held like wands to direct smoke around the shaman and his patient and into areas of the room where more shadowy forces need to be dispelled.

Kneeling before his mesa, Raphael began to pray, in a tongue which was not Spanish or Quechua but more the sort of meta-language that shamans sometimes use to speak with their angels and allies in spirit.

Rocking gently backwards and forwards, at certain stages in his prayer he would point to the North, South, East and West, until all the directions of the four winds were covered, then to the sky and earth. Finally, he made a clockwise circling motion of Palo Santo smoke over the centre of the mesa: the place where the energies of the four directions were to be brought, spiralled down into the altar itself.

At last his petitions ended and he picked up a bottle of reddish-black liquid from the arrangement of objects on his mesa. Opening it, he blew tobacco smoke into it.

From the colour of the liquid, I anticipated – correctly – that this was tobacco juice, and I began to prepare myself for the ritual of singado: the snorting of tobacco for removing negative energies and imparting positive new ones. I have never enjoyed this ritual but it is part of many San Pedro ceremonies and I had resigned myself to it. The fact that Raphael had picked up a cup and not a shell, however – the customary vessel for singado – was something new.

He offered me the cup, motioning for me to drink not snort the contents. 'You will certainly vomit,' he said. 'But this is good. The negative energies hidden in your soul will be expelled and your stomach will be cleared so San Pedro has a clean vessel.'

With contrachisa, the emetic formula offered by some shamans prior to drinking San Pedro, there is a delayed effect and it can take half an hour or so for the potion to work. Drinking tobacco and aguardiente, however, as Raphael presented it here, is more immediate. I had barely swallowed the bitter sickly-sweet liquid and registered its acrid, searing, taste – and Raphael had barely motioned to the bucket at my side – than I was spewing it back up as a stream of equally noxious fluid.

I couldn't imagine what spiritually healing effects it might have. Unlike the contrachisas of the past, it hardly had time to reach my stomach yet alone conduct an exploration of my soul before it was exploring the bottom of a bucket.

Raphael looked pleased with the result, however, and I supposed that, on a physical level, at least, it – and the fast I had undertaken the day before – would ensure that there was no food left in my stomach to get in the way of San Pedro.

Raphael allowed a few minutes to pass in silence until we were both sure there would be no more vomiting, then he blew tobacco smoke into a large cup before filling it with San Pedro and blowing smoke into that too. He handed it to me and I drank it in three gulps.

The taste and consistency were the same as ever, although San Pedro has a certain kindness to it, in that every time I drink, it somehow enables me to forget how unpleasant the process can be until I have almost finished the cup. Then there is a brief reminder, a retch or two and a short battle to finish the rest, after which my body tolerates it. With ayahuasca it is a little different and I would normally have to fight for several minutes against my desire to vomit.

'We have a little time now,' said Raphael, 'so here is some advice for your journey…

'You have a desire to meet God, for whom you have some questions, it seems. This appears to be a big ambition but, frankly, it is not. Everyone, after all, will – and must – make this journey at some point in their lives, even if it takes a lifetime and their first step is from their deathbeds. We must all make peace with God.

The sadness for some is that they do not do so earlier so the lives they were blessed with could have been different.

'This conference with God is one that all shamans must also hold because we cannot diagnose or treat an illness until we know His plans for our patient. We can *heal*, but not *cure*; not until we know the desires of God and, therefore, what it means for our patients to be cured so they are brought into balance and their destiny can unfold.

'The way to take this journey,' he continued, 'is to hold your objective in mind – or, rather, to feel it *here* [he patted his stomach] as if it is a living force. But do not cling to it so rigidly that you miss your opportunity when it comes. By this I mean: do not have a prescribed notion of who – or what – you mean by 'God' or you may be led off-course. Also keep in mind that the true nature of God bears little similarity to the quaint ideas you may have heard in schoolrooms and churches.

'When you feel the medicine start to work concentrate and follow it, then forget your mind – without losing sight of your question, of course. Do not believe for one second that you *must* have an answer either, or a solution and a logical outcome, because the more you try to control this medicine, the more it will fight back! You have told it your purpose and it will use its powers in your interests but it will not be controlled by you. The best thing you can therefore do is get out of its way and let it do its work.

'Don't be distracted by the things you see either and don't *think* about them. That is why God gives us evenings: so we can reflect on our todays and why He gives us tomorrows: so we can act on our reflections. So don't wallow in your thoughts . Just let the journey take you.

'Since it is only us here you may speak out loud if you must, or laugh, or scream, or cry! You may also leave the room and walk in the land around you. If you speak, I will not answer you though, unless you call for me directly. If you leave, I will not stop you, though I will watch over you. In short, I will not volunteer my help in any way because this is a journey we must all make alone. If you need my help, however, and if you call me, I will come to sweep your fears away.'

The room went silent for a moment as I considered what Raphael had said and he thought about what advice to give me next. It seemed also to gather darkness.

'God sometimes grants us a vision,' he said, after a while. 'This is different from a hallucination like some other plants may give you. Hallucinations have their value too, as bubblings-up from the waters of our souls: the drifting to the surface of events from our lives that have a message or a lesson for us, so also pay attention to them. But it is a *vision* you are seeking: a direct communication from God – so you must discriminate and be extra vigilant.

'True visions are rare, and you will know them because they hit you first in the stomach, not the head. You will recognise their truth because it is beautiful and terrifying, awe-inspiring and incontrovertible, like a punch to your gut, and it will reach you long before your mind can try to explain it away. This punch to the gut is what will stay with you, even when your mind interferes, as it eventually will. So if you feel the fist of spirit in your belly make sure you pay special attention.

'You are alone now and I am with you. Lie down if you wish and dream.'

Maybe forty minutes had passed. Everything seemed familiar at first: the same physical sensations, the same realisation that I was no longer human but energy, like something as-yet unformed; the same desert too. That part of me that watches recognised it all.

The great white wall of Paradise was there before me again as well, but this time its gates were unguarded and open. I walked inside and no cosmic gatekeeper or horde of angels questioned my motives or tried to stop me. It felt odd inside, like one of those ghost towns that cowboy heroes ride into in films: a place where families raised kids and everyone once knew their neighbour but which has been strangely abandoned and nobody quite knows why. In those films, the reason usually turns out to be terrible and I had a sense of foreboding here too, like a punch to the gut.

I suppose I was expecting a garden. That, after all, is the original idea of Paradise – a 'walled garden' – and what we imagine Eden must be. But not even a flower grew here. Instead, everything was white and gold and silent, with row upon row of white stone pillars, none of which seemed to serve any purpose. Yet, there were hundreds of them, towering above me, going on for miles, like markers of some kind.

At the end of one of the avenues they made was a palace, also white and gold, and inside it a gigantic throne made of the same bleached stone. The God who occupied this temple must have been a colossus because everything was massive compared to human scale. But now it was completely empty.

I began (in both 'real' and 'visionary' time) to feel uneasy. If Paradise was empty (even the words sounded strange) was it empty just for me or for everyone?

With nothing to see, I returned to the desert, where the San Pedro spirit was waiting, dressed as before, sword in hand, looking out over the sand to a distant row of mountains. He said nothing but raised his sword to point at the horizon. I began walking in that direction.

The sun above me was white and high and the journey through sand and nothingness seemed to take forever. I was sweating but I didn't feel hot and, in fact, that part of me that lay on Raphael's floor was shivering.

I arrived at a low cave and had to bend to enter its darkness. I felt cobwebs on my face and, as I wiped them away, a sense that I was not alone here.

Only a faint light penetrated but, as my eyes adjusted to the gloom, I noticed an old man among the rocks. He seemed familiar too, dressed in sackcloth, with a matted grey beard and wild hair that fell over his shoulders and chest and, I realised, He was God. He barely looked up as He spoke. 'I see I am not what you expected,' he said.

It was a statement of fact, not a question, and it was true: if I'd had a notion of God – or if I could have chosen a God for myself – it would have been a magnificent and radiant being, not an old man like this. Then I remembered Raphael's words: 'Do not have a prescribed notion of who – or what – you take God to be, or you may be led off-course. The true nature of God must not be trivialised.'

No other words were spoken. Instead, the old man lifted a handful of dust from the cave floor and let it spill from his fingers. As it drifted down it became diamonds, illuminating the cave and casting rainbows on its walls. The light was blinding where the diamonds landed and a sort of vortex opened up there to create a three-dimensional screen where I watched history unfolding.

At the same time the old man spoke – not in words exactly, but more as a kind of 'information download' from His mind to mine: 'People have been searching for God for thousands of years,' he said. 'Always they look outwards – to 'Paradise', 'Heaven', or 'out there' into the universe. They have a million names for the place that God will be found; all of them outside of themselves and all of them wrong.

'They are always 'big places': some grand destination they can go to and escape their mundane world... or a vast force that will save them and make everything right – because they do not want that responsibility for themselves. But, in fact, their responsibility is even greater than they imagine, which they would see if they chose to look *inwards* instead.'

I am not sure whether the old man was speaking again or whether a memory had come to me from somewhere but I was suddenly aware of something I was certain I'd always known and which seemed incongruous but totally pertinent to the moment: that 90% of the cells in our bodies are bacteria.

It was a strange thought but, as if to emphasise its importance, the vortex in the cave floor became a window into my body and I could see the bacteria within me with such vivid intensity that, for a moment, I knew what it was to be one of them.

All of these bacteria, these cells, the microscopic make-up of life, were as conscious and aware as I was. In fact, there was no 'I'. Instead, my body – or what I thought of as 'I' – was an amalgam; a community of life forms. It felt overwhelming: a buzz of information and activity in the teeming of life within and around me, as if I was formed of insect-song and the choir could at any moment fly away, leaving me as pure consciousness, not flesh and blood at all. To the singers of my cells, I *was* the 'something bigger than themselves'... the universe... God.

It occurred to me – and this is surely what the old man had meant – that we humans look outwards for our answers, hoping to catch a glimpse of something divine, while the life within us does the same, looking to *us* for answers. If they – or we – looked inwards however we would all see the same thing: that we are all composed of smaller lives who regard us as their mysterious and distant God.

Perhaps our search for a magnificent and 'out there' God is no more than arrogance, then: that only a 'big and important answer' could satisfy a 'big and important human' – or 'big and important bacteria'. Or maybe it is desperation and frailty which causes us to look beyond ourselves for answers when, really, we are more than enough or, at least, all that we have and know to be true.

'Look again,' said the old man. I stared into the vortex once more and saw a succession of Gods – like the rows of white pillars in the empty Paradise I had come from. All of them were, by a human scale, vast, but just as I thought there could be no greater God another would grow from the ground to dwarf the first and then another even greater until I was surrounded by giants. At the same time, they were all tiny too, like bacteria. All of us – including the Gods – were nothing more than life forms in the gut of something so gigantic that it simply couldn't be known.

Great blocks of stone fell around us then, crashing into the dust, and I knew that they were prayers sent by the needy. They assembled themselves into white and gold temples in which these multiple Gods became entombed. The prayer-stones walled them in until the Gods themselves became stone, then dust, then sand and only the temples remained, silent and empty.

'People have always created Gods,' said the old man, 'and then they kill them with their prayers. Prayer also makes God your servant – and what use is a God who is a slave? I was one of those created Gods and to survive your prayers I quit.'

My journey was taking on qualities of the bizarre, like a mad dream you can't wake up from. Then I remembered Raphael's advice: 'Forget your mind and do not believe for one second that you *must* have an answer, a solution, a logical outcome… There is no sense to be made.'

Again I tried not to. For years I had understood – in my mind, at least – that what the old man was saying was true: that we hunger for salvation from external forces – whether Gods or lovers, parents or politicians – and that time and again we give away our power by not taking responsibility for ourselves. What I was experiencing now, however, was beyond an intellectual understanding. It was delivered viscerally and I felt it rather than thought it.

I suppose I had assumed that we could *choose* or not choose to take the responsibility for our lives that was rightfully ours and that there would always be someone – some heavenly father - there to save us if we didn't. Now, though, there *was* no choice. The decision had already been made. God had quit.

Raphael's last words had been: 'You are alone and I am with

you.' Now they took on new meaning. In a world without God we *are* all alone – and all in this together: universes of life dependent on each other with no one and nothing but ourselves to rely on for survival. It was not that we had been excluded from Paradise; there *was* no Paradise and never had been.

I began to laugh at the great joke of life and opened my eyes to see Raphael fanning my body with feathers and blowing smoke around me, sweeping my body free of fears, as he said he would if he sensed that I needed him.

I was instantly calm again, both from the healing and the knowledge that there are people like Raphael who *will* take care of others. This was the meaning of reciprocity, the *real* connection between us. Now it was Raphael taking care of me but later it might be me looking after him or someone else; it didn't matter who as long as care *was* taken and the energy of love and compassion could circulate and return to those who had given it. I closed my eyes again and returned to the God who had quit.

He was standing outside the cave now, looking at the desert. 'All this sand is what became of your Gods,' he said. 'They knew that to be free – and for *you* to be free – they had to remove themselves from Paradise. They became sand, sky, sun, rain, trees… They are all around you, in everything. They are in you too, so you see, there is really no need to look beyond yourself.'

As if to emphasise his words, giants began to grow from the sand until we were surrounded by thousands of Gods, all of them crackling with energy. At the height of their power, with electricity screaming around us, they burst into sand once more and crashed down in a storm around us.

Poetry began to circle in my head; this time lines from Blake's *Auguries of Innocence*:

To see a world in a grain of sand
And a heaven in a wild flower;
Hold infinity in the palm of your hand

And eternity in an hour...

What did it matter that God had 'quit'? From what He said, He never existed in the first place, except as a thought-form, a construct projected by us onto the cosmos to save us from ourselves, our power and our loneliness.

I opened my eyes again and Raphael was there, offering me water. I took it and sat up, less shaky and more aware of my body than after some San Pedro journeys.

He returned to his mesa and began to pray, offering thanks to the spirits for their protection and guidance. I wondered if his prayers were directed to God – and where they would end up in a Godless universe – and whether Raphael knew what I did.

Calmly, he extinguished the candle on his altar and lit a mapacho. He blew the smoke around me and then sat back to enjoy the rest. 'The ceremony is over,' he said. 'Tell me when you are ready to talk.'

Thirty minutes later and my mood had changed entirely as Raphael laughed at my description of the God who had quit.

'Yes, that God quit a long time ago!' he said, wiping his eyes. 'There is always some God or other threatening to walk out on us, but even if they all left it would not mean the end of God!'

Still a little dizzy, I was puzzled at his reaction. How could a God 'quit' and 'not quit' at the same time and, irrespective of either decision, still continue to exist?

'I told you at the beginning not to go looking for answers because there is no sense to be made,' said Raphael in response. 'What you heard and saw may best be described as an allegory. San Pedro will never lie to you but it may talk in poetry or symbols because that is how the soul best understands its message.

'There are many things to consider here. Firstly, there is what you bring to San Pedro: your beliefs, concerns, or, let us say, your mythology. You are from the West and in your culture there *is* no

God or, if He exists, He is a commodity for sale in churches or a government advisor to matters of war and invasion: something to be 'had' or taken, in other words – and that, of course, is no God at all.

'Your belief in this commodity-God, distant and unavailable but capable of being bought and sold, is ingrained in your soul because it is what your culture has taught you and so you hear what San Pedro has to say and take it literally since the absence of God is all you have ever known.

'A Peruvian hearing the same words would have laughed at God's joke and looked for the real meaning in what was being said because we *know*, without doubt, that God exists and always will. It is impossible for Him not to.

'So what does it mean that God has 'quit'? To me it means that He never existed in the first place according to your definition of Him. So you must ask yourself, well then, how *does* God exist? And you were given the answer to that question too: He exists in the sand, the sky, in your skin and the germs in your gut – in nature, that is – and not in great palaces or fortresses that we are excluded from.

'How did this God appear to you? As a hermit in a cave, locked away in darkness and tired of the world. Think of this in terms of your culture too and its impoverished view of the world... We get the Gods we deserve.

'For God to exist – and for us to have a better and more meaningful future – we have therefore to change our minds about God so we see the divine in the world around us: in the rocks, plants, mountains, and the people who share our planet with us.

'This is another way of seeing or understanding, where we are conscious that all things are alive and have spirit – and this is the true meaning of Pachamama: that the world itself is ensouled and made of the thoughts, hopes and dreams of all who live or have ever lived and attained a certain level of knowledge.

'It is like saying that what we regard as the lowest puddle of slime is God, just as much as the Holy man. They are one and the same. This is what God meant when He said that He is present in even the sands and he has resigned from being 'God' so that humans may evolve.

'We evolve, after all, through awareness of God in *all* things and we will reach the next stage of our development when we understand that we are God too: the pond slime *and* the priest. The first step in this evolution is simple: to look at a flower... an insect... or your life... and see it as beautiful, precious and soulful. Everything is sacred – *todos es sagrado* – Do you see?'

What Raphael was talking about was the distinction between the Christian God and the one which more traditional peoples know which, for want of a better word, is *nature*, and the spirit it contains. The Andean God is immediate, visible and present. He is revealed in the candle glow whose light illuminates a ceremonial room, bringing more than luminescence but comfort. He is there in the trees and plants which heal us and in the breath of life contained in the four winds too. As Tracie says, He is present in 'every curve of the mountain range, every boulder, rock, stone, and blade of grass... all of it part of the same incredible tableau and all of equal importance.'

By contrast our Western God is as distant from us as the stars. Perhaps we adopted this vision of God because His very remoteness gave us something to aspire to morally and spiritually at a time in our evolution when that was most needed: some distant quality we could reach for and hope to realise one day for ourselves. By making God invisible and placing Him so far away, however, we ensured that we could never attain what we desired because we have no measure of whether or not we have succeeded and so we will always be unhappy and striving for more.

God has indeed become a commodity: something to be yearned for, aspired to and worked towards, but never attained.

And yet the truth is that God has never gone away: 'He' was always right there in the flowers and the breeze.

'Do you know the story of the condor and the hummingbird?' Raphael asked suddenly. I did, of course. It was the same story I had told in the Amazon all those months ago: the story of the tiny bird who so loved God that he hid away in the condor's feathers to make his journey to the divine.

'And so, finally, the hummingbird got what he wanted: he met with God,' said Raphael. 'But why is it, then, do you think, that this little bird continues to dance among the flowers? You would think, would you not, that if his devotion was so great, he would have long ago vanished from the Earth and made his home in God's great palaces? But, no, he continues his dance, visiting each garden and kissing every bright flower in turn.

'Why? Because he was informed by God through his journey and given the greatest secret of all: that the *divine world* is *our world* and its most beautiful expression is nature.

'This, too, is how we will find our peace and an end to suffering: by following the hummingbird's journey to God and knowing that Paradise is all around us. That is really our only task as human beings. From that our health and our happiness flows, like nectar from a flower: always hopeful and sweet.'

I have wondered for some time about a God who would choose to live like a hermit in a cave and, in fact, it was only recently that this mystery was solved for me, when I read in Bonnie Glass-Coffin's book[1] that the original inhabitants of the Andes 'claimed descendence from the god *Huari*, a cave dweller who was part of a race of giants.' It stands to reason, I suppose, that the God who would speak to me would be one native to the land and not a concept I had brought with me.

In terms of my intentions for this journey – to know God and myself a little better – His message was simple: that the world itself is composed of spirit and gives itself freely to us, but what we make of that is up to us.

As Michael also discovered during his San Pedro experience, 'We have the power to create our own heaven or hell with every passing thought' because 'our thoughts are *things* and create our reality in the physical world.'

There is never anything to fear, however, because 'we are all part of God.'

Chapter 11

The Journey of the Hummingbird
The Lessons of San Pedro

Man makes holy what he believes
Ernest Renan

It had started simply, with the telling of a lullaby-story about a hummingbird while dreaming by a river one day. The journey I had taken from there had led me to some of our deepest and most enduring questions: What is healing? Who or what is God? What is our relationship to the world? And how should we act within it?

I had travelled from the rainforest basin to the high mountains of Peru and into the spiritual universe and the knowledge locked away in the soul without hardly a pause, guided at all stages, in some strange and synchronous way, by the spirit of a hummingbird and the cactus of vision with which it is so entwined.

Along the way I had met remarkable people who had been gracious with their time and who had helped me understand San Pedro's lessons. Now it was time to make sense of things. 'God gives us evenings so we can reflect upon our todays,' Raphael had said; 'He gives us tomorrows so we can act on our reflections.' What truths, then, do these reflections reveal?

The first is that human beings are more powerful than we know. We have the ability, by changing our thoughts or flexing our will, to cure illness, to become fulfilled and whole, to know who we are and how we fit with the universe and to act on all of this so that the world evolves as we wish it. San Pedro is our ally in this. It provides us with the insight, visions and awareness to know where we stand and what is at stake.

Don Juan, in the books of Castaneda, describes an ally as a spirit which must be fought with and forced to yield its secrets. 'The man must wrestle the spirit to the ground and keep it there until it gives him power' he says.[1] It is then that the ally offers him strength, knowledge and the ability to perform miracles.

How the ally appears will be unique to each individual. For Castaneda, Mescalito was a moth; for Donna and I, it was a matador; for Mark, a hummingbird; for Jamie, Michael and Kane, the Earth itself; and for Kyle, maybe, a stone dog.

For others it may take some other completely different form. As don Juan says: 'I cannot say that it is really a moth, the way we know moths [any more than it is really a matador or a hummingbird]. Calling the ally a moth is again only a way of talking; a way of making that immensity out there under-standable.'[2]

How the spirit of San Pedro appears to us may therefore have new information for us about who we are. Castaneda was a man who flitted between intellectual conceits (or, at least, that is how he was regarded by don Juan) and who often, in his work with the Yaqui shaman, came close to the light and then, in fear of what he might discover, vanished back to the shadowed cloisters of academia and did not see his mentor again for months. In this, he was like a moth drawn to a candle but constantly withdrawing from its flame and it seems wholly understandable, therefore, that Mescalito would appear to him in a similar form which represented his psychology and way of engaging with life.

In my encounters with San Pedro my issues had been an unconscious fear of the world, a need for new strength and a desire to know what is true. It is no wonder, then, that I perceived (or received) an ally in the form of a strong and dignified man who was able to face the world with courage and power and who could offer me a new understanding of life.

Shamans say that once we have established a connection to

our allies they never leave us; that, with one drink of San Pedro, we absorb the spirit of the teacher and can draw forever from its wisdom, strength and healing.

Others believe that the change is even more profound: that what we ingest can alter the structure of our DNA. The scientist Jeremy Narby did not go quite that far in his book *The Cosmic Serpent* but, as a result of his experiences with ayahuasca and the people of the Amazon, he did suggest that shamans can perform their healings because their ally-plant enables them to enter into contact with their patient's DNA. Through ayahuasca, they merge with 'the global network of DNA-based life.'[3]

Intrigued by this possibility, Narby began to study the characteristics of DNA and found that it emits electromagnetic waves corresponding to the narrow band of visible light. It is a weak signal, equivalent only to the intensity of a candle at a distance of 10 kilometres, but it is surprisingly coherent; like a laser. It is just possible that this is the waveform of consciousness itself and that allies like San Pedro and ayahuasca provide a means of making it tangible. By drinking them, therefore, we also gain access to fundamental wisdom about ourselves: the absolute truth of who we are at a cellular level, beneath the beliefs, conditioning and assumptions that we have grown up with over the years.

By going back to the source in this way and reconnecting to our pure consciousness, we not only discover the origins of our problems and illnesses and can heal them then and there, we erase our personal histories and do away with our habitual responses and ways of seeing the world that have been layered on top of who we are. We emerge from this inner journey not only with better health, but in a different state; one which ensures that our new-found power stays with us and can lead to other changes in our lives, as Simon and Tracie have found, among others.

There is another, associated, possibility for how ally-plants work: that they open our eyes to the infinite within and without us and once we know the real facts of life, we can never go back to our limited worlds or forget what we have seen.

This is the suggestion of Kane, who says that: 'The experience I had will *never* leave me!' and of Donna, who reflects that: 'I now dedicate my life to honour and integrity in every action I take; I accept life's path rather than trying to dictate it ... My world has become better already.'

We live such narrow lives most of the time. Told by governments, school teachers, employers and parents what to think, feel, believe, and what to do, we accept who we are – or who we have been given – and rarely question things anymore.

The benefits are a safe, secure and 'known' world, a predictable future and a certain destiny. The downside is that we are only living half-lives and half-truths, for nothing is actually known or ever can be. Science and politics make it seem that way but once we scratch the surface there is always another mystery left to beguile us.

All the time that we subscribe to the myths of a known and ordered world, however, we are malleable and easily controlled. This is also why, no doubt, there are few governments on Earth which support the use of mind-expanding psychedelics but only the drugs of docility like alcohol and anti-depressants.[4] San Pedro takes us out of this mind-set, shows us new possibilities and reveals a world of choice not servility. Because we are not used to this, the understanding that we are more powerful than we think can be frightening when it first comes. But then we learn to cope with it and to make the most of what our awareness of a new and myth-free world can bring.

As Kane put it: 'My main problem was understanding that thoughts create things. I was actually horrified when I first learnt this. But I think I was just scared of how much power and influence I have over my own life... Over time I have learned to love this part of me... I am happy with the way things are turning out.'

Once we have the experience we begin to understand, like Kane, that it is our worldviews which are killing us and that by changing our outlook and reclaiming our power, we can not only survive but be happy.

Where this leads is to the realisation that the ally is also an aspect of ourselves: that the inner is the outer. This aspect, normally hidden from consciousness and suppressed within our psyches, is the strength of our souls given the freedom to express themselves and to lead us towards a positive future.

We are multiple personalities, after all. This is not a 'disease' or a 'condition' to be labelled[5] and treated, as we tend to regard such things in the West, but a fact of life and a perfectly natural expression of who we are. So it is that, faced with the same challenge on two different days we either flourish and shine or crumble under pressure, depending on which of 'us' is in charge.

We rarely get to know these other selves because exploration like this is not encouraged in the West. As a consequence, we do not know how to recognise our strengths within ourselves, to work with them, or to benefit from what they might offer. A psychologist might show them to us or years of therapy might reveal them, but San Pedro takes us straight there so we experience directly the range of powers we have and, once we know them, we can draw on them forever. They become our guides, our mentors, our 'higher selves' who can lead us, in the words of the psychologist, Abraham Maslow, to 'self-actuali-sation': the ability to become all that we are capable of being by making fuller use of our true and perhaps infinite resources.

Various studies have shown how powerful these inner states can be. The oncologist Carl Simenton, for example – recent winner of the Humanitarian Award from the Cancer Control Society – has demonstrated that cancer patients can regulate the progression and effects of their illnesses and even achieve states of spontaneous and otherwise unexplainable remission by meeting their inner guides and imagining themselves well.[6]

Studies of the power of prayer and good intentions (or 'good ideas', as Andean shamans say) also show that people who are prayed for after operations achieve better and faster recoveries than those who are not. To pray effectively for another – or for ourselves – a trance-like state of connection to our higher powers and an absolute belief in our abilities to work wonders is important. Then we have the power to perform miracles.[7]

San Pedro is another route to opening the door behind which our true capabilities have been locked away by our culture.

In contrast to don Juan's views, however, my experience of San Pedro (and that of others) is that its spirit does not have to be fought with and 'made' to give up its power. Its intention is more gracious than that. And I doubt, in any case, that it ever could be 'wrestled to the ground'; its strength is too immense. Instead, it is we who must yield.

I interpret Castaneda's words to mean therefore that we must wrestle *ourselves* to the ground so we let go of the ego's resistance to change in its encounter with the spirit. To fight San Pedro would have got me nowhere – literally – but by trusting it to lead me where I needed to go its secrets were given freely.

Kane says something similar: 'My San Pedro journey became very dark at times.' Simon, too, 'felt sad and grieved and like crying' at his memory of the loss of his sister. Cara had to relive a difficult relationship with her father which had caused her problems with love and intimacy. But by going with it, they all found something of importance and a healing could take place.

At the end of his journey what Kane learned was his 'greatest lesson'. For Simon, it was that 'the little things are really the big things' and that to laugh at ourselves instead of wearing our masks of suffering is often the greatest medicine. 'I am ever-grateful to San Pedro for these insights,' he said later.

Cara had to 'dissolve' to see 'the beauty in all things, including myself' and to be sufficiently 'changed' that within two weeks of drinking she had met the man who would become her husband. 'There's no bigger way to say that it healed my relationship problems.' This willingness to be dissolved is the way of the peaceful warrior: not to fight but to yield; to wilfully lose a battle so we can win a war.

The God that San Pedro takes us to in order for these lesson to be learned is a curious one, though - although no more so than the other plant-Gods that humans have met with from time-to-time. Certainly He is not the 'loving Father-God' of Christian invention, but ambivalent and matter-of-fact in His directness.

In many of my encounters with this spirit there was no sense of being welcomed and wrapped up in love, for example, but, rather, an emotionless downloading of information and the reali-sation that 'this is how things are, and you may take it or leave it. It is your choice'.

A similar quality has been noticed by others too. Thus, Rick Strassman's DMT volunteer, Elena, said of her encounter that 'There was no benevolent god, only this primordial power... It was 'amoral'.' To it (and to herself) 'All of my ideas and beliefs seemed absurdly ridiculous.'[8]

Shanon's ayahuasca drinkers also found a God who was less 'human' and more 'a force that is the ground for all Being'; a 'non-material substance which is identified as Cosmic Consciousness.'[9]

Terence McKenna, writing under the pseudonym, O T Oss, captures something of the nature of this God – straightforward, plain-talking and ambivalent – when, under the influence of magic mushrooms, he channelled some of the teachings embodied in this plant-ally:

I am old, older than thought in your species, which is itself fifty times older than your history. Though I have been on earth for ages I am from the stars. My home is no one planet, for many worlds scattered through the shining disc of the galaxy have conditions which allow my spores an opportunity for life... there lie richer and even more baroque evolutionary possibilities.'[10]

Jim DeKorne in *Psychedelic Shamanism* remarks that:

To understand the entity [including the 'God'] phenomenon it is useful to lay aside the concept of monotheism in general and of universally benevolent, well-intentioned deities in particular. Popular Christianity has generally conditioned Westerners to the idea of a single, all-loving Father-God. Based on empirical facts [however], it may be more productive to re-examine the ancient notion of a pantheon of 'gods' coming in as many kinds and dispositions as we do.

San Pedro shamans are, of course, familiar with the popular Christian view and many include its notion of God in their work although they tend, in the main, to regard the divine as a force or energy which flows throughout the universe in a way similar to the God who spoke through McKenna. If we build our connections to this force, they say, it comes to inhere in us too and lends us its power and potential. In this way, we have choice and freewill so we are not just subject to divine 'laws' which must be followed but have an opportunity to find healing, meaning and balance for ourselves. The San Pedro God is the 'Cosmic Consciousness' which Shanon's participants also experienced and He does, indeed, come 'in as many kinds and dispositions as we do', as DeKorne concludes.

This shamanic view of God also helps us to understand His ambivalent nature for, if God is energy – like electricity, for example – then of course it is also amoral and un-loving. So is electricity. In human hands it can be put to good use, such a powering a hospital or making food for family and friends, or it can be used to power an army or put someone to death in an

electric chair. 'It just was' – or is – as one of Strassman's participants put it.

Beneath this surface-ambivalence, however, there is often a
deeper and more profound truth, for what the audience with
God also teaches us is that everything is sacred (*todos es sagrado*
as Raphael had said), that there is power in everything and that,
within *this*, there is love.

Hence another of Strassman's participants, Cleo, concluded
finally that 'God is in everything and we are all connected... God
dances in every cell of life, and every cell of life dances in God.'
She goes on, in a description of her journey which is not
dissimilar to my own when I met the God of the cave and experienced the life within me, that 'I was trying to look out, but they
[the spirits she met] were saying, "Go in". I was looking for God
outside. They said "God is in every cell of your body"... The
euphoria goes on into eternity. And I am part of that eternity.'

God is within us and He is in nature, too. 'The contemplation
of these different forces invokes a deep appreciation of the
bounty of nature and the essential dependence of life upon it'
along with the realisation that 'there is sense and reason to all
things and that reality is invested with deep, heretofore
unappreciated meaningfulness.'[11] In Jamie's words, it is the
realisation that there is 'no suffering; there is only, ever, the
pursuit of truth' and in Tracie's that 'the world is an exceptionally beautiful place'.

With these gifts that San Pedro offers us, I wondered what it
gets in return and why it should give so freely of itself when, on
the face of it, it receives so little back from us. The notion of
reciprocity, so important to Andean thinking, would suggest that
there should be an exchange of some kind.

It was a question I put to several shamans. My long-time
friend and ayahuascero, Javier Aravello, answered it in his
familiar and gentle way: 'The plants love us and it is their
pleasure to help us because they want us to understand what is

important.'

Don Raphael was more forthright:

What is important to the plants is our evolution. Human beings stand at a pivotal place in history. We have grown through our intellect to a point where we are in great danger of irreversibly harming not just ourselves but our planet, including the animals and plants who are our brothers and sisters. That is the nature of power when it is driven only through the mind: we gain the technology to become destroyers of worlds without the wisdom or morals to know this is wrong. Now we must evolve through the heart, so we understand where we have come from and where we are going unless we use our power to change. We must see that we have a place in the Kingdoms of the Earth and that we do not stand apart from our surroundings. We need to return to nature – to see God in the sand and flowers – so we can make our peace with the world.

When we drink San Pedro, no matter what healing we wish from it or what problems we think we are dealing with, a subtle awareness grows in us too that life and beauty are all around us. From this inspiration we take our rightful place in the world and learn to act responsibly.

I was again reminded of Kane. He had come to Peru on a 'healing mission' to mend his broken heart but what he found was something greater: 'I met mother earth and suddenly realised that I've been standing on her my entire life. I felt ashamed and stupid for not knowing that she's always right there.' When he drank San Pedro again, he said, he would be doing so 'to increase my awareness and communication with Pachamama, to assist and to heal her.'

Once we heal ourselves, that is, we see the connections between us and our planet-home so we also become healers with a desire to give something back to the Earth. This, then, is what the plants get from their partnership with us: the possibility of a peaceful and positive world where we co-exist and share a future. 'Nature is alive and is talking to us; this is *not* a metaphor', Terence McKenna once wrote. What nature is saying now is that we can live in peace together if we wish.

The visionary painter and shaman, Pablo Amaringo, says much the same thing[12]:

My most sublime desire is that every human being should begin to put as much attention as they can into the knowledge of plants because they are the greatest healers of all. And they should also put effort into the preservation and conservation of the rainforest and care for it and the ecosystem because damage to these not only prejudices the flora and fauna but humanity itself. This expression of love must be a sincere and altruistic interest in the lasting well-being of others. We are not here simply to exist but to enjoy life together with plants, animals and loved ones and to delight in contemplation of the beauty of nature.

His words are reminiscent of Jamie's after her San Pedro experience:

This is how it feels to be in balance, as a human who is part of the larger race of humans, a simple creature like any other on this planet we have called Earth. This is how it feels, with the quiet mountainsides, the green grass, the song of the wind, the gray of ceremonial stone. This is how it feels to be one among a family of bird and flower and dog and other people in their own quiet moments of search and wonder, each of us unto ourselves, each of us belonging, each of us at home.

This is the real message of San Pedro and the real vision it offers

233

us no matter what else we may ask of it or how we find our ways to it: that we can live in a perfect world if we choose; indeed, that we already do if we open our eyes and see it.

We do not need to seek perfection or look elsewhere for God because He (or she or it) is there in the beauty around us. We just need to step forward and play our part in the magic which is unfolding. The world is perfect as it is and will remain so if we are brave, creative and dignified, not running to hide in its shadows and if we treat it, ourselves and each other with the respect we all deserve.

Through realisations like this, the hummingbird leads our journey to God.

Notes

Introduction

1. See, for example, Rick Strassman's account of the struggles he went through to gain approval and funding for his research into the psychedelic, healing, and mystical qualities of DMT, the active ingredient of ayahuasca. In *DMT: The Spirit Molecule*. Rick Strassman, MD. Park Street Press, 2001.
2. Again, see Strassman for a discussion of this.

Chapter 1

1. For those interested, a good book on the history of Iquitos is *Iquitos: Gateway to the Amazon*, by John Lane.

    The story of Carlos Fitzcarrald is told in Werner Herzog's 1982 film, *Fitzcarraldo*, with the title role played by the equally eccentric Klaus Kinski.
2. Bantam Books, 1994

Chapter 2

1. *Dance of the Four Winds: Secrets of the Inca Medicine Wheel*. Inner Traditions, 1995
2. There is an interview with Juan in my book, *Plant Spirit Shamanism*. Destiny Books, 2006. According to another San Pedro shaman, Eduardo Calderon, in *Eduardo El Curandero: The Words of a Peruvian Healer* (North Atlantic Books, 1999), *singado*, also known as *tabaco*, contains 'dried black unprocessed leaf tobacco, three perfumes – agua cananga, agua florida, and Tabu – sweet lime juice, cane alcohol, white sugar, and boiled San Pedro. *Tabaco* is 'raised' (imbibed through the nostrils) by the *curandero*, his two assistants, and all patients and observers at certain intervals during a session. It is the auxiliary catalyst of a séance.'
3. University of New Mexico Press, 1998
4. In *Eduardo El Curandero*. Ibid

5. This length of brewing is, again, confirmed more or less by Glass-Coffin, who says of the San Pedro preparations she has seen, that 'the cactus is prayed over and put on the stove to boil for anywhere from two to seven hours.' *The Gift of Life.* Ibid.

Chapter 3

1. *The Cosmic Serpent: DNA and the Origins of Knowledge.* Phoenix, 1999.
2. *The Antipodes of the Mind: Charting the Phenomenology of the Ayahuasca Experience.* Oxford University Press, 2002
3. I say 'strangely enough' because DMT is a chemical, administered in a sterile lab; a situation I railed against in my Introduction because it is, in my view, wholly unnatural and inconducive to spiritual experience. And yet, I cannot deny the comparison.

Chapter 4

1. In Bonnie Glass-Coffin, *The Gift of Life.* Ibid. 'Subconscience' does not exist as a word but it is appropriate to the spirit of this quotation. It implies a combination of 'subconscious': that God is within us and part of our deeper selves, and '*sub-conscience*': i.e. that our sense of God exists at a fundamental level beneath even human conscience, as a sort of moral barometer or innate guide to right and wrong to which good and bad health are also connected. On this latter point, see for example Chapter 8.
2. Possibly the most useful book on the subject is Douglas Sharon's *Wizard of the Four Winds: A Shaman's Story* (Free Press, 1978). This, however, is more or less the story of a single individual, Eduardo Calderon, who Sharon, an anthropologist, spent a couple of seasons witnessing and helping, supported by grants from UCLA. As such, it focuses on one person operating within the traditions of one part of Peru (the

north) rather than providing a more global or general perspective. It is also a study of curanderismo (Andean healing) rather than San Pedro, per se. These limitations aside, however, it is certainly worth reading – if you can find a copy, since it has been out of print for a while now, and is hard to come by, with copies on the web often selling for several hundred dollars.

3. Irene Silverblatt, *Moon, Sun, and Witches: Gender Ideologies and Class in Inca and Colonial Peru* (Princeton University Press, 1987). Quoted in Bonnie Glass-Coffin, *The Gift of Life*. Ibid.

4. In *Plants of the Gods: Their Sacred Healing, and Hallucinogenic Powers* by Richard Evans Schultes, Albert Hoffman, and Chritian Ratsch. Healing Arts Press, 2001.

5. In *Plants of the Gods*. Ibid

6. In Douglas Sharon, *Wizard of the Four Winds*. Ibid.

7. Breakout Productions, 1994.

8. In Stafford, P, *Psychedelics Encyclopaedia*. Ronin Publishing, 1992.

9. In *Sacred Plants of the San Pedro Cult*. Harvard University: Botanical Museum leaflets, 1983.

10. In *Psychedelic Shamanism*. Ibid.

11. *Peru seeks tribal cure for addiction*, by Javier Lizarzaburu. BBC Radio 4, *Crossing Continents*, at http://news.bbc.co.uk/2/hi/programmes/crossing_continents/3243277.stm. Retrieved on April 26 2008.

12. Destiny Books, 2003.

13. Literally, 'penis of God'.

14. In Bonnie Glass-Coffin, *The Gift of Life*. Ibid.

15. In Cowan, Sharon and Sharon: *Eduardo El Curandero*. Ibid.

16. *Plants of the Gods*. Ibid.

17. In *Eduardo El Curandero*. Ibid.

18. Wade Davis, *Sacred Plants of the San Pedro Cult*. Ibid.

19. This more neutral perspective, beyond 'good' and 'evil', is supported by the shamans that Bonnie Glass-Coffin worked

with. In their view, simply, 'The right side of the mesa is frequently called *banco curandero* (curing bench or bank), while the left side of the mesa is frequently called the *banco ganadero*. *Ganadero* has several meanings in Spanish, including the occupational name given to those who herd livestock (*Ganado*) and the nominative reference given to 'one who wins or dominates' (from the verb *ganar*)'. In *The Gift of Life*. Ibid.

20. This broadly reflects the fields of the mesa, where the left contains the essence of 'negative' energies (i.e. those which do not serve the patient so well), and the right, 'positive'.

21. What I have come to call 'old school shamans', who employ far more ritual and have a much more rigid structure to their ceremonies than 'new wave' practitioners like Miguel, who are content to play a secondary role to the plant.

22. In *The Gift of Life*. Ibid.

23. Peter T Furst, *Flesh of the Gods: The Ritual Use of Hallucinogens*. Waveland Pr Inc, Reprint edition, 1990.

24. The energetic power of the ancient sites themselves.

25. http://blogs.thetimes.co.za/greeff/about/, retrieved in January 2008

26. In *The Gift of Life*. Ibid.

Chapter 5

1. www.erowid.com.

2. See, for example, DeKorne, *Psychedelic Shamanism*. Ibid. Chapter 9.

3. In *DMT: The Spirit Molecule*. Ibid.

4. In *DMT: The Spirit Molecule*. Ibid.

5. *Miserable Miracle: La Mescaline*. Schoenhofs Foreign Books, 1991.

6. 'Supposed' powers of the brain since, until recently the structure of the brain has not really been known and, even today, many of its functions are not clearly understood.

7. I have heard it suggested that this 'dreaming state' was itself

aided by a plant, although I don't know how factual this is.

8. In *Flesh of the Gods*. Ibid.

9. Aldous Huxley, *The Doors of Perception and Heaven and Hell*. Perennial; Reissue edition, 1990.

10. Donna's grandson, Freddie, was born almost on schedule and is a healthy and happy baby. Donna's other daughter, meanwhile (who has no ambitions of her own for a baby yet), continues to plead with her mother not to have visions about her!

11. Including tyramine, hordenine, 3-methoxytyramine, anhalaninine, anhalonidine, 3,4-dimethoxyphen-ethylamine, 3,4-dimethoxy-4-hydroxy-B-phenethylamine, and 3,5-dimethoxy-4-hydroxy-B-phenethylamine.

12. Other plants that might be added include perejil (*Petroselinum crispum*) for overcoming *dano* (sorcery) and *susto* (fright), or for 'forgetting love or trauma', and apio cimarron (*Apium graveolens*) for curing nervous disorders, insomnia and anxiety, as well as physical problems such as bronchitis and colic. See *Plantas de los Cuatrovientos* (*Plants of the Four Winds: The Magic and Medicinal Flora of Peru*) by Rainer W Bussmann and Douglas Sharon (Peru, 2007) for others.

13. See my book, *Plant Spirit Shamanism* (Destiny Books, 2006) for more information on this.

14. Although he is best-known for his accounts of working with the shamans of Mexico in books like *The Teachings of Don Juan*, Carlos Castaneda was, in fact, born in Cajamarca in the northern highlands of Peru, on December 25, 1925.

15. *Breaking Open the Head: A Psychedelic Journey into the Heart of Contemporary Shamanism*. Broadway, 2003.

16. See Chapter 2.

Chapter 6

1. In *Las Lagunas de los Encantos: Medicina Tradicional Andina del Peru Septenrional*. Lima: Grifica Bellida.

2. A *bruja* is a female sorcerer.
3. La Gringa's stairway of light photograph is reproduced in the photo section of this book.
4. Agua florida, or Florida Water, is a plant-based perfume with healing properties.
5. This is a point also made by Cowan et al, in *Eduardo El Curandero*. Ibid. '*Curanderos* and *brujos* [male sorcerers]... are very individualistic, and each sets up his mesa according to his own idiosyncratic needs and inspiration.'
6. Artes are magical objects of power, such as stones or shells or crystals, that are used for healing and protection.
7. There is a photograph of La Gringa's mesa in the photo section of this book.
8. Chonta are wooden staffs that San Pedro shamans sometimes use to lightly beat participants and move their spiritual energies around.
9. This is interesting and appears to be a departure from more commonly-held beliefs these days. Based on a comment by Eduardo Calderon, recorded by Cowan et al in *Eduaro El Curandero* (ibid), many Western healers and 'psychonauts' actively seek out four-ribbed cactuses for their use. Perhaps this is a misunderstanding on their part, however, because Calderon never said that four-ribbed cactuses deliver a wonderful or desirable experience. What he actually said was: 'There are San Pedros of twelve, eight, seven, six, five, and of four ribs. One with four is very difficult to find, but he who finds a four-ribbed San Pedro can cure all sicknesses and maladies. Four-ribbed San Pedro is the mystical San Pedro: it was used in time immemorial, and is depicted in Mochica photography, in the sculpture of Chavin de Huantar, in the Sierra, and in the north coast region, where its application to curing is essential up to the present.' There is nothing in this that suggests a 'divine experience'; rather, it is consistent with La Gringa's observation that four-ribbed cactus will cure the

most difficult of cases ('all sicknesses and maladies', in Calderon's words) – those where even an exorcism may be necessary. But, if that is the case, it also stands to reason that the effects of the plant and the healing journey that the patient and curandero embark on are unlikely to be pleasant. What is more likely, in fact, is that the cactus will, indeed, 'take you to Hell'.

10. Donna and I had both experienced ourselves as 'the breath of the world', flowing, like a sentient wind, across the landscapes of the planet during our ceremony with Miguel. During this I also became aware of the thoughts and intelligence contained in the air around us and it was interesting for me to reflect on this, therefore, as I listened to La Gringa's words which followed.

11. The Q'ero are the first people of Peru. They live at high altitudes and, because of this, managed to escape detection by the invading Spanish so they were able to preserve their original culture and beliefs. For centuries nobody knew they existed at all, and it was only about twenty years ago that they came down from the mountains to deliver the prophecies which had been given to them by spirit for the future of humankind.

12. As previously noted, Wade Davis points out, in his description of a ceremony performed in 1981, that participants sometimes do exhibit ailments like those La Gringa describes. Because of the nature of San Pedro, however, health precautions are recommended. San Pedro can raise blood pressure, for example, and some of its compounds may also act as mild MAOIs (monoamine oxidase inhibitors) which affect serotonin levels (Source: www.erowid.com). Medical consultation is therefore suggested for people taking serotonin selective re-uptake inhibitors (SSRIs) in the form of antidepressants or drugs affecting serotonin levels as these do not combine well with MAOIs. Non-prescription medicines,

such as antihistamines, dietary aids, amphetamines and their derivatives, and some herbal remedies (especially those containing ephedrine, high levels of caffeine, or other stimulants) should also be discontinued before you drink San Pedro.

13. Cowan et al write, for example, in *Eduardo El Curandero*, that 'besides his intelligence, the single most important ingredient in Eduardo's healing is [not San Pedro, but] his profound humanity and charismatic personality. We know from personal experience that this is the key to his success with his patients, and suspect that such is the case with shamans in general.'

14. Chatting afterwards, however, and describing the matador-spirit that Donna and I had both seen, La Gringa confirmed that she had also seen this entity or ally in her own visions, though she couldn't say that it was *the* spirit of San Pedro rather than *a* spirit attendant to the plant.

Chapter 7

1. La Gringa would, of course, dispute the description of these experiences as solely physical *or* emotional. In her view, the two are intimately connected and every disease is psychosomatic: of the body *and* the mind. There is more on this in the chapter which follows.

2. *DMT: The Spirit Molecule*. Ibid.

3. 'Set' refers to the mind-set, attitudes and intentions of the people involved and 'setting' to the environment in which the event took place.

4. That is, relative to the changes that most of us make.

5. This is the Temple of the Moon.

6. Simon has posted a video containing images of his experiences in Peru, including ayahuasca and San Pedro-related ceremonies, at
http://www.youtube.com/watch?v=RGYMw0qzfDE.

Retrieved on December 25, 2008.

7. Ibid.

8. *The Antipodes of the Mind*. Ibid.

9. It may well have arisen for others too and been at least one aspect of their journey, but here I am including only those reports where fear and suffering were specifically mentioned.

10. In *The Antipodes of the Mind*. Ibid.

Chapter 8

1. Oxford University Press, 2004.

2. Where those who suffer from asthma tend also to be suscep-tible to eczema, both conditions brought on by a common set of circumstances, often described as 'stress'.

3. Joan Parisi Wilcox, *Masters of the Living Energy: The Mystical World of the Q'ero of Peru*. Inner Traditions, 2004.

4. Stan Gooch, *Creatures from Inner Space*. Rider & Co, 1984.

5. In *Eduardo El Curandero*. Ibid.

6. Mass hysteria – Telling the truth to the terrified, *The Economist*, May 20, 2006.

7. Richard Gross, *Psychology: The Science of Mind and Behaviour*. Lawrence Erlbaum, 1996.

8. David G Myers, *Social Psychology*. McGraw-Hill, 2006.

9. In *The Gift of Life*. Ibid.

10. David Adam, *Meditation 'leads to longer life'*, May 2, 2005, The Guardian newspaper.

11. In *Creatures from Inner Space*. Ibid.

12. R L Moody, Bodily Changes During Abreaction, *Lancet*, vol. 251, no. 2, 1946; and vol. 254, no. 2 1948.

13. In fact, Bertha Pappenheim, an Austrian-Jewish feminist.

14. See, for example, Milgram's studies on obedience to authority, which are also described in my book, *The Way of The Lover*. Llewellyn, 2007.

Chapter 9

1. This is not Eduardo Calderon, but one of Cusco's less-celebrated healers, who I met when I received a healing treatment from him almost ten years ago.

2. A hex or curse.

3. Ibid.

4. For a discussion of the other healing influences on it see, for example, Robert T Trotter II and Juan Antonio Chavira, *Curanderismo: Mexican American Folk Healing.* University of Georgia Press, 1997.

5. Trotter and Chavira, *Curanderismo.* Ibid.

6. Jean-Pierre Chaumeil, *Varieties of Amazonian Shamanism. Shamans and Shamanisms: On the Threshold of the Next Millennium*, in *Diogenes*, Summer 1992, No. 158.

7. In *Plant Spirit Shamanism* by Ross Heaven. Destiny Books, 2006.

8. The Andean equivalent of the chakras. In Quechua, the word is ñawi, and in Aymara, naira. Both literally mean 'eye' but refer to energy centres in the body.

9. Another name for San Pedro.

10. Many shamans say the same thing: that they, as healers, are the agents or ambassadors for God, that they have a *don* or a healing gift, but that God is the real doctor.

11. *les données immédiates de la conscience.*

12. In his summary of the literature as part of the research proposal he shared with me for his study of the psychic potentials of San Pedro.

13. Vollenweider, F X & Geyer, M A, 2001. *A systems model of altered consciousness: integrating natural and drug-induced psychoses.* In *Brain Research Bulletin*, 56(5), 495-507.

14. Psi is a term used in para- (or transpersonal) psychology which derives from the 23rd letter of the Greek alphabet and comes from the Greek for 'psyche': 'mind' or 'soul'.

15. Quoted in *Plants of the Gods*. Ibid.

Notes

16. Quoted, again, in *Plants of the Gods*. Ibid.

17. See, for example, Marti-Ibanez, F (1965, June). *The gates to paradise*. In *MD Medical News magazine*, 11.

18. Osmond, H, *Variables in the LSD setting*. In Anon, *Proceedings of Two Conferences on Parapsychology and Pharmacology*. Parapsychology Foundation, 1961.

Chapter 10

1. *The Gift of Life*. Ibid.

Chapter 11

1. Carlos Castaneda, *A Separate Reality*. Washington Square Press, 1991.

2. Carlos Castaneda, *Tales of Power*. Simon & Schuster, 1974.

3. *The Cosmic Serpent*. Ibid.

4. In 2008, however, the Peruvian government declared that the traditional use of ayahuasca would be regarded as a cultural treasure. The decision was signed by the Director of the National Institute of Culture, Javier Ugaz Villacorta, and published in the country's official daily newspaper, *El Peruano*. Villacorta noted the 'religious, therapeutical and cultural purposes' of ayahuasca, and its 'therapeutical virtues.' 'There is a need for protection of the traditional use and the sacred aspect of the ayahuasca ritual,' he said, 'differentiating it from the Occidental use, which is out of context, consumerist and with commercial purposes.'

5. For example, as 'bipolar' or 'Dissociative Identity Disorder'.

6. For more information on Simenton's work see my book *The Journey to You*. Bantam, 2001.

7. For more information on the power of prayer see my book *Spirit in the City*. Bantam, 2002.

8. In *DMT: The Spirit Molecule*. Ibid.

9. In *The Antipodes of the Mind*. Ibid.

10. In *The Entities of the Imaginal Realm*, chapter 5 of *Psychedelic*

245

Shamanism by Jim DeKorne. Ibid.

11. Shanon, in *The Antipodes of the Mind.* Ibid.

12. In the introduction to my book, Plant Spirit Shamanism. Destiny Books, 2006.

Glossary

Agua florida: Perfumed 'water for flourishing'. A fragrant mix of herbs and scents used by shamans for healing

Aguardiente: Alcohol in which flowers and plants are often preserved by Andean healers

Ally: Shamanically-speaking, a helpful spirit contacted through teacher plants such as San Pedro

Artes: Ritual power objects used on altars for healing

Ayahuasca: The 'vine of souls'. The visionary brew of Amazonian shamans

Ayahuasceros: Shamans who work with ayahuasca

Ayni: The Andean principle of reciprocity; a form of giving without the desire to receive in return but in the awareness, nonetheless, that we will be rewarded for our actions as the energy they create continues to circulate

Bilis: 'Rage'. A disease arising from emotional causes but which is strong enough to lead to physical problems such as stomach upsets and ulcers

Bruja: A sorceress

Brujo: A sorcerer

Chonta: Wooden sticks, often placed on or around altars, which are used in healing ceremonies

Contrachisa: An emetic plant mixture used by healers to help their patients purge negative energies and spiritual toxins from their bodies

Curanderismo: The art of healing. The word derives from the Spanish *curar*: to heal

Curandera: Female healer or shaman

Curandero: Male healer or shaman

Daño: 'Harm'. A spiritual attack or magical illness often sent by a sorcerer working on behalf of a client

Don: A title, like doctor. Also a healing gift which is said to be sent by God

El Dorado: In Peru, the fabled city of gold

Empacho: A spiritual or emotional illness which causes a blockage in the stomach and leads to digestive disorders

Entheogen: A visionary plant, such as ayahuasca or San Pedro, used in shamanic rituals

Envidia: A spiritual attack arising from envy or jealousy

Field of Evil: According to Eduardo Calderon, the right side of the mesa (altar), which contains positive and life-giving energies

Field of Justice: According to Eduardo Calderon, the left side of the mesa (altar), where illness is diagnosed and dealt with

Hallucinations: As distinct from visions, 'bubblings-up from the waters of our souls' in the words of don Raphael. 'The drifting to the surface of events from our lives that have a message or a lesson for us'

Hanaqpacha: In Andean spiritual cosmology, the upper, or divine, world

Huachuma: San Pedro

Huachumera: Female San Pedro shaman

Huachumero: Male San Pedro shaman

Icaro: The prayerful song of the ayahuasca shaman, sung to the spirits of the plants or to patients as part of a healing and visionary ceremony

Jatun: The 'great force of life'. The spiritual dimension from which all things are made manifest

Kawsay: The principle of respect for all life in the awareness that we are connected

Kaypacha: In Andean spiritual cosmology, the middle world, which includes physical reality as we know it and its spiritual counterpart

Las Huaringas: The sacred lakes of Peru that have been revered for their healing properties since the earliest civilisation

Llankay: The principle of taking appropriate, wise and

compassionate actions

Mal aire: 'Bad air'. A bad atmosphere surrounding an individual or family, which can lead to illness

Mal ojo: The 'evil eye': staring intently at someone and projecting energy through the eyes with the intent to harm

Mal puesto: A hex or curse

Mal suerte: 'Bad luck' arising from a spiritual cause

Mapacho: Cigars made from pure jungle tobacco which are used by shamans in healing rituals to direct prayers and good intentions through the smoke they produce

Mesa: An altar containing healing tools and power objects

Munay: The principle of acting with compassionate and loving intent

Pachamama: The spirit of the Earth

Palo Santo: Incense used to freshen and sweeten ceremonial spaces

Peyote: A mescaline cactus native to Mexico

Placebo effect: A medical phenomenon where a healing is produced through the power of belief or suggestion alone

Placitas: A therapeutic consultation described as a 'heart-to-heart, soul-to-soul discussion' with a patient

Planta maestros: 'Master teacher plants', such as ayahuasca and San Pedro

Psychedelic (e.g. drugs or plants): Producing visionary effects. Literally, 'mind-manifesting'

Psychosomatic: Mind and body. E.g. where thoughts or emotions produce physical effects and lead to illness

Pulsario: A physical illness arising from an emotional cause, usually presenting as a digestive disorder

Purge: The removal of negative energies through vomiting

Q'ero: The first people of Peru, who live at high altitudes and, because of this, managed to escape detection by the Spanish and preserve their original culture and beliefs

Saladera: 'Bad luck' arising from a spiritual cause. Also see *mal suerte*

San Pedro: The Peruvian mescaline 'cactus of vision'

Seguro: Bottles of magical herbs used in healing

Singado: Tobacco macerated in alcohol which is snorted to purify and cleanse the body and soul

Soul retrieval: The shamanic healing practice of restoring lost energy or spirit

Susto: 'Soul loss'; a condition where part of the spirit or energy is lost so the patient does not have access to his full power. Also see *soul retrieval*

Ukupacha: In Andean spiritual cosmology, the lower world

Virote: A magical 'evil thorn' or dart of energy which is sent as a spiritual attack

Vision: As distinct from an hallucination, the experience of knowledge or healing in the form of 'a direct communication from God', according to don Raphael

Wirococha: In Andean spiritual cosmology, described by some as a lake of memory and wisdom, similar to the collective unconscious imagined by Jung

Yachay: The principle of living according to informed wisdom which is greater and deeper than simple 'knowledge'

About The Author

Ross Heaven is a therapist, healer, and the director of The Four Gates Foundation, one of Europe's leading organisations for the teaching, promotion and application of spiritual wisdom and freedom psychology.

He is the author of several books on shamanism, healing and spiritual plant medicines, including *Plant Spirit Shamanism: Traditional Techniques for Healing the Soul, The Sin Eater's Last Confessions, Plant Spirit Wisdom, The Way of The Lover,* and *Love's Simple Truths: Meditations on Rumi and The Path of The Heart.*

He offers courses and retreats in healing, self-awareness and indigenous wisdom and spiritual journeys to work with the healers and plant spirit shamans of Peru. His Magical Earth journeys take place in the Amazon with ayahuasca, the vine of souls, each year and his Cactus of Vision journeys are to the Andes for healing work with San Pedro.

For details of these journeys as well as information on new books, workshops and healing events, email ross@thefourgates.com or visit The Four Gates website at www.thefourgates.com.

Disclaimer

The techniques and approaches in this book are for interest purposes only. It is important that you proceed with caution and take responsibility for your actions when pursuing any spiritual or shamanic plant practices. Double-check all plant formulas and recipes for legality and safety before you use them internally or externally and if you are in any doubt take medical or other advice to reassure yourself that there are no contraindications before you begin.

Any application of these practices is at the reader's own risk and the author and publisher disclaim any liability arising directly or indirectly from them.

Index

W
Wachuma 52
Wade Davis 49, 55, 56
William Blake 3, 217
Wirococha 190

Y
Yolanda (shaman) 27

BOOKS

O is a symbol of the world, of oneness and unity. In different cultures it also means the "eye," symbolizing knowledge and insight. We aim to publish books that are accessible, constructive and that challenge accepted opinion, both that of academia and the "moral majority."

Our books are available in all good English language bookstores worldwide. If you don't see the book on the shelves ask the bookstore to order it for you, quoting the ISBN number and title. Alternatively you can order online (all major online retail sites carry our titles) or contact the distributor in the relevant country, listed on the copyright page.

See our website **www.o-books.net** for a full list of over 500 titles, growing by 100 a year.

And tune in to myspiritradio.com for our book review radio show, hosted by June-Elleni Laine, where you can listen to the authors discussing their books.

MySpiritRadio